The Saving and Investing Workbook

937 Questions and Answers To Financial Literacy

Michael Fischer

This book is a work of non-fiction. Unless otherwise noted, the author and the publisher make no explicit guarantees as to the accuracy of the information contained in this book.

The author does not want to take credit nor does he assume responsibility for anyone's investment successes or failures, although he clearly believes that financial education and financial literacy are the keys to achieving good saving and investing results and that this book will provide a huge step forward along the journey towards achieving this goal.

This book is a workbook of questions. For the original content and full discussions, please see the book by the same author entitled 'Saving and Investing - Financial Knowledge and Financial Literacy that Everyone Needs and Deserves to Have!'

While the materials have been put together over a long time period and using personal experience, education, professional experience as well as publicly available information on each subject which we believe to be reliable, it can not be guaranteed, nor does it purport to treat each subject exhaustively.

Copies of this Book are for the personal use of the purchaser of the materials. Examples and illustrations are not to be regarded as recommendations for investment purchase or sale nor construed as investment advice. This publication is designed to provide accurate financial literacy and financial education information on the subjects covered. It is made available with the understanding that savingandinvesting.com LLC is not engaged in providing investment recommendations or investment advice, nor is it providing legal or accounting advice.

AuthorHouse™ UK Ltd.
500 Avebury Boulevard
Central Milton Keynes, MK9 2BE
www.authorhouse.co.uk
Phone: 08001974150

First published by AuthorHouse 9/21/2010

ISBN: 978-1-4520-4891-8 (sc)

This book is printed on acid-free paper.

PREFACE

- ➡ DOES THE WHOLE SUBJECT OF MONEY, SAVING AND INVESTING BAFFLE YOU?
- ➡ HAVE YOU EVER WISHED THAT YOU COULD UNDERSTAND FINANCIAL MATTERS BETTER?
- ➡ HAVE YOU EVER WISHED THAT YOU COULD BETTER SEE WHAT WAS GOING ON IN THE FINANCIAL MARKETS?
- ➡ HAVE YOU EVER FELT THAT THIS INFORMATION WOULD BE USEFUL IN THINKING ABOUT YOUR FUTURE, YOUR FAMILY'S FUTURE OR THE FUTURE OF INVESTMENT OPPORTUNITIES THAT MIGHT BE PRESENTED TO YOU OR THAT YOU MIGHT BE CONSIDERING?
- ➡ HAVE YOU EVER WISHED THAT PERHAPS HAVING AN UNDERSTANDING OF THE FUNDAMENTALS WOULD ALLOW YOU TO HAVE A BETTER DIALOGUE WITH A FINANCIAL ADVISER OR CONSIDER YOUR OPTIONS MORE INTELLIGENTLY?
- ➡ ARE YOU A STUDENT OF BUSINESS, FINANCE OR ECONOMICS, WITH A DESIRE TO LOOK AT THE SUBJECT FROM A FRESH PERSPECTIVE?
- ➡ ARE YOU CONSIDERING A CAREER IN FINANCIAL SERVICES?
- ➡ WILL YOU BE INVOLVED WITH INVESTMENTS AS A PART OF YOU WORK?
- ➡ ARE YOU A FINANCIAL ADVISER STARTING IN THE PROFESSION?
- ➡ ARE YOU A FINANCIAL ADVISER THAT WANTS TO REFRESH A FEW TOPICS?

THE PURPOSE OF THIS BOOK IS TO PROVIDE THE NECESSARY INSIGHT TO FEEL COMFORTABLE WITH THIS SUBJECT MATTER AND ALL OF THE ABOVE QUESTIONS.

THE BOOK IS A WORKBOOK COVERING A VAST ARRAY TOPICS THAT RELATE TO SAVING AND INVESTING - FUNDAMENTAL CONCEPTS, TERMINOLOGY AND REAL-WORLD INTERACTIONS, STRATEGIES AND TOPICS THAT READERS OF ANY NEWSPAPER, WATCHERS OF ANY NEWS PROGRAM, AND ANY POTENTIAL SAVER OR INVESTOR WOULD BE PRESENTED WITH. A COMPREHENSIVE RANGE OF TOPICS, TERMINOLOGY, AND CONCEPTS IS APPROACHED FROM MULTIPLE ANGLES - THROUGH SPECIFIC TARGETED QUESTIONS WITH ANSWERS. THIS ISOLATES SPECIFIC DETAIL, IN AN INTERACTIVE MANNER, WITHOUT LIMITATIONS OF SPACE OR WRITING STYLE.

GETTING ALL OF THE QUESTIONS RIGHT ON A SINGLE RUN IS NOT IMPORTANT - READING THE QUESTIONS AND THINKING ABOUT THE ANSWERS - AND ULTIMATELY UNDERSTANDING THE MAIN TOPICS, OR AT LEAST FEELING MORE COMFORTABLE WITH THEM, IS. QUESTIONS THAT TOUCH ON COMPLICATED TOPICS ARE SET UP TO COMMUNICATE THE KEY CONCEPT AS CLEARLY AS POSSIBLE EITHER IN THE QUESTION, OR IN THE AVAILABLE MULTIPLE CHOICES AND VIA THE ANSWER (AND POTENTIALLY THE FURTHER EXPLANATION THAT IS PROVIDED WITH THE ANSWER).

THE CONCEPTS ALONG WITH OTHER EXAMPLES AND INFORMATION ARE ALSO PROVIDED IN A READABLE NON-QUESTION AND ANSWER FORMAT IN THE BOOK 'SAVING AND INVESTING - FINANCIAL KNOWLEDGE AND FINANCIAL LITERACY THAT EVERYONE NEEDS AND DESERVES TO HAVE!' BY THE SAME AUTHOR.

FINANCIAL MARKETS ARE DYNAMIC, AND ONLY BY HAVING AN UNDERSTANDING OF THE CORE CONCEPTS CAN WE ATTEMPT TO MANEUVER IN DIFFERING MARKET ENVIRONMENTS, INTERPRET NEW INFORMATION, AND CONSIDER THE IMPACT OF NEW DEVELOPMENTS. **THIS BOOK FOCUSES ON FINANCIAL LITERACY - TO BE ABLE TO UNDERSTAND AND INTERPRET NEW INFORMATION AND CONSIDER DIFFERENT OPTIONS IN WHAT WILL UNDOUBTEDLY CONTINUE TO BE EVOLVING MARKETS AND DIFFERING FINANCIAL ENVIRONMENTS.**

THIS SAVING AND INVESTING WORKBOOK SEEKS TO PROVIDE THE FINANCIAL KNOWLEDGE AND FINANCIAL LITERACY THAT EVERYONE NEEDS AND DESERVES TO HAVE.

Saving and Investing Introduction

1. **Over the past decades, we have become:**
   a. less responsible for our finances - governments have become more responsible
   b. more responsible for our finances - governments and employers less so
   c. we are equally responsible - nothing has changed
   d. totally irresponsible - in fact no one should be responsible for our finances

2. **Money usually becomes an issue when:**
   a. there is not enough of it
   b. we have been saving and investing diligently
   c. we have been planning properly
   d. we make a lot of it and save intelligently

3. **Understanding finance and money is important because:**
   a. it can improve the quality of our lives
   b. it is a very important part of the world around us
   c. if we do not understand it, we are much more likely to make financial mistakes
   d. all of the above

4. **Which of the following are good reasons for learning about saving and investing:**
   I. it is a big part of the world around us
   II. it is spoken about in the press all day long
   III. we are putting ourselves at a disadvantage without some knowledge of this material
   IV. we can have a better understanding of our financial options
   V. we can have better dialogue with financial advisers

   a. I only
   b. I and II only
   c. I, II and III only
   d. I, II, III and IV only
   e. I, II, III, IV and V

5. **Which of the following are good reasons to save some money:**
   I. to have an emergency fund
   II. for a house
   III. for education
   IV. for retirement
   V. for unforeseen circumstances

   a. I only
   b. I and II only
   c. I, II and III only
   d. I, II, III and IV only
   e. I, II, III, IV and V

6. **The best time to save money is:**
   a. in retirement
   b. during high earning years
   c. never
   d. as a student

7. **When it comes to understanding finance and the world around us, one of the keys is to get:**
   a. just the sound-bites
   b. a few interesting facts for use at social events

c. the complete picture - to be able to interpret new information and potentially have a view
d. none of the facts - because the subject is not important

8. <u>Saving and investing can be best described as:</u>
   a. putting money aside and putting in place structures with a view to letting it grow slowly
   b. taking large risks and hoping for the best
   c. following other people's advice blindly
   d. speculation

9. <u>Which of the following is not a result of being financially literate:</u>
   a. it can help assess which investments could not possibly be a good idea
   b. it can assist in understanding financial advice
   c. it will ensure that we never have a risk of a loss in any investment
   d. it can reduce risk, partly by ensuring that all of our eggs are not in one basket

10. <u>We should think of saving and investing as:</u>
    a. the main way of generating wealth
    b. a way of retaining and accumulating funds that can complement an income
    c. a way of winning the lottery with more work
    d. a waste of time

11. <u>Saving, investing and financial markets can be thought of as:</u>
    a. a fad that is not going to last
    b. things that affect only a small part of the population
    c. things that only bankers need to think about
    d. one of the backbones of developed civilization that affect almost everyone

12. <u>Potentially the worst time to start thinking about saving and investing matters is when:</u>
    a. we have money to save and invest
    b. we are in a very bad financial situation
    c. everything is going well with our jobs
    d. we are planning for the future

13. <u>When people start talking about stocks and bonds we should:</u>
    a. shut off completely as matter of principle
    b. at least have some clue as to what these two things are
    c. scream and leave the room
    d. tell them that stocks and bonds don't exist

14. <u>True or False: Our financial system is built on a few very fundamental concepts and most products and ideas follow from these concepts.</u>

15. <u>True or False: Learning about saving and investing can only be justified by greed.</u>

16. <u>True or False: Saving and investing is so complicated that we are better off not knowing anything about it.</u>

17. <u>True or False: Saving and investing is a long-term project.</u>

18. <u>True or False: Knowing about saving and investing will help us understand what is being spoken about in the media.</u>

19. <u>Which of the following is the best definition of investing:</u>
    a. saving money
    b. trial and error
    c. gambling

d. committing money with a view to gaining a financial return

20. Which of the following is most closely tied to the study and science of money, the management of money and financial markets:

a. accounting
b. finance
c. bookkeeping
d. administration

21. The topics of saving and investing and finance are frequently discussed:

I. in the money or financial section of the newspaper
II. on the evening news
III. on the front page of the newspaper
IV. at the bank
V. amongst friends and in relationships

a. I only
b. I and II only
c. I, II and III only
d. I, II, III and IV only
e. I, II, III, IV and V

22. Saving money can be best described as:

a. investing money
b. buying mutual funds
c. putting money in a pension plan
d. spending less than one is earning

23. A difference between saving and investing is:

a. there is none
b. saving is higher risk than investing
c. saving money is not a good idea - investing is
d. saving relates to keeping money, investing relates trying to get a return

24. Which of the following statements is true:

I. saving money can form the basis for subsequent investments
II. investing is higher risk than saving
III. not saving can lead to financial problems
IV. not saving can lead to excess leverage
V. saving is an easy first step, investing can require a bit more thought

a. I only
b. I and II only
c. I, II and III only
d. I, II, III and IV only
e. I, II, III, IV and V

25. Potential problems that could arise if we do not play a role in our finances and investments are:

I. it leaves room for abuse
II. we are not well positioned to monitor how things are going
III. we would not be well-placed to have a dialogue regarding our investments
IV. we would not be able to assess what financial advisers are saying
V. we would not be well-positioned to understand investment alternatives presented to us

a. I only
b. I and II only

c. I, II and III only
d. I, II, III and IV only
e. I, II, III, IV and V

26. <u>Victims of investment scams are most likely going to be:</u>
a. informed investors
b. professional investors
c. gullible and uniformed individuals
d. no one - there are no investment scams

TOTAL: 26 QUESTIONS

COMPOUNDING

27. Compounding money can be best described as:
a. adding return to a sum of money, getting return on new larger sum - repeating again, again and again
b. repeatedly earning a return on sums of money that grow with each incremental return
c. gaining an increasingly larger return as prior returns are added to the existing amount
d. all of the above

28. The most important single concept behind compounding is:
a. getting a very large return once
b. repeatedly getting a return
c. removing the return each time it is earned
d. being very active in moving the money around

29. Compounding, by definition, can only take place if:
a. the return each year is very high
b. the return is added to the existing amount and future returns added to consequently larger amounts
c. the return of any given year is removed each year
d. the returns are the same each year

30. True or False: Compounding can take place in a bank account as well as with many other investments.

31. Compounding is a powerful concept, because it can:
a. allow large sums to be saved with relatively small regular contributions
b. allow small sums to be saved with large regular contributions
c. multiply our savings many times almost overnight
d. result in lottery like winnings that have no basis in any financial reasoning

32. True of False: With compounding, the amount that we can compound our money to over the long term can be much larger than the sum of the amounts contributed.

33. Earning a 5% annual return on $100, after one year will mean a new sum of:
a. $105.00
b. $150.00
c. $100.50
d. $500.00

34. If we add this first-year return to the $100, and let this new amount grow at 5% for a second year, the dollar amount by which the new sum grows by in the second year will be:
a. less than in the first year
b. more than in the first year
c. same as the first year
d. either more or less than in the first year

35. Compounding has been described as the 8th wonder of the world. Why is this likely to be the case?
a. no one can understand it
b. it can not be analyzed on a simple spreadsheet
c. it ensures that no investment can ever fall
d. it can make savings grow so much over the long term

36. Compounding is sometimes described as, or can be thought of as:
a. a snowball rolling down a hill and getting bigger and bigger
b. a snowball being thrown against a wall
c. snowflakes melting on the ground

d. a snowman that is being built

37. **Because compounding with a positive return means that money grows by a larger amount with each year that it is being done, we should be aware that:**
a. starting late is fine because we can always catch up at the end
b. someone that starts early will not save more than someone that starts late
c. it does not matter when we start
d. starting early is theoretically best because it allows more returns to be added, the sum to be larger, and the returns each year to be larger

38. **When it comes to compounding, which of the following will we be least likely have control over, and/or where should we be most aware of the risk:**
a. the amount we contribute
b. the length of time that save for
c. when we start
d. the return that we get in any given year

39. **Which of the following is/are important factor(s) affecting how much our money grows to:**
a. the amount we save
b. the return we get
c. the length of time that the money compounds for
d. all of the above

40. **True or False: Getting a slightly higher return without taking more risks, is sometimes possible at the bank by committing to leaving the money on deposit for a longer period of time.**

41. **The saying 'pay yourself first' refers to:**
a. spending money on luxury items for yourself first
b. setting some money aside for saving and investing before we do anything else
c. going to the bar for a good time with every paycheck
d. an illegal activity

42. **The interest rates that we pay on debt, versus the interest rate we get on savings are usually:**
a. higher
b. lower
c. the same
d. none of the above

43. **Which of the following statements is true:**
I. a borrower borrows money
II. a lender lends money
III. lenders and borrowers can transact with one another
IV. a borrower lends money
V. a lender borrows money

a. I only
b. II only
c. I, II, III only
d. I, II, IV and V only
e. I, II, III, IV and V

44. **Interest rates on borrowed money are typically higher, when:**
a. the likelihood of getting the money back is lower for the lender
b. the likelihood of getting the money back is higher
c. when the loan is risk free
d. the borrower is buying a house

45. Which of the following do lenders typically consider to be the least risky type of borrowing, and where correspondingly interest rates are usually lowest:

a. when we borrow to make high risk investments
b. when borrowing for something that we do not need
c. when borrowing for a house to live in
d. for property speculation

46. Borrowing at high interest rates, means that the money we owe grows:

a. more slowly
b. more quickly
c. at the same speed
d. none of the above

47. A company might believe that it is justified in borrowing because:

a. the return that it can get on the borrowed money is higher than the cost of borrowing
b. the return that it gets is lower than the cost of borrowing
c. it is never done - companies never borrow money
d. it is bad for the company

48. Which of the following could be used to calculate how money compounds:

a. a spreadsheet program like Excel
b. a compound interest calculator on the web
c. a financial calculator
d. all of the above

49. The nature of compounding makes a strong case for:

I. starting early
II. getting a reasonable return
III. trying to get a consistent return
IV. trying to save taxes on the returns
V. taking huge bets

a. I only
b. I and II only
c. I, II and III only
d. I, II, III and IV only
e. I, II, III, IV and V

50. Unpaid credit card debt often compounds like savings, but differs in that:

a. this debt usually grows more slowly
b. this debt usually does not grow
c. this debt usually grows much more quickly
d. they both grow randomly

51. A valid reason that might partly explain the extremely high typical interest rates on credit card debt might be:

a. the loans are low-risk
b. the loans are risk-free
c. the loans are always against solid assets
d. the loans are very risky and the risk of default is higher - they are often against assets that can not be resold easily and that will typically be worth much less as soon as purchased

52. Having an outstanding credit card balance is most often:

a. a good idea
b. a bad idea

c. a terrible idea
d. an excellent idea

53. **Making only the minimum payment on a credit card is:**
a. going to pay off the card very quickly
b. still going to cost us a lot in interest on the debt
c. a good idea because we are letting our money grow
d. a bad idea because it will decrease our outstanding balance

54. **Buying consumables on a credit card and not paying the interest or principal is:**
a. a good idea because it will make the money that we owe grow very quickly
b. a bad idea because it will mean that we don't owe any money
c. a bad idea because the amount that we owe will grow quickly, effectively making the purchased items much more expensive
d. a good idea because we want the credit card companies to make a return at our expense

55. **In 2005, bank regulators and advocacy groups in the United Stated proposed a revised set of guidelines to raise the minimum payment on a credit card from 2% of the outstanding balance to 4% of the outstanding balance. These guidelines were most likely put forward in order to:**
a. help credit card companies
b. help retailers
c. help the government
d. protect consumers

56. **Paying as much as possible, or ideally the total balance each month, on a credit card means:**
a. higher costs over the life of the credit card because monthly payments have risen
b. higher payments over the life of the card because more interest would have to be paid
c. the same level of payments over the life of the card
d. significantly lower payments over the life of the card because of lower accumulated interest

57. **Credit card companies are likely to make the most money when:**
a. consumers pay off their balances each month
b. consumers keep an outstanding balance for a long period
c. consumers default on their credit card debt
d. consumers do not use their credit card

58. **True or False: A credit card charges 26% interest on any outstanding balance from month end - this is a guaranteed after-tax cost. Since the likelihood of finding an investment that will provide a guaranteed after-tax return of over 26% is virtually zero, paying down the credit card first is always the best investment option.**

59. **If a sum of money was left to compound for 20 years at 10% compounding annually, the amount the saver would have at the end, when compared to the sum he or she started with would be:**
a. about twice as much
b. about five times as much
c. almost seven times as much
d. about ten times as much

60. **Which if the following would result in a higher amount saved:**
a. $1,000 compounding for 5 years at 10% annually
b. $1,000 compounding for 10 years at 5% annually
c. $100 compounding for 50 year at 10% annually
d. $100 compounding for 100 years at 5% annually

61. **Saving $5.00 every day for 10 years, with the money compounding at 8% every year (annually) will result in overall savings closest to:**
    a. $5,000
    b. $10,000
    c. $20,000
    d. $30,000

62. **True or False: The Rule of 72 can be used to calculate how long approximately it would take for money to double with a given return. For example - with a return of 6%, it would take roughly 72/6=12 years for the money to double.**

63. **Someone with $1,000 is able to grow their money at 4%. Which of the following statements is true:**
    I. the return in the first year will be $40
    II. the return in the second year, if the first-year return is removed will be $40
    III. the return in the second year if the first-year return is added to the $1,000 will be higher than $40
    IV. if the money were left to compound at the same rate, it would double in approximately 18 years
    V. if each year's return is added to the existing sum, the money will grow by the same percentage each year, but by a larger dollar amount each year

    a. I only
    b. I and II only
    c. I, II and III only
    d. I, II, III and IV only
    e. I, II, III, IV and V

64. **What is the interest per year on an outstanding credit card balance of $5,000 if the credit card company charges interest of 20%:**
    a. $100
    b. $500
    c. $600
    d. $1,000

65. **An investor expects the stock market to return 12% on average. She is paying 20% on her $5,000 credit card balance. She has $4,000 of cash that she does not need right now and would like to invest, or use to pay down debt. Which decision would make sense:**
    a. invest the money in the stock market to get the 12% return
    b. spend the money and increase the credit card debt
    c. repay credit card debt - the effective 'return' at about 20% is much higher than the 12% (expected)
    d. borrow more on the credit card and invest the $4,000 as well as the additional borrowing

66. **True or False: Compounding, either on our debts or on our savings, often takes place automatically and without manual intervention from us.**

TOTAL: 40 QUESTIONS

Debt, Equity and Financial Markets - Providers and Users of Capital

67. **True or False: When an individual, a company or a government borrow money and pay interest on this money, an entity on the other side of that transaction is likely to be getting a return for having made it available.**

68. **True or False: Savers and investors can also be thought of as providers of capital in the context of financial markets.**

69. **Which of the following can be considered key principles of our capitalist saving and investing system:**
    I. goods that are economically viable are provided; they are purchased by those able to pay
    II. companies that can deliver returns should have access to capital
    III. generally companies that are not economically viable will fail
    IV. all goods are provided to all consumers
    V. the government should and will usually compete with companies in most industries

    a. I only
    b. I and II only
    c. I, II and III only
    d. I, II, III and IV only
    e. I, II, III, IV and V

70. **In which of the following situations could we consider ourselves a provider of capital in the context of debt, either directly or indirectly:**
    a. buying a car
    b. keeping a balance in a bank account
    c. borrowing on a credit card
    d. buying a stock

Questions 71 & 72 are linked.

71. **A provider of capital can compound their money by:**
    a. lending it
    b. buying it
    c. spending it
    d. renting it

72. **True or False: The other way (other than way of previous question) for providers and users of capital to interact is through equity or ownership.**

73. **As a saver and an investor, our foremost consideration should be:**
    a. providing capital where it is needed
    b. helping out
    c. getting a positive return and managing risk
    d. helping the needy

74. **Providing capital in the interest of benevolence or goodwill, and without a desire or expectation of a financial return, is known as:**
    a. speculation
    b. short-selling
    c. investing
    d. charity

75. **True or False: Investors are providers of capital in the context of users and providers of capital.**

76. **Which of the following are often considered major providers of capital:**
   I. private investors or high net worth individuals
   II. investment funds
   III. pension funds
   IV. insurance companies
   V. sovereign wealth funds

   a. I only
   b. I and II only
   c. I, II and III only
   d. I, II, III and IV only
   e. I, II, III, IV and V

77. **One of the core ideas behind debt, equity and financial markets relates to an interaction between:**
   a. providers and users of capital
   b. speculators and gamblers
   c. hedging companies and insurance companies
   d. short-selling companies and newspapers

78. **Providers and users of capital can potentially interact, because**
   I. the user of capital requires capital
   II. the provider of capital is looking for a return
   III. the user of capital may be able to offer a return
   IV. one has money looking for a return, the other needs it
   V. providers of capital rely on returns to compound their money

   a. I only
   b. II only
   c. II, III only
   d. I, II, IV and V only
   e. I, II, III, IV and V

79. **True or False: Whether an agency is a provider or user of capital relates to their role in a specific situation - they might fulfill a different role in a separate transaction.**

80. **Which of the following statement(s) relating to equity and debt is/are correct?**
   I. one side of a debt transaction is lending money for a return
   II. a user of capital in a debt-based transaction borrows money
   III. a provider of capital that owns a part of a company is involved in an equity transaction
   IV. debt and equity can be thought of as two main ways by which providers of capital (savers and investors) and users of capital (companies and governments) can interact
   V. debt and equity are the same thing

   a. I only
   b. I and II only
   c. I, II and III only
   d. I, II, III and IV only
   e. I, II, III, IV and V

81. **In which of the following situations could we consider ourselves a provider of capital in the context of equity, either directly or indirectly:**
   a. buying a car with cash
   b. keeping a balance in a bank account
   c. borrowing on a credit card
   d. buying a stock

82. **Lending money involves:**
   a. debt
   b. equity
   c. shares
   d. stocks

83. **A lender is:**
   a. someone that lends money
   b. someone that borrows money
   c. someone that has no money
   d. someone that wants money

84. **A borrower is:**
   a. someone that lends money
   b. someone that borrows money
   c. someone that has no money
   d. someone that wants money

85. **When we are talking about lending and borrowing money, we are talking about:**
   a. debt
   b. equity
   c. options
   d. stocks

86. **A bank that lends money is seeking a return through:**
   a. an equity investment
   b. a debt investment
   c. a stock investment
   d. a commodity investment

87. **When we are talking about ownership, we are talking about:**
   a. debt
   b. bonds
   c. equity
   d. lending

88. **Anyone that owns a piece of a company, owns a piece of the:**
   a. debt
   b. equity
   c. bonds
   d. liabilities

89. **Investors that buy the equity of a company, can also be referred to as:**
   I. debtholders
   II. equityholders
   III. bondholders
   IV. owners or part-owners of a company
   V. lenders

   a. I only
   b. I and II only
   c. I, II and III only
   d. II and IV only
   e. I, III and V only

90. **Two major distinct groups of providers of capital are:**

a. debtholders and equityholders
b. debtholders and bondholders
c. equityholders and shareholders
d. stockholders and shareholders

91. **The equity of a large company is often split into smaller pieces. This statement is:**
a. true, and these pieces are known as stocks or shares
b. true, and these pieces are known as debt
c. true, and the pieces do not have a name
d. not true

92. **Someone that owns a share in a company, owns:**
a. a part of the equity of that company
b. a part of the debt of the company
c. bonds of the company
d. the liabilities of the company

93. **An investor that buys a bond is effectively:**
a. lending money
b. borrowing money
c. taking an ownership stake
d. buying equity

94. **True or False: The owner of a stock in a company is an equityholder in that company.**

95. **True or False: Shareholders are the owners of a business.**

96. **True of False: Stockholders can also be referred to as shareholders in a company.**

97. **True or False: When the amount of money that companies borrow gets very large, the way in which the providers of capital provide the money is often through bonds.**

98. **Which of the following statements is/are true:**
I. the equity of a company can be split into stocks or shares for large companies
II. the equity of a company can be split into bonds for large companies
III. the debt of a company can be split into stocks or shares for large companies
IV. the debt of a company can be split into bonds for large companies
V. equity and debt are never parceled into smaller slices

a. I only
b. II only
c. I and III only
d. I and IV only
e. V only

99. **The owners of a company are seeking a return through:**
a. an equity investment
b. a debt investment
c. a bond investment
d. a commodity investment

100. **Which of the following is not an advantage of having the equity of a company split into stocks or shares that can be bought and sold on a stock exchange:**
a. it makes owning a part of the company easier
b. it makes it easier for investors to sell an ownership stake
c. it allows companies to raise capital by selling more stocks/shares

d. it allows an investor to buy the whole company by buying a single stock

101. Which of the following statements provides the same information as saying that a company is fully financed through equity:

I. the company has no debt outstanding
II. the company only has equityholders
III. the company has bondholders
IV. the company has no bondholders or other debt
V. the company has borrowed money

a. I only
b. II only
c. I and II only
d. I, II and IV only
e. II and IV only

102. True or False: When a company goes public, equity that was held privately becomes more publicly available.

103. If a company raises money by borrowing more, it will have:

a. more equity outstanding
b. less equity outstanding
c. more debt outstanding
d. less debt outstanding

104. Which of the following is true:

a. a company can finance itself via equity and debt
b. a company can only finance itself via debt
c. a government can finance itself via equity and debt
d. a government can only finance itself via equity

105. True or False: The holder of a government bond has effectively lent money to the government.

106. True of False: Smaller slices of debt are known as stocks.

107. Two major, distinct ways in which providers and users of capital interact are:

a. stocks and shares
b. equity and debt
c. equity and stocks
d. debt and bonds

108. True or False: Smaller slices of equity are known as bonds.

109. True or False: The return to debtholders is generally more variable than the return to equityholders.

110. True or False: When we borrow money to purchase an asset, we are employing leverage.

111. Which statement(s) with respect to leverage is/are true:

I. leverage typically involves borrowing money to purchase an asset
II. leverage increases the riskiness for equityholders
III. leverage can mean that we lose our money (our equity) more quickly
IV. leverage is often used in home purchases
V. too much leverage is very dangerous

a. I only
b. I and II only

c. I, II and III only
d. I, II, III and IV only
e. I, II, III, IV and V

112. **True or False: Debt and equity are the two main forms through which providers of capital and users of capital can interact.**

113. **Which of the following statements is false:**
   a. the debt of a company is generally considered less risky than the equity of the same company
   b. United States or United Kingdom government debt is considered very low risk, if not risk-free
   c. if a company goes bankrupt, equityholders are considered first in terms of repayment
   d. United States government bonds are lower risk than a US company's bonds since the company is more likely not to be able to make an interest or principal payment

114. **Which of the following is the best definition of a security:**
   a. an investment instrument issued by a government or corporation that offers evidence of equity or debt and that represents financial value
   b. a pool of money that is going to be managed by a portfolio manager
   c. a legal entity that is set up to conduct a certain business
   d. an unregulated investment pool that is typically set up to generate absolute returns for sophisticated investors

115. **True or False: Stocks and bonds are sometimes more generally referred to as being examples of securities.**

116. **Which of the following can not issue stocks:**
   a. a US company
   b. a UK company
   c. a German company
   d. a US government

117. **Equity can also be thought of as:**
   a. the amount that an asset can be sold for
   b. the amount that remains when we sell an asset and have repaid all of the liabilities
   c. revenues
   d. net income

118. **The primary difference between stocks and bonds is:**
   a. stocks go up, bonds might go up
   b. stocks should be considered better investments
   c. stocks are issued by companies, bonds can not be issued by companies
   d. stocks represent ownership, bonds are typically lending instruments

119. **Which of the following can not be considered an equity or ownership instrument:**
   a. a stock
   b. a share
   c. private equity
   d. a corporate bond

120. **In order for a company to have its shares listed on a stock exchange, it has to:**
   a. go public
   b. go private
   c. go bankrupt
   d. go insane

121. **The more money an investor borrows to purchase an investment, the higher the:**

a. equity
b. leverage
c. ownership
d. dividend

122. **True or False: Stocks are considered equity or ownership securities.**

123. **A provider of debt capital can also be referred to as a:**
a. borrower
b. lender
c. shareholder
d. revenues

124. **It would be correct to say that:**
a. leverage has no impact on an investor's return
b. leverage magnifies returns for equityholders on the upside but not the downside
c. leverage magnifies returns for equityholders on the downside but not the upside
d. leverage magnifies returns/losses for equityholders both on the downside and the upside

125. **A common form of leverage for many people is:**
a. paying for a car in full
b. paying for a house in full
c. a mortgage
d. paying for groceries with cash

126. **It would be more sensible to argue for the use of leverage when:**
a. we expect the value of the asset to drop
b. we have no idea where the asset will go
c. we expect the value of the asset to be stable and slowly rising (although we can always be wrong)
d. the asset is very risky

127. **An individual buys a home by putting down 20% of the purchase price and borrowing the rest. The cost of selling the house is 5% of the sales price. If the asset falls in value and she was forced to sell it 20% below the purchase price, which of the following statements would be true with respect to the investor after the sale:**
a. she would have made money
b. the investor would have broken even
c. the investor would have lost a small part of the down payment
d. she would have lost more than the entire 20% down payment

128. **Leverage makes the equity of a company:**
a. less risky
b. more risky
c. more stable
d. more certain to go up

129. **When the equity of a company is held by a small group of investors/founders and it is not traded on an exchange, it is known as:**
a. private equity
b. public equity
c. stocks
d. bonds

130. **The equity of a company before the company has gone public and sold shares on a stock exchange is known as:**
a. public equity

b. negative equity
c. private equity
d. brand equity

131. **Which of the following is not considered a characteristic of private equity:**
a. illiquidity
b. it can be difficult to value
c. it trades on the stock exchange
d. it is riskier than equity of larger companies

132. **Which of the following would be the least likely investor in private equity:**
a. the founders of the company
b. family and friends of the founders
c. a small circle of sophisticated high net worth individual investors
d. an investor that invests in stocks only

133. **True or False: The most common way for most investors to have ownership stakes in large companies is through stocks on a stock exchange either directly, or indirectly though funds.**

134. **True or False: We can become a part-owner in many of the largest companies in the world by buying stocks in these companies.**

135. **True or False: Every investor that owns a share or stock in a company is a part-owner of that company.**

136. **The event that takes place when a company goes from having private equity, to having public equity, is known as:**
a. the graduation
b. the initial public offering (IPO)
c. the bond issue
d. the debt issue

137. **Which of the following refer to the same event:**
I. going public
II. the initial public offering (IPO)
III. listing the shares
IV. selling bonds
V. selling shares to the public for the first time

a. I only
b. I and II only
c. I, II and III only
d. I, II, III and IV only
e. I, II, III and V only

138. **Advantages of listing their shares on a stock exchange for a company typically include:**
I. access to more investors
II. increased exposure for the firm
III. consumers of their products can also be shareholders/owners of the firm
IV. increased ability to raise additional capital
V. a liquid ownership interest that could be used for acquisitions

a. I only
b. I and II only
c. I, II and III only
d. I, II, III and IV only

e. I, II, III, IV and V

139. **True or False: Stock markets and exchanges exist around the world, and a public company will often have its shares listed on an exchange in its home country.**

140. **True or False: Companies and governments need investors, and investors need profitable investment opportunities - hence the opportunity for a structure that benefits both sides.**

141. **History has shown that:**
   a. the fastest growing companies or sectors will always be the fastest growing going forward
   b. companies often go through different stages of growth, and because of innovation, the future is likely to be different than the past
   c. nothing ever changes
   d. a company that is growing quickly today, might slow when it gets larger but it is almost certain to be the fastest growing company again

142. **When a company goes bankrupt and it appears that they can only meet a small part of their debt obligation, which of the following is likely to happen:**
   I. the share price will go to zero, or very close to zero
   II. the equity of the company will be worth nothing or very close to nothing
   III. the very junior debt is going to be worth nothing or very close to nothing
   IV. the most senior debt that is repaid first might still have some value
   V. the company would restructure by selling assets or restructuring their financing

   a. I only
   b. I and II only
   c. I, II and III only
   d. I, II, III and IV only
   e. I, II, III, IV and V

143. **Which of the following are generally recognized as phases of a company's life cycle:**
   I. start-up
   II. growth
   III. maturity
   IV. decline
   V. fraud

   a. I only
   b. I and II only
   c. I, II and III only
   d. I, II, III and IV only
   e. I, II, III, IV and V

144. **Stocks can be described as:**
   a. slices of ownership in companies
   b. slices of ownership in governments
   c. slices of debt in companies
   d. slices of debt in governments

145. **Corporate bonds can be described as:**
   a. slices of ownership in companies
   b. slices of ownership in governments
   c. slices of debt in companies
   d. slices of debt in governments

146. **Government bonds can be described as:**

a. slices of ownership in companies
b. slices of ownership in governments
c. slices of debt in companies
d. slices of debt in governments

147. **When one company wants to buy another company and issues shares to finance the transaction, the services that it might draw on in this context are most likely to relate to:**
a. commercial banking
b. investment banking
c. commodities trading
d. bond trading

TOTAL: 81 QUESTIONS

Financial Statements

148. The analysis and study of a company's assets, liabilities, cash flows and income falls into an area of study known as:

a. economics
b. accounting
c. biology
d. derivatives

149. Having some idea regarding financial statements is useful because:

I. they are spoken about very frequently
II. they provide a lot of insight into how stocks and bonds might behave
III. it helps understand how companies make money
IV. they help illustrate leverage
V. an investor has to prepare them very regularly on behalf of the company

a. I only
b. I and II only
c. I, II and III only
d. I, II, III and IV only
e. I, II, III, IV and V

150. True or False: The Annual Report for a company will provide a summary of what happened in a given year for a company and of the status of the company at the end of the reporting period - it will typically include the three most common financial statements - the balance sheet, the income statement and the cash flow statement.

151. True or False: The financial statements that are found in the Annual Report often come with footnotes that can be very important in understanding the company.

152. A company's annual report could be of interest to:

I. investors
II. employees
III. mutual fund managers
IV. hedge fund managers
V. stock analysts

a. I only
b. I and II only
c. I, II and III only
d. I, II, III and IV only
e. I, II, III, IV and V

153. The __________ checks a company's finances for accuracy in the annual report.

a. stock trader
b. bond trader
c. auditor
d. investment bank

154. True or False: Stock analysts can calculate a large number of ratios based on the income statement, balance sheet and cash flow statement to gain further insights into a company's financial state.

155. Which of the following is not a typical financial statement:

a. the balance sheet

b. the income statement
c. the cash flow statement
d. the overall statement

156. **True or False: The income statement provides a summary of a company's revenues, costs and expenses, leading to the income for the company.**

157. **Which of the following are other words for a company's income or net income:**
I. net profit
II. profit
III. earnings
IV. revenues
V. sales

a. I only
b. I and II only
c. I, II and III only
d. I, II, III and IV only
e. I, II, III, IV and V

158. **The sales of a company are also known as the company's:**
a. cash flow
b. net income
c. costs
d. revenues

159. **The income statement from top to bottom typically contains:**
a. revenues minus all expenses to give a figure for the net income
b. assets and liabilities
c. cash flows
d. stocks and bonds

160. **The income statement could be summarized as:**
a. stocks minus bonds
b. revenues minus cost of goods sold minus operating expenses minus non-operating expenses, such as interest and taxes, to arrive at the net income
c. revenues minus operating expenses minus taxes minus dividends minus cash flows
d. assets minus liabilities

161. **One of the key principles of the income statement is that it is intended to show the company as:**
a. historical entity - it is intended to capture the distant past
b. a going concern - a company that is in business and will continue operations
c. a company in liquidation - a company that will finish operations with no need to reinvest
d. a dormant company - a company that is currently not active

162. **The terms 'top line' and 'bottom line' correspond to where the items appear on the:**
a. balance sheet
b. income statement
c. cash flow statement
d. annual report

163. **A company's 'top line' refers to:**
a. its earnings
b. its revenues
c. its cash flows
d. its dividends

164. A company's 'bottom line' refers to:
a. its earnings
b. its revenues
c. its cash flows
d. its dividends

165. When a company makes a loss, which of the following is certain to be true:
a. the revenues are negative
b. cash flow will be negative
c. earnings will be negative
d. earnings will be up

166. True or False: We can capture a company's sales over a given period and subtract all expenses including interest and taxes to find out how much profit the company is making.

167. True of False: When a company has sales, the income statement illustrates that debtholders get paid interest before earnings are calculated.

168. True or False: The earnings of the company are more relevant for equityholders than they are for debtholders.

169. True or False: The structure of the income statement typically gives a very clear indication as to whether bondholders or equityholders get paid first.

170. True or False: Whether debtholders or equityholders get paid first is relevant to the discussion of risk and returns.

171. Companies can do all of the following with their earnings except:
a. retain them
b. pay them as dividends
c. show them on their income statements
d. call them revenues

172. The income statement is:
a. a snapshot at a point in time
b. a summary of events over a period of time
c. not usually in the annual report
d. the same thing as a balance sheet

173. Which one of the following terms is not like the other three:
a. net income
b. earnings
c. profits
d. revenues

174. The income statement would contain the following entries:
I. revenues
II. operating expenses
III. earnings
IV. assets
V. liabilities

a. I only
b. I and II only
c. I, II and III only

d. I, II, III and IV only
e. I, II, III, IV and V

175. **True or False: Companies can choose to pay out a part of their profits or net income in the form of a dividend.**

176. **Which of the following could cause higher earnings, all other things being equal:**
I. revenues were higher
II. taxes were lower
III. the company had a one-off gain
IV. the interest expense was lower
V. material costs/cost of goods sold were lower

a. I only
b. I and II only
c. I, II and III only
d. I, II, III and IV only
e. I, II, III, IV and V

177. **True or False: The income statement balances.**

178. **The net margin of a company is defined as the net income divided by the revenues. The net margin indicates which of the following for the period:**
I. the earnings generated per dollar of revenues
II. the company's profitability
III. how much of every dollar of sales made it to earnings for that period
IV. the company's balance sheet structure
V. the number of shareholders in the company

a. I only
b. I and II only
c. I, II and III only
d. I, II, III and IV only
e. I, II, III, IV and V

179. **True or False: Earnings that are retained within the company (i.e. not paid out as dividends) would end up in the shareholders' equity portion of the balance sheet.**

180. **True or False: The choice of depreciation method can affect a company's earnings.**

181. **Companies that have earnings of zero are:**
a. bankrupt
b. not making revenues
c. breaking even
d. having large losses

182. **True or False: The income statement is intended to show a company as a going concern.**

QUESTIONS 183 & 184 ARE LINKED.

183. **True or False: When a company purchases a major piece of equipment to be used for a number of years, it might pay for it all at once or over time. In either case, the income statement would not show the entire cost in any one year, but instead show an annual expense to reflect the use of the item.**

184. The cost of this asset would typically be spread as annual expenses over the useful life of the item. This expense is known as:
a. cost of goods sold
b. tax expense
c. depreciation
d. earnings

185. The entry on the income statement that reflects the material costs of items sold is:
a. operating expenses
b. cost of goods sold
c. interest expense
d. taxes

186. Depreciation can also be described as:
a. the cost of employees
b. the cost of renting an office
c. an expense for wear and tear that is intended to capture the reduction in value of an item over its useful life
d. company sales

187. A company with costs that are fixed in the short-term, sees its revenues decline very suddenly by 10% - the earnings of the company are likely to be down:
a. less than 10%
b. 10%
c. significantly more than 10%
d. not at all

188. A sudden 10% rise in the revenues of a company is likely to cause:
a. earnings to rise by less than 10%
b. earnings to also rise by exactly 10% always
c. earnings to stay the same
d. earnings to rise by potentially much more than 10%

189. Company 'RED' supplies paint to the car manufacturer 'WHEELS'. This paint would be recognized as follows:
I. revenues for the company RED
II. revenues for the company WHEELS
III. cost of goods sold for the company RED
IV. cost of goods sold for the company WHEELS
V. assets for both companies

a. I only
b. II only
c. II and III only
d. I and IV only
e. V only

190. Which of the following would not impact the earnings of a company:
a. a decline in revenues due to a slowing economy
b. a rise in material costs
c. an increase in the tax rate the company has to pay
d. an increase in the company's dividend

191. **True or False: The net margin is a measure of the profitability of a company and is intended to show how much each dollar of revenues or sales provides in terms of net income. It is calculated by dividing net income by revenues (in %).**

192. **True or False: We could prepare an income statement for our personal financial situation by summarizing a typical month or year. A detailed statement of this type could show where our money is going and how much is left over, and could be used to figure out how much more we could theoretically save.**

193. **True of False: We could schematically and logically represent a company by showing its assets on the left side, and the way that it has funded itself on the right side.**

194. **True or False: By showing a company's assets, liabilities and shareholders' equity, we can get a very good sense for the amount of leverage in the company.**

195. **True or False: Showing the assets of a company on the left side, and how these assets are funded on the right side is known as a balance sheet.**

196. **If the assets are found on the left side, which of the following would typically be found on the right side of a balance sheet:**
   a. cash
   b. shareholders' equity and liabilities
   c. revenues
   d. cash flow

197. **Companies are financed, in general, by:**
   a. assets and liabilities
   b. equity and debt
   c. debt and bonds
   d. assets and stocks

198. **On a balance sheet, the assets are shown typically on:**
   a. the left side
   b. the right side
   c. the top
   d. the bottom

199. **On a balance sheet, the right side typically shows:**
   a. the assets
   b. shareholders' equity and liabilities
   c. the income
   d. the revenues

200. **True or False: The assets on the left side of the balance sheet equal the value of the shareholders' equity and liabilities on the right side.**

201. **The balance sheet is:**
   a. a snapshot at a point in time
   b. a summary of events over a period of time
   c. not usually in the annual report
   d. the same thing as an income statement

202. **Which items on the balance sheet balance:**
   a. assets on one side and debt on the other
   b. assets on one side and equity on the other
   c. assets and debt on one side and equity on the other

d. assets on one side and equity and debt on the other

203. When the value of the assets of a healthy company go up greatly:
a. the liabilities do not change that much - but the shareholders' equity goes up greatly
b. neither shareholders' equity nor liabilities go up
c. the liabilities go up greatly
d. the cost of goods sold of the income statement reflects this increase

204. The main beneficiaries of a rise in the value of the assets of a healthy company are:
a. lenders to the company
b. bondholders of the company
c. shareholders or owners of the company
d. government bondholders

205. Bonds that a company has issued to finance itself would appear in:
a. the assets portion of the company's balance sheet
b. the equity portion of the company's balance sheet
c. the liabilities portion of the company's balance sheet
d. they would not be shown

206. If a company buys a factory, that factory would appear on:
a. the asset portion of that company's balance sheet
b. the equity portion of that company's balance sheet
c. the liabilities portion of that company's balance sheet
d. nowhere

207. Stocks that a company issues would appear where on the balance sheet:
a. the assets side (left side)
b. as shareholders' equity (right side)
c. the liabilities side (right side)
d. as revenues (top of income statement)

208. If a company invested some of its surplus cash in government bonds, these bonds would appear where on the balance sheet:
a. the assets side (left side)
b. as shareholders' equity (right side)
c. the liabilities side (right side)
d. as revenues (top of income statement)

209. True or False: When a company issues new shares to the market for cash, the right side of the balance sheet would show the equity getting larger and the left side would show the cash that was taken in from the sale.

210. If a company buys back its own shares with cash, the balance sheet will reflect:
a. a decrease in liabilities
b. a decrease in liabilities on the right side and a decrease in inventory on the left side
c. a decrease in equity on the right side and a decrease in debt on the right side
d. a decrease in cash on the left side and a decrease in equity on the right side

211. True or False: After a new item is added to the balance sheet such as a new asset, the balance sheet will still be required to balance.

212. Which of the following is true:
I. Assets = Equity + Liabilities
II. Equity + Liabilities = Assets
III. Equity = Assets - Liabilities

IV. Liabilities = Assets - Equity
V. Assets - Liabilities = Equity

a. I only
b. I and II only
c. I, II and III only
d. I, II, III and IV only
e. I, II, III, IV and V

213. The value at which things are recorded on the balance sheet is known as:
a. the book value
b. the market value
c. the loss value
d. the liquidation value

214. True or False: The balance sheet shows the capital provided by the owners the lenders.

215. True or False: If a company buys a piece of equipment using cash, cash on the left side of the balance sheet would go down and the item would be recorded on the left side of the balance sheet as an asset. The balance sheet would still balance.

216. True or False: If a company buys a piece of equipment using debt, the item would be recorded on the left side of the balance sheet and the debt on the right side. The balance sheet would still balance.

217. A company has financed itself through debt and equity (which also includes retained earnings). The ratio of debt to equity is a measure of:
a. the profitability of the company
b. the leverage on the balance sheet
c. the sales of the company
d. the cash flow of the company

218. In order to raise cash on its balance sheet, a company can do which of the following:
I. sell new shares
II. sell new bonds
III. borrow money from a bank
IV. sell assets for cash
V. retain more of its earnings

a. I only
b. I and II only
c. I, II and III only
d. I, II, III and IV only
e. I, II, III, IV and V

219. In the above example, which of the actions that the company could take would not increase the size of the balance sheet (i.e. make the left side larger and the right side larger).
I. sell new shares
II. sell new bonds
III. borrow money from a bank
IV. sell assets for cash
V. retain more of its earnings

a. I only
b. II only
c. III and V only

d. IV only
e. I, II, III, IV and V

220. **True or False: We can use the concept of a balance sheet to look at our own finances.**

221. **True or False: We can prepare a balance sheet for our personal finances showing our assets, our debt and the equity. The equity in such a balance sheet would also be our net worth.**

222. **True or False: The concept of a balance sheet - the equity, the leverage, and their sensitivity to moves in the price of an asset can be used to think about many different investment situations.**

223. **The equity in our homes can be calculated by taking:**
a. the value of the home less any debts or mortgages against the home
b. the value of the home plus any debts or mortgages against the home
c. the amount of the mortgages on the home
d. the amount of rent that we pay

QUESTIONS 224 - 230 ARE LINKED.

224. **An investor buys an asset using 50% equity (own money) and borrowing the rest. The interest rate on the borrowed money is 8%. The amount borrowed is closest to:**
a. 10% of the asset
b. 20% of the asset
c. 50% of the asset
d. 100% of the asset

225. **The purchaser of the asset can also be referred to as:**
I. the owner
II. the provider of equity capital
III. the provider of debt capital
IV. the bondholder
V. the lender

a. I only
b. I and II only
c. I, II and III only
d. I, II, III and IV only
e. I, II, III, IV and V

226. **If the asset price rises by 20%, the return to the provider of the debt capital is closest to:**
a. 8%
b. 10%
c. 20%
d. 40%

227. **If the asset price falls by 20%, the return to the provider of the equity capital is closest to:**
a. 8%
b. -8%
c. -20%
d. -40%

228. **If the asset price falls by 20%, the return to the provider of the debt capital is closest to:**
a. 8%
b. -8%
c. -20%
d. -40%

229. **If the value of the asset rises by 20%, the return for the owner will be:**
   a. 8%
   b. 10%
   c. 20%
   d. 40%

230. **By how much would the value of the asset have to fall for the owner to lose all of his or her money:**
   a. 10%
   b. 20%
   c. 50%
   d. 100%

231. **True or False: The capital structure of a company refers to the structure of the company's financing on the right side of the balance sheet. These sources of capital have different 'seniorities' in terms of which receive interest first, and which are paid off first in the event of a bankruptcy or liquidation.**

232. **What is the correct order (from most senior to least senior) for the following sources of funding:**
   I. senior debt
   II. subordinated debt
   III. equity

   a. I, II, III
   b. III, II, I
   c. II, I, III
   d. III, I, II

233. **True or False: One of the main objectives of the cash flow statement is to calculate the change in cash levels over a given year.**

234. **True or False: The cash flow statement typically starts with the net income from the income statement and then makes certain adjustments to calculate cash flow from operations. Cash flow from investing and financing are also looked separately at in the cash flow statement.**

235. **True or False: Depreciation on the income statement is a non-cash charge.**

236. **True or False: A share issue would not be shown on the income statement but it impacts the company - in particular cash levels and the equity on the balance sheet. A share issue would be shown on the cash flow statement and the balance sheet.**

237. **Cash flow statements are useful because:**
   I. there are non-cash entries on the income statement such as depreciation
   II. income statements focus on operations and not financing or investing
   III. the income statement might recognize revenues even though the cash has not been received
   IV. monitoring the cash position of a company is very important to ensure survival
   V. income statements show the company as a going concern but might not show all cash flows exactly as they take place

   a. I only
   b. I and II only
   c. I, II and III only
   d. I, II, III and IV only
   e. I, II, III, IV and V

238. **A cash flow statement is typically split into the following categories to reflect where the cash flows took place:**
   a. operating, investing and financing activities
   b. buying and selling
   c. assets and liabilities
   d. revenues, costs and income entries

239. **True or False: The net change in cash that is calculated from the cash flow statement would be reflected in the balance sheet over time.**

240. **True or False: Depreciation is reflected (and accumulated) on the balance sheet showing how assets are depreciating over time by allowing a net book value to be calculated.**

241. **Earnings are more relevant for equityholders than debtholders because:**
   I. debtholders are paid interest before earnings are even calculated
   II. earnings can be paid out as dividends which equityholders receive
   III. if the earnings are retained they become a part of shareholders' equity
   IV. equityholders own the company; whatever is left over after expenses and liabilities is effectively theirs
   V. equityholders are always paid all earnings in cash every year in all cases

   a. I only
   b. I and II only
   c. I, II and III only
   d. I, II, III and IV only
   e. I, II, III, IV and V

242. **A company buys a major piece of equipment that has a useful life of 10 years using cash. Which of the following would be expected to happen:**
   I. the cash flow statement would show the outgoing cash flow
   II. the balance sheet would reflect a decrease in cash and the acquisition of this equipment
   III. the income statement would reflect a deprecation charge each year over the useful life
   IV. the balance sheet over time would reflect the accumulated depreciation to show the reduction in book value since purchase
   V. the full cost of the piece of equipment would be recorded as a cost in the income statement

   a. I only
   b. I and II only
   c. I, II and III only
   d. I, II, III and IV only
   e. I, II, III, IV and V

TOTAL: 95 QUESTIONS

Financial Markets

243. **True or False: Stocks and bonds trade on financial markets.**

244. **True or False: One of the main benefits of a market is that it allows many different entities to come together to do business.**

245. **Financial markets exist to:**
    a. provide a place for gamblers
    b. allow governments to have an IPO
    c. allow providers and users of capital to interact
    d. allow private equity to trade

246. **True or False: Investors come to the financial markets seeking a return.**

247. **True or False: The return that financial markets provide can be a key element of how savers and investors compound their money.**

248. **Ideally, financial markets:**
    a. provide a place for investors to earn returns
    b. allow companies that need capital to raise it
    c. provide transparent and liquid trading in securities
    d. all of the above

249. **True or False: Financial markets have been around for hundreds of years.**

250. **True or False: Financial markets offer advantages to both providers and users of capital.**

251. **Advantages of financial markets for users of capital can include:**
    I. access to more investors
    II. a higher profile for firm
    III. an externally determined price for equity and debt
    IV. easier access to capital
    V. less reporting requirements

    a. I only
    b. II only
    c. I,III and V only
    d. II and IV only
    e. I, II, III and IV

252. **True or False: One of the key roles of the financial markets is to figure out to whom money should be provided based on the expected ability to provide a return.**

253. **The financial markets can provide which of the following advantages to providers of capital or savers and investors:**
    I. choice
    II. centralization of transactions
    III. improved transparency
    IV. improved liquidity
    V. no risk in any investment

    a. I only
    b. II only
    c. I,III and V only
    d. II and IV only

e. I, II, III and IV

254. Which of the following is/are function(s) of the financial markets:

I. to make appropriate allocations of capital possible
II. to allow good firms to get access to funding
III. to provide a place for savers and investors to seek returns
IV. to allow buying and selling of stocks and bonds
V. to give investors choice

a. I only
b. I and II only
c. I, II and III only
d. I, II, III and IV only
e. I, II, III, IV and V

255. Financial markets in principle allow all of the following except:

a. providers of capital the potential to compound their money
b. users of capital access to capital via investors that also participate there
c. investors to have access to a broad selection of investments
d. a guaranteed return for providers of capital or investors in all cases

256. Financial markets are intended to ensure that there is:

a. capital for all companies
b. capital for bad companies
c. an efficient allocation of capital
d. a random allocation of capital

257. Which of the following trade on financial markets:

I. stocks
II. bonds
III. commodities
IV. derivatives
V. currencies

a. I only
b. I and II only
c. I, II and III only
d. I, II, III and IV only
e. I, II, III, IV and V

258. Securities including stocks and bonds trade in the financial markets at:

a. the book value
b. the market value
c. the loss value
d. the liquidation value

259. True or False: There are many different types of financial markets that we can speak about - for example, the stock market, the bond market etc.

260. The market for government debt that has been split into smaller slices to facilitate trading is known as the:

a. government bond market
b. government equity market
c. corporate bond market
d. stock market

261. The market for securities that represent ownership in companies is known as the:

a. government bond market
b. government equity market
c. corporate bond market
d. stock market

262. A large publicly traded company would most likely raise equity capital via the:

a. commodities market
b. corporate bond market
c. government bond market
d. stock market

263. A large publicly traded company that has a large number of bonds outstanding, would most likely raise large sums of additional debt capital via the:

a. commodities market
b. corporate bond market
c. government bond market
d. stock market

264. Well-functioning financial markets benefit from:

I. transparency - the ability to see prices and get information readily
II. liquidity - it is easy to buy and sell securities
III. many participants
IV. choice for investors in terms of investments
V. a regulatory structure - in terms of how information is disclosed, insider trading laws etc.

a. I only
b. I and II only
c. I, II and III only
d. I, II, III and IV only
e. I, II, III, IV and V

265. The stock market has something in common with which of the following other markets:

a. the government bond market - both are for debt
b. the corporate bond market - in both cases the users of capital/issuers are companies
c. the market for government debt - they both have the same users of capital
d. the market for government securities - in both the government is the user of capital

266. True or False: In financial markets like major stock exchanges, large numbers of investors buy and sell large numbers of securities during market trading hours, and sometimes even after the market closes.

267. Financial markets are important because they facilitate:

a. the interaction between governments and shareholders
b. the interaction between accountants and lawyers
c. the interaction between shareholders and bondholders
d. the interaction between providers and users of capital

268. A privately held company first sells stock to the public and lists itself on the stock exchange at the:

a. company formation
b. first bond sale
c. initial public offering
d. private equity placement

269. A company that already has its shares trading on the stock market issuing more shares is referred to as a(n):

a. initial public offering
b. IPO
c. secondary offering
d. bond sale

270. **True or False: The market that comprises initial public offerings is sometimes also referred to as the primary market. The market for stocks that have already been issued can also be referred to as the secondary market.**

271. **An investor that buys a stock on a stock exchange is most likely to be buying it from:**
a. the government
b. the company that issued it
c. another investor
d. the tax authorities

272. **An investor might sell a stock for which of the following reasons:**
I. the investor believes the stock will go down
II. the investor needs cash
III. the stock has reached a price target
IV. the investor is unsure about the stock market
V. the investor owned the stock as part of a hedge against another position and is getting out of the overall position

a. I only
b. I and II only
c. I, II and III only
d. I, II, III and IV only
e. I, II, III, IV and V

273. **The expression a 'zero-sum game' refers to:**
a. a game where no one wins
b. a game where no one loses
c. a situation in which the gains of the winners equal the losses of the losers
d. a situation in which the same winners always win and the same losers always lose

274. **Which of the following is generally considered a zero-sum game or situation:**
a. communication and cooperation
b. gambling
c. saving and investing
d. the stock market

275. **True or False: A market in which securities trade by phone or computer is known as an OTC (over-the-counter) market.**

276. **True or False: Because of their importance to society, to investors and to companies and governments, securities markets are often regulated.**

277. **True or False: The fact that a securities market is regulated ensures that no investment can lose a significant amount of value.**

278. **Well-designed securities laws in developed countries are intended to:**
a. allow very few players to get rich
b. allow a small group to benefit from insider information
c. level the playing field between different investors and promote broad participation in saving and investing
d. turn securities markets into a place where no one can gain any benefit

TOTAL: 36 QUESTIONS

INVESTMENTS - DEBT AND BONDS

279. **True or False: The issuer of a bond is typically borrowing money, the purchaser of a bond is typically lending money.**

280. **Debt investments and bonds relate to:**
    a. ownership
    b. lending
    c. equity
    d. shareholding

281. **True or False: When we keep money in a bank account, the bank typically pays interest because the money has value to the bank. They are able to pay interest because they can do something with the money that allows them to get interest (of which they pay us a part).**

282. **True or False: When we keep money in a bank account, we can think of ourselves as having lent money.**

283. **True or False: We can think of bonds as loans that have been converted into securities.**

284. **Differences between stocks and bonds include:**
    I. stocks represent ownership, bonds do not
    II. stocks are typically more volatile than bonds
    III. there are more different bonds than stocks available
    IV. stocks trade on the stock market, bonds do not
    V. bonds often have a limited life or maturity, stocks do not

    a. I only
    b. I and II only
    c. I, II and III only
    d. I, II, III and IV only
    e. I, II, III, IV and V

285. **Which of the following could be an issuer of bonds:**
    I. a foreign car company
    II. a pharmaceutical company
    III. a technology company
    IV. a foreign government
    V. our government

    a. I only
    b. I and II only
    c. I, II and III only
    d. I, II, III and IV only
    e. I, II, III, IV and V

286. **Debt investments like bonds are also generically often referred to as:**
    a. equities
    b. fixed income investments
    c. commodities
    d. convertibles

287. **True or False: Most governments are very large issuers of bonds.**

288. **Which of the following is not a typical characteristic of bonds:**

a. maturity
b. coupon
c. dividend
d. face value or par value or principal

289. **Which of the following can not be considered a form of debt, or a debt instrument:**
a. a bank loan
b. a savings account
c. a stock
d. a government bond

290. **The payment to bondholders by the issuer made periodically (for example twice a year) is:**
a. the dividend
b. the liability
c. the coupon
d. the revenues

291. **True or False: Bonds can be thought of as a series of cash flows.**

292. **True or False: Governments borrow money through the bond markets for major expenditures that they might have in one year. They are in a position to pay interest in large part as a result of the money they take in through taxes.**

293. **Investors that hold bonds are going to get a cash return while holding the bonds from:**
a. the coupon
b. the dividend
c. capital gains
d. depreciation

294. **The amount of money that an investor would receive on maturity of a bond is known as the:**
a. depreciation
b. face value or par value
c. coupon
d. price

295. **The periodic payments that bonds make, which represent a form of interest, are known as:**
a. the maturity
b. coupons
c. principal
d. duration

296. **The time to repayment of the principal of the bond is known as the bond's:**
a. maturity
b. coupon
c. principal
d. duration

297. **Which of the following terms is not like the other three:**
a. maturity value
b. face value
c. par value
d. coupon

298. **A measure of the time it takes an investor to receive payments both through coupons and the principal payment is known as the:**
a. coupon

b. duration
c. maturity
d. face value

299. True or False: One definition of duration is that it is the cash-weighted average time to maturity of a bond.

300. True or False: Most bonds in the United States make semi-annual payments.

301. If a bond makes semi-annual payments, it would:
a. make a payment every two years
b. make two payments per year
c. make two payments per month
d. make payments every two months

302. Which of the following best describes what typically happens when an investor sells a bond:
I. the investor is reducing his ownership in the company
II. the investor is reducing the amount lent
III. the company repays the investor
IV. the investor that buys the bond directly or indirectly pays the seller
V. nothing happens

a. I only
b. II only
c. I and III only
d. II and IV only
e. I and V only

303. True or False: In the United States, the US Department of the Treasury is responsible for issuing government debt.

304. True of False: Debt issued by the US Treasury includes T-Bills, T-Notes and T-Bonds.

305. A T-Bill in the Unites States is:
a. a form of equity
b. short-term debt (maturity up to one year) issued by corporations
c. short-term debt (maturity up to one year) issued by the US Treasury on behalf of the government
d. long-term debt issued by the US government

306. Debt securities with maturities of up to one year issued by the US Treasury are known as:
a. Treasury Bills
b. Treasury Notes
c. Treasury Bonds
d. Treasury Inflation Protected Securities (TIPS)

307. Debt securities with maturities of between one year and ten years issued by the US Treasury are known as:
a. Treasury Bills
b. Treasury Notes
c. Treasury Bonds
d. Treasury Inflation Protected Securities (TIPS)

308. Debt securities with maturities of over ten years issued by the US Treasury are known as:
a. Treasury Bills
b. Treasury Notes
c. Treasury Bonds

d. Treasury Inflation Protected Securities (TIPS)

309. **Debt securities where the principal is adjusted by changes in the consumer price index (CPI) that are issued by the US Treasury are known as:**
a. Treasury Bills
b. Treasury Notes
c. Treasury Bonds
d. Treasury Inflation Protected Securities (TIPS)

310. **Which of the following have the longest maturity:**
a. Treasury Bills
b. Treasury Notes
c. Treasury Bonds
d. Certificates of Deposit

311. **US government bonds are considered 'risk-free' because:**
a. they can never go down in price
b. if interest rates go up, they rise in value
c. there is considered to be no risk of default
d. US Stocks are also considered 'risk-free'

312. **A bond that is issued at a discount, that does not pay a coupon and where the return comes from the appreciation of the bond towards its principal or par value is known as:**
a. a stock
b. a dividend-paying bond
c. a zero-coupon bond
d. a government bond

313. **Commercial paper is:**
a. an unsecured short-term debt issued by a corporation
b. debt issued by the government
c. a deposit for a period of time offered by a bank
d. a form of equity

314. **True or False: Corporations are able to issue different types of debt, with different maturities, depending on how they would like to repay it, market conditions, and what the funds are to be used for.**

315. **Certificates of deposit (CDs) are:**
a. an unsecured short-term debt issued by a corporation
b. debt issued by the government
c. a deposit for a period of time offered by a bank
d. a form of equity

316. **In the United States, certificates of deposit are:**
I. saving products offered by banks
II. insured by the FDIC if the bank is insured by the FDIC
III. typically for a certain time frame - they are also often referred to as 'time deposits'
IV. potentially interesting for savers as alternatives to keeping money in a savings account
V. potentially able to offer a higher rate of interest than a savings account where the money can be withdrawn on demand

a. I only
b. I and II only
c. I, II and III only
d. I, II, III and IV only

e. I, II, III, IV and V

317. **True or False: Because there are so many different agencies that want to borrow money, and so many different situations for which they want to borrow money, and because there are also so many different ways of repaying the money, in the end there are many different types of bonds that exist and that can be created, and there is correspondingly a very large and diverse bond market.**

318. **Stocks trade on a stock exchange which often has a physical location where the stocks are traded or where records are kept. Bonds trade:**
   a. on a bond exchange
   b. on the same stock exchange
   c. over-the-counter: meaning by telephone and computers largely
   d. on the stock market

319. **To categorize bonds, bonds have different ratings that are assigned by:**
   a. investors
   b. rating agencies like Moody's and S&P
   c. governments
   d. tax authorities

320. **True of False: Rating agencies rate bonds in terms of credit worthiness.**

321. **True of False: Rating agencies analyze bonds to the best of their abilities, but the bonds of an issuer can be downgraded when the outlook for that firm or bond changes.**

322. **True or False: A bond's rating is fixed and can not change.**

323. **The yield or implied interest rate that longer-term government bonds provide is set by:**
   a. the central bank
   b. companies
   c. governments
   d. investors who buy and sell the bonds in the market

324. **True or False: A benefit, like a cash payment is typically worth more to us the sooner we receive it.**

325. **True or False: Valuing bonds, and valuing investments in general, has a lot to do with assessing today's value of future expected cash flows.**

326. **True or False: A cash flow that we receive today is worth more than the same amount received in the future under normal circumstances.**

327. **When interest rates for a certain period rise, the value of a fixed amount of cash to be received in the future, would be worth _________ to us today than before the interest rate rise.**
   a. more
   b. less
   c. the same
   d. an equivalent amount

328. **Normally, when the maturity of a bond or loan is longer, the interest or return is:**
   a. lower
   b. higher
   c. the same
   d. all loans have the same maturity

329. **Banks are theoretically able to offer a higher rate of interest when they know that they will have our deposit for longer.**

a. this is true and is one of the principles behind certificates of deposit
b. this is not true
c. this is true and is one of the principles behind equity investing
d. this is true and is one of the principles behind foreign exchange

330. **True or False: A bond can trade at a premium to par if interest rates change from the time the bond was issued.**

331. **The price of a bond could fall when its yield rises because:**
I. investors in new similar-risk bonds would expect a higher yield, making a bond that had a lower yield issued previously worth less
II. the discount factor that we would use to discount the bond's future cash flows rises meaning that future cash flows are worth less
III. bond prices do not fall when yields rise - the question is irrelevant
IV. the yield is a reflection of the risk of the bond -the higher yield could be caused by an increase in risk and the bond would therefore be worth less
V. when the yield rises, companies immediately cut dividends making bonds worth less

a. I only
b. II only
c. III only
d. I and V only
e. I, II and IV only

QUESTIONS 332-334 ARE LINKED.

332. **A 5-year bond is issued with a par value of $1,000 and with a 7% semi-annual coupon. How many coupons would an investor expect to receive per year:**
a. 0.5
b. 2
c. 24
d. 6

333. **Each coupon payment that the investor would expect to receive would be:**
a. $70
b. $14
c. $7
d. $35

334. **In total, how many coupon payments would an investor expect to receive over the entire life of the bond:**
a. 2.5
b. 24
c. 10
d. 1

335. **When a bond becomes more risky, the return or yield that investors require is:**
a. higher
b. lower
c. the same
d. not present

336. **Most investors that are saving and investing would have exposure to bonds by:**
a. buying and selling individual bonds actively
b. buying and holding bonds to maturity
c. investing in a bond mutual fund

d. they should not have any bond exposure

TOTAL: 58 QUESTIONS

EQUITY AND STOCKS, INDICES AND VALUATION

337. **True or False: Equity relates to ownership, and stocks are slices of equity or ownership of a company, where the equity has been split into smaller pieces.**

338. **True or False: The equity of a company can either be private or public depending on how widely it is available, and in particular whether it is available through a stock market.**

339. **A private company is typically owned by:**
    a. investors through the stock market
    b. a limited group of investors, often including the founders of the company
    c. investors who have bought bonds
    d. the stock market traders

340. **Which of the following statements regarding private equity is true:**
    I. private equity through a financial services company is typically reserved for professionals or high net worth investors
    II. private equity is very illiquid and is often considered higher risk
    III. private equity is equity that is not directly available through a stock exchange
    IV. owners of private equity are often the founders of the company, their family and friends, perhaps some high net worth investors and potentially later on private equity funds
    V. it is typically more difficult to get information regarding private companies

    a. I only
    b. I and II only
    c. I, II and III only
    d. I, II, III and IV only
    e. I, II, III, IV and V

341. **The equity of a company that is operating normally (and not close to bankruptcy) is riskier than the debt of the same company because:**
    I. when a company makes money, bondholders are paid first
    II. when the assets of a company go down, equity is affected more
    III. when the assets of a company go down, the debt is affected less
    IV. in case of company bankruptcy, bondholders are typically repaid first
    V. equity is considered less senior in the capital structure

    a. I only
    b. I and II only
    c. I, II and III only
    d. I, II, III and IV only
    e. I, II, III, IV and V

342. **True or False: Investing directly or indirectly (through funds) in stocks or shares is the most widespread way for investors to invest in the equity of companies.**

343. **Which of the following could be an issuer of stocks:**
    I. a foreign car company
    II. a pharmaceutical company
    III. a technology company
    IV. a foreign government
    V. our government

    a. I only
    b. I and II only

c. I, II and III only
d. I, II, III and IV only
e. I, II, III, IV and V

344. <u>True or False: A shareholder is a part-owner of a company.</u>

345. **Professional stock investors seek to allocate money:**
a. to companies that will not deliver a return
b. to companies that need it
c. based on a desire to be helpful
d. to companies that can deliver a return

346. **As shareholders we might care about:**
I. company earnings
II. company profitability
III. sales growth
IV. cash flows
V. the quality of the company's management

a. I only
b. I and II only
c. I, II and III only
d. I, II, III and IV only
e. I, II, III, IV and V

347. **While holding stocks, investors often get a return from:**
a. the coupon
b. the dividend
c. capital gains
d. depreciation

348. **The total return to a shareholder between purchase and sale comes from:**
a. the bond yield
b. the dividend yield
c. the capital appreciation
d. the dividend yield and capital appreciation

349. **True or False: Investors in the equity of a business should think about whether it makes sense for them to be owners or part-owners of that business.**

350. **When a healthy business does very well, the ones that will benefit the most are the:**
a. owners or shareholders
b. lenders or bondholders
c. corporate bondholders
d. government bondholders

351. **True or False: Although equityholders as a group can play a role in getting the management of a company replaced over a medium-term timeframe, for the most part they are dependent on the management to make decisions that are in the best interests of the company and its shareholders.**

352. **The management of a company:**
I. plays a major role in determining returns for investors
II. could be corrupt and steal from the company at the expense of shareholders
III. plays a major role in determining if the company is a winner or a loser in the industry
IV. might make very bad acquisitions
V. might have shareholders' interests at heart - or they might not

a. I only
b. I and II only
c. I, II and III only
d. I, II, III and IV only
e. I, II, III, IV and V

353. Bad company management can hurt returns for shareholders by:

I. paying themselves too much - taking money out of the company that does not make it to earnings
II. making bad investment decisions
III. not retaining key staff
IV. acquiring other companies at prices that are too high
V. focussing on the wrong business activities

a. I only
b. I and II only
c. I, II and III only
d. I, II, III and IV only
e. I, II, III, IV and V

354. True or False: Predicting exactly what management is going to do next is very easy.

355. A company should care about its share price for which of the following reasons:

I. it creates positive publicity
II. management compensation is often linked to the share price
III. if the company wants to sell more shares, having a high share price allows more capital to be raised for the same percentage of the company that is sold
IV. if the company wants to make an acquisition, having a strong share price can be beneficial
V. companies never care about their share price

a. I only
b. I and II only
c. I, II and III only
d. I, II, III and IV only
e. I, II, III, IV and V

356. In a well-functioning securities market, companies and their managements should care about the performance of their shares alongside shareholders because:

I. often their compensation is linked to the performance of the shares
II. they are also often shareholders
III. if the share price does not perform, the management is at risk of being relieved of their duties by shareholders as a group
IV. strong share price performance can create positive momentum for a business and affect the operations positively as well
V. the company might want to make an acquisition and use its shares to do so, in which case having highly valued shares is a big plus

a. I only
b. I and II only
c. I, II and III only
d. I, II, III and IV only
e. I, II, III, IV and V

357. Which of the following best describes what typically happens when an investor sells a stock:

I. the investor is reducing their ownership in the company

II. the investor is reducing the amount lent to the company
III. the company repays the investor
IV. the investor will receive cash proceeds from whoever buys the stock via an intermediary system
V. nothing happens

a. I only
b. II only
c. I and III only
d. I and IV only
e. I and V only

358. Which of the following statements regarding equity investing is true:

I. investing in the equity of a company is typically considered riskier than investing in its debt
II. investing as an owner should be based on understanding the company and its business
III. many professional equity investors spend most of their time analyzing companies
IV. the companies that are the winners in an industry often have the best share price performance
V. companies that are in a bad industry, or that are the losers in an industry, over time can go bankrupt and see their share prices go to zero

a. I only
b. I and II only
c. I, II and III only
d. I, II, III and IV only
e. I, II, III, IV and V

359. True or False: There are significant groups of investors that believe that the analysis of public companies is a waste of time even for professional investors because markets have become so efficient.

360. Good sources of information with respect to companies include:

I. annual reports
II. company websites
III. industry websites
IV. research reports
V. company press releases and filings

a. I only
b. I and II only
c. I, II and III only
d. I, II, III and IV only
e. I, II, III, IV and V

361. Typical rights of a common shareholder in a company include:

I. a vote for company directors
II. the right to assets during a liquidation after bondholders are paid
III. a right to vote on major company issues
IV. the right to the company's revenues
V. a first claim on the company's assets

a. I only
b. I and II only
c. I, II and III only
d. I, II, III and IV only
e. I, II, III, IV and V

362. **True or False: A corporate raider can be described as an investor that buys the securities of a company with a view to enhancing value through some sort of action.**

363. **The difference between a very large shareholder and the holder of a single stock is:**

I. a very large shareholder is likely to have more influence on management
II. a very large shareholder has more shareholder votes
III. a very large shareholder might have to declare the shareholding to regulatory authorities
IV. a very large shareholder will take longer to sell shares and/or might move the share price more when selling
V. a very large shareholder can make day-to-day decisions in the company

a. I only
b. I and II only
c. I, II and III only
d. I, II, III and IV only
e. I, II, III, IV and V

364. **Holders of a single common stock can influence a company by:**

I. having a shareholder vote at the annual meeting
II. voting during the election of a board of directors
III. deciding on corporate strategy
IV. making hiring decisions
V. firing employees

a. I only
b. I and II only
c. I, II and III only
d. I, II, III and IV only
e. I, II, III, IV and V

365. **True or False: The dividend is typically a periodic cash payment by companies to shareholders, that provides a return while the shares are held.**

366. **An investor in a single stock receives:**

a. the earnings per share of the company
b. the revenues per share of the company
c. the cash flow of the company
d. the dividends, and any capital appreciation between purchase and sale, minus taxes

367. **The amount that a company pays out from it earnings to shareholders is known as:**

a. the dividend
b. the shares
c. the earnings
d. the revenues

368. **True or False: Instead of paying a dividend, companies can choose to retain earnings, in which case they would be kept within the company.**

369. **True or False: Companies that have less of a need to reinvest, or that are in industries that are not growing as quickly, often pay out more of their earnings in the form of dividends.**

370. **When a company's earnings drop significantly and the stock market is performing poorly, a company that wants to retain cash is most likely going to:**

a. cut its dividend
b. raise its dividend
c. buy back shares

d. decrease borrowing

371. **Companies that do not pay a dividend are:**
   a. bankrupt
   b. corrupt
   c. cheating shareholders
   d. retaining earnings

372. **The dividend per share divided by the earnings per share, is also known as:**
   a. the dividend yield
   b. the current yield
   c. the payout ratio
   d. the net margin

373. **The dividend per share divided by the share price, is also known as:**
   a. the dividend yield
   b. the current yield
   c. the payout ratio
   d. the net margin

374. **The dividend yield is:**
   a. a bond yield
   b. the percentage capital appreciation
   c. the percentage return received in the form of dividends based on the current share price
   d. the dividend divided by the earnings

375. **A company has a payout ratio of 30%; what percentage of the earnings is the company retaining:**
   a. 30%
   b. 50%
   c. 70%
   d. 100%

376. **Which of the following is not a reason for a company to retain earnings:**
   a. it wants to reinvest in its business
   b. it wants to avoid raising more equity or debt capital in the future
   c. it has a lot of investment opportunities
   d. it wants to increase its dividend yield

377. **It would make sense for a company to pay a larger dividend when:**
   I. it does not require these earnings for investment in its industry
   II. shareholders have more profitable investment opportunities than the company does
   III. the firm is operating in a mature industry where investment needs are low
   IV. the company has more capital than it needs
   V. the company is considering ways of raising capital

   a. I only
   b. I and II only
   c. I, II and III only
   d. I, II, III and IV only
   e. I, II, III, IV and V

378. **Which of the following companies would be most likely to pay a dividend:**
   a. a technology company
   b. a fast-growing company
   c. a utility
   d. a bond

379. **The percentage return that an investor would receive in the form of dividends is:**
   a. the dividend yield - it is the dividend divided by stock price
   b. the percentage capital appreciation - it is the percentage increase in the stock price divided by the original price
   c. the bond yield - it is the coupon divided by the bond price
   d. the yield to maturity - it is the bond yield realized if the bond is held to maturity

380. **True or False: Companies sometimes buy back their own shares.**

381. **True or False: When companies buy back shares they are giving money back to shareholders. When companies pay dividends they are also giving money back to shareholders.**

382. **True or False: If a company feels that the market is not valuing its shares highly enough, it can buy its shares back in the market.**

383. **If a company makes a large extraordinary gain and it does not need or want to retain the capital, it would most likely:**
   a. raise its dividend permanently
   b. pay an extraordinary dividend
   c. raise equity capital
   d. raise debt capital

384. **Companies might buy back shares for all of the following reasons:**
   I. they believe the shares are undervalued
   II. they want to signal to the market that the shares are undervalued
   III. they have excess capital
   IV. they see this as an alternative to paying a dividend
   V. they are trying to raise capital

   a. I only
   b. I and II only
   c. I, II and III only
   d. I, II, III and IV only
   e. I, II, III, IV and V

385. **Which of the following terms might commentators use to group stocks:**
   I. blue-chip stocks
   II. growth stocks
   III. cyclical stocks
   IV. defensive stocks
   V. no-ownership stocks

   a. I only
   b. I and II only
   c. I, II and III only
   d. I, II, III and IV only
   e. I, II, III, IV and V

386. **The stock of a large and well-established company could be referred to as a:**
   a. blue chip stock
   b. growth stock
   c. defensive stock
   d. cyclical stock

387. **The stock of a company that has strong earnings and revenue growth might be referred to as a:**

a. blue chip stock
b. growth stock
c. defensive stock
d. cyclical stock

388. A stock that is very sensitive to the state of the economy could be referred to as a:
a. blue chip stock
b. growth stock
c. defensive stock
d. cyclical stock

389. A stock that analysts expect to be resilient in an economic downturn could be referred to as a:
a. blue chip stock
b. growth stock
c. defensive stock
d. cyclical stock

390. True or False: Categorizing stocks as 'growth' or 'blue-chip' stocks is not without risks since companies can change quite dramatically.

391. The specific area that concerns itself with how a company is run and how certain checks and balances are put in place to monitor management is known as:
a. government
b. corporate action
c. corporate governance
d. accounting

392. Public companies typically have external boards whose principal responsibility it is to:
a. help the company with its accounting
b. sell the company
c. act as a check on management
d. invest in the company

393. True or False: Public companies often have investor relations departments that communicate with investors and securities analysts, with a view to communicating information about the company, and keeping the company on investors' radar screens.

394. Which of the following statements about share prices and equity values is/are true:
I. a company can split its shares two for one - the number of shares outstanding would double (and the price would halve)
II. a share price does not capture all of the information regarding a company's equity market value
III. a low share price does not imply better value than a high share price
IV. the share price multiplied by the number of shares gives the market value of the equity
V. when share prices rise (and the number of shares is unchanged), equity market values rise

a. I only
b. I and II only
c. I, II and III only
d. I, II, III and IV only
e. I, II, III, IV and V

395. The market-cap or market capitalization of a company can be summarized as the:
I. share price times the number of shares
II. market value of the company's equity
III. market value of the company's debt and equity
IV. book value of the company

V. value of the company's assets

a. I only
b. I and II only
c. I, II and III only
d. I, II, III and IV only
e. I, II, III, IV and V

396. Which of the following does not capture the market value of the equity of a company:
a. the share price multiplied by the number of shares
b. the company's market-capitalization
c. the market value of all of the outstanding shares
d. the company's outstanding debt

397. A large-cap stock, is a stock that:
a. has a high share price
b. has strong revenues
c. has a large market-capitalization
d. has strong earnings

398. Terms that relate to stocks which one might find in the newspaper on a daily basis include:
I. price
II. dividend yield
III. P/E ratio
IV. name of the company
V. price change from the prior day

a. I only
b. I and II only
c. I, II and III only
d. I, II, III and IV only
e. I, II, III, IV and V

399. Which of the following could move a stock in the near-term:
I. statements by the company
II. rumors
III. a large seller
IV. a major decision by the company management
V. a change in the economic outlook from a well-recognized agency

a. I only
b. I and II only
c. I, II and III only
d. I, II, III and IV only
e. I, II, III, IV and V

400. If a stock has gone down recently, we can say that:
a. it will go up again soon
b. it will probably continue to go down
c. it should stabilize next
d. we should not draw conclusions about future performance from past performance

401. A company that reported their quarterly earnings and 'beat earnings estimates':
a. reported better than expected earnings
b. delivered very poor earnings
c. grew earnings over a long period

d. delivered earnings that were higher than revenues

402. **An investor who buys a stock 'on margin' is:**
I. borrowing money to buy the stock
II. using leverage
III. increasing the risk of the position
IV. magnifying returns both on the upside and downside
V. lending money

a. I only
b. I and II only
c. I, II and III only
d. I, II, III and IV only
e. I, II, III, IV and V

403. **When an investor buys a stock on margin, the amount that the investor is putting in of his or her own money is known as:**
a. the debt
b. the leverage
c. the margin
d. the stock price

404. **Buying a stock on margin involves:**
I. leverage
II. borrowing
III. a higher percentage loss for a given move in the stock
IV. trying to buy a fraction of a stock
V. short-selling the stock

a. I only
b. I and II only
c. I, II and III only
d. I, II, III and IV only
e. I, II, III, IV and V

405. **True or False: The stocks that we typically speak about are also known as a common stocks. Some companies have additional share classes beyond common stocks - such as preferred shares.**

406. **Which of the following are characteristics of preferred shares:**
I. they are more senior than common stock
II. they often have a negotiated dividend amount
III. they do not carry voting rights
IV. they are not as senior as bonds
V. they can never go down

a. I only
b. I and II only
c. I, II and III only
d. I, II, III and IV only
e. I, II, III, IV and V

407. **A company is considered bankrupt when:**
a. the company misses a dividend payment
b. it can not pay creditors and files for bankruptcy
c. the stock price loses 50% or more
d. the company loses a lot of money

408. <u>When a company files for bankruptcy, which of the following will typically end up with more control and a greater share of the assets:</u>

a. equityholders
b. bondholders
c. management
d. stockholders

409. <u>A company if the United States that files for bankruptcy will often be said to be:</u>

a. going into 'Chapter 0' - it refers to the chapter on very low stock prices
b. going into 'Chapter 10' - it refers to chapter 10 of the bankruptcy code
c. going into 'Chapter 11' - it refers to chapter 11 of the bankruptcy code
d. going into 'Chapter 12' - it refers to chapter 12 of the bankruptcy code

410. <u>True or False: Under US law, if a company is so far in debt that it does not want to seek protection from creditors and try to reorganize itself, then it can elect to cease operations entirely and have a trustee sell assets - this is known as Chapter 7 of the bankruptcy code.</u>

411. <u>When a company goes bankrupt:</u>

I. equityholders should expect to lose all of their money
II. bondholders/creditors might be involved in the restructuring process
III. bondholders/creditors could recover some of their money
IV. there is no chance that the company will be able to continue any form of operations
V. the company will always disappear completely very shortly thereafter

a. I only
b. I and II only
c. I, II and III only
d. I, II, III and IV only
e. I, II, III, IV and V

412. <u>If we believed that picking stocks was going to help us beat the market - things that we would probably look at to determine the outlook for a company's stock would include:</u>

I. the quality of the management of the company
II. whether we trusted the management of the company
III. the prospects for the company
IV. the earnings and future cash flows for the company
V. the valuation of the company on various metrics

a. I only
b. I and II only
c. I, II and III only
d. I, II, III and IV only
e. I, II, III, IV and V

413. <u>Fundamental stock analysis typically involves:</u>

a. financial ratios, financial statement analysis, and modeling
b. charts, price information, and price and volume ratios
c. an analysis of macroeconomic factors and economic forecasting
d. a quantitative analysis of government spending

414. <u>Technical stock and market analysis typically involves:</u>

a. financial ratios, financial statement analysis, and modeling
b. charts, price information, and price and volume ratios
c. an analysis of macroeconomic factors and economic forecasting
d. a quantitative scoring of management and key employees

415. **True or False: Securities laws are set up to try and ensure that all investors have access to the same information at the same time in order to make equally informed decisions.**

416. **In a properly functioning securities market, which of the following is not a common reason for which an investor might sell shares in a company:**
   a. his or her target price has been reached
   b. they need cash
   c. their view is that the shares will not perform that well
   d. they know exactly what will happen in the future and no one disagrees

417. **One of the big conceptual elements of the Glass-Steagall act pertained to:**
   a. investors not being able to invest
   b. an investor in stocks not being able to hold bonds
   c. a separation between commercial banking and the securities industries
   d. trading on insider information

418. **A well-functioning securities market has which of the following characteristics:**
   I. efficiency
   II. prices do not jump around by large amounts without substantial news
   III. a good regulatory framework
   IV. it is easy to buy and sell assets quickly
   V. timely and accurate information

   a. I only
   b. I and II only
   c. I, II and III only
   d. I, II, III and IV only
   e. I, II, III, IV and V

419. **Transactions in the stock market are most likely to take place when:**
   a. all investors have the same view
   b. all investors have the same time horizon
   c. different investors have different views and/or time horizons
   d. all investors are on holiday

420. **True or False: Investors can get a sense for the movement of an entire stock market by looking at a relevant stock market index.**

421. **True or False: A stock market index might combine information on many companies to provide a picture of how a certain market or segment of the market is behaving.**

422. **True or False: Different indices are calculated using different methods - the differences in methods relate to how security prices are combined to arrive at the index level.**

423. **Price-weighted and market-capitalization weighted refer to:**
   a. two different ways of calculating indices and hence two different types of indices
   b. two different types of companies
   c. two different types of bonds
   d. two different types of governments

424. **True or False: In a price-weighted index, companies with higher share prices have a higher weighting in the index.**

425. **True or False: In a market-capitalization weighted index, companies that are typically considered larger will have a higher weighting.**

426. Which of the following is not a stock market index:
a. the S&P 500
b. the Dow Jones Industrial Average
c. the Nasdaq Composite Index
d. the Lehman Aggregate Bond Index

427. True or False: A majority of the commonly used stock market indices are market capitalization weighted as opposed to price-weighted.

428. Which of the following is probably the best known example of a price-weighted index, with all of the other ones being market capitalization weighted:
a. the S&P 500
b. the Dow Jones Industrial Average
c. the Nasdaq Composite Index
d. the FTSE 100 Index

429. Which of the following are examples of stock market indices around the world:
I. the FTSE 100 Index
II. the CAC 40 Index
III. the Nikkei 225 Index
IV. the DAX Index
V. the Hang Seng

a. I only
b. I and II only
c. I, II and III only
d. I, II, III and IV only
e. I, II, III, IV and V

430. If the S&P 500 is up strongly, which of the following is a safe conclusion:
I. the market value of every US company has increased
II. the market value of all non-US companies is down
III. the share prices of the largest US companies in aggregate, weighted by size, has gone up
IV. the bond market is down
V. commodities are up

a. I only
b. I and II only
c. III only
d. I, II, III and IV only
e. I, II, III, IV and V

431. True or False: Some indices capture a country's stock market performance, other indices might capture the performance of a certain industry such as the semiconductor industry.

432. True or False: The up and down movement of a technology index captures information regarding the performance of the corresponding technology sector.

433. A short-term down movement in a stock index could be caused by:
I. many of the largest companies in the index having their stock price decline
II. more sellers than buyers
III. news that the economy is much worse than people expect, and inflation higher
IV. investors becoming more risk-averse
V. profit warnings from a number of the largest companies in the index

a. I only
b. I and II only
c. I, II and III only
d. I, II, III and IV only
e. I, II, III, IV and V

434. **True or False: A stock market index captures the performance of a single company's equity.**

435. **The concept that pertains to the value of cash flows received today and those received in the future is known as:**
a. the delay of money
b. the cash flows of time
c. the time value of money
d. the money value of money

436. **All future returns or yields stated for bonds or stocks are:**
a. certain
b. expected
c. already realized
d. based on rumors

437. **Security and market analysis that starts with the economy and works its way down to an individual company's financial statements is known as:**
a. bottom up analysis
b. top-down analysis
c. sideways analysis
d. upside down analysis

438. **Security analysis that starts with, and that focuses on, the company is known as:**
a. bottom up analysis
b. top-down analysis
c. sideways analysis
d. upside down analysis

439. **An investor might argue that valuing bonds is easier than valuing stocks because:**
I. bondholders are more certain to be paid, since bonds are more senior in the capital structure
II. bonds have a defined coupon and principal payment, so we have more certainty on the size of the expected cash flows and their timing
III. the value of the stock is more dependent on the decisions of the management of the company
IV. if we were to value both by discounting future cash flows, the discount factor would be easier to determine, or at least less variable, for the bond
V. a stock will go to zero much earlier than the bond of the same company

a. I only
b. I and II only
c. I, II and III only
d. I, II, III and IV only
e. I, II, III, IV and V

440. **True or False: Valuing a bond (especially a low-risk bond or risk-free bond such as a government bond) is typically easier than valuing a stock because the cash flows are easier to project.**

Questions 441 - 453 are linked.

441. **A 5-year bond is issued with a par value of $1,000 and with a 7% annual coupon. What is the face value of the bond:**

a. $700
b. $70
c. $1,000
d. $35

442. **What is the principal of the bond:**
a. $700
b. $70
c. $1,000
d. $35

443. **What would be the payment be that the investor would expect to see annually:**
a. $700
b. $70
c. $1,000
d. $35

444. **This annual payment that the bond is expected to make is known as:**
a. the bond's par value
b. the bond's nominal value
c. the price
d. the coupon

445. **What would happen if 5-year market interest rates rose substantially:**
a. the price of the bond would fall
b. the price of the bond would rise
c. the price of the bond would not change
d. the price of the bond would go to 0

446. **What would happen if 5-year market interest rates fell substantially:**
a. the price of the bond would fall
b. the price of the bond would rise
c. the price of the bond would not change
d. the price of the bond would go to 0

447. **With the substantial rise in interest rates, the coupon would:**
a. fall substantially
b. rise substantially
c. go to 0
d. remain unchanged

448. **True or False: The coupon and principal repayment are all expected payments. If the issuer of the bonds runs into difficulty, the payments might not be realized.**

449. **True or False: The bond would be expected to make coupon payments for 5 years, and in year 5 pay the principal back along with the final coupon(s).**

450. **True or False: An investor that bought this bond some time after issue for $950 would expect a higher than 7% yield if the bond was held to maturity and all expected payments were made - he or she would expect the same annual payments - and the fact that the bond was bought below the face value of $1,000, would provide a further source of return.**

451. **True or False: With the bond trading at $900, it can be said to be trading at a discount.**

452. **A year after the bonds were issued interest rates have risen substantially. An issuer that comes to the market now and that wants to issue attractively priced bonds with a face value of $1,000 would have to offer coupon payments that are:**
   a. lower - investors expect less
   b. higher - investors would expect a higher payment reflecting higher interest
   c. the same - investors would not have changed their expectation
   d. 0 - investors would not expect a payment any more

453. **If this bond became a lot more risky, its price would:**
   a. rise
   b. fall
   c. stay the same
   d. go to 0 immediately

454. **Which of the following completes the phrase best - the shares of a good company will be:**
   a. certainly a good investment
   b. certainly a bad investment
   c. possibly a good investment subject to valuation
   d. a good investment if the valuation is high enough

455. **True or False: The value of a stock can be calculated which allows all investors to know with certainty where the stock price will go to.**

456. **True or False: There are different levels of market efficiency that professionals talk about.**

457. **A market in which historical price data can not be used to predict future prices is said to be:**
   a. strong-form efficient
   b. semi-strong form efficient
   c. weak-form efficient
   d. totally efficient

458. **A market in which publicly available information can not be used to earn an excess return is said to be:**
   a. strong-form efficient
   b. semi-strong form efficient
   c. weak-form efficient
   d. totally efficient

459. **A market in which insider/non-public information can not be used to earn an excess return is said to be:**
   a. strong-form efficient
   b. semi-strong form efficient
   c. weak-form efficient
   d. totally efficient

460. **Which of the following would be most likely to have insider information about a company:**
   a. an outside investor
   b. a day trader
   c. the government
   d. the company's management

461. **True or False: Insider information is relevant (or material) non-public information that the company has not disclosed to investors broadly.**

462. **True or False: Trading on insider information is illegal in many countries.**

463. Calculating the right value for a stock is:

a. very easy
b. just a matter of crunching a few numbers
c. filled with uncertainly - we never know exactly what will happen in the future
d. easier than calculating the value for a bond

464. Valuing stocks is complicated by which of the following factors:

I. future earnings are difficult to forecast
II. company management decisions can be unpredictable
III. different valuation methods can lead to different results
IV. the competitive landscape can change dramatically
V. the future is never certain

a. I only
b. I and II only
c. I, II and III only
d. I, II, III and IV only
e. I, II, III, IV and V

465. True or False: Analyzing companies and stocks is a complicated process and one can never be sure exactly what will happen - by conducting detailed analysis, proponents of stock analysis try to figure out what is happening in an industry, a sector, and with a company, to determine whether the stock should be purchased.

466. Valuation ratios that analysts might look at in assessing a company's valuation include:

I. the Price-to-Earnings (P/E) Ratio
II. the Price-to-Sales (P/Sales Ratio)
III. the EV/EBITDA Ratio
IV. the Price-to-Book Ratio
V. the Dividend Yield

a. I only
b. I and II only
c. I, II and III only
d. I, II, III and IV only
e. I, II, III, IV and V

467. The main advantage of the P/E ratio is:

a. it is always accurate
b. it takes into account many years of earnings
c. earnings capture all of the characteristics of a firm's operations
d. it is very easy to calculate

468. The 'P' in the P/E ratio is a:

a. price
b. profit
c. earnings
d. revenues

469. The 'E' in the P/E ratio refers to:

a. price
b. extraordinary profit
c. earnings
d. revenues

470. Earnings per share are calculated by:

a. dividing revenues by net income
b. dividing earnings by the number of shareholders
c. dividing profit or earnings by the number of bonds outstanding
d. dividing earnings by the number of shares outstanding

471. **The P/E ratio is typically calculated by taking the price of a share and dividing by the earnings per share. It could also be calculated by taking:**
a. the revenues and dividing by the net income
b. the operating expenses divided by the revenues
c. the market capitalization of the company and dividing by the net income of the company
d. the net income divided by the number of shares

472. **One stock trades on a P/E ratio of 6, the other on a P/E ratio of 8. Which of the following is a prudent conclusion:**
a. the stocks with a P/E ratio of 6 is a better buy
b. the stock with a P/E ratio of 8 is a better buy
c. both stocks are equally valued
d. the P/E ratio alone is not enough information to draw any of the above conclusions

473. **The P/E-to-Growth ratio might be preferable to the P/E ratio when:**
a. two firms have the same growth rate
b. firms have different growth rates that might help explain a part of the P/E difference
c. when P/E ratios are not available
d. when the growth is unclear

474. **The Price-to-Sales ratio might be useful when:**
I. a company does not yet have earnings
II. a company has abnormally depressed earnings
III. a company has poor earnings which should normalize to an industry average over time
IV. the company has no sales
V. the company has sales that are growing quickly

a. I only
b. I and II only
c. I, II and III only
d. I, II, III and IV only
e. I, II, III, IV and V

475. **Which of the following is not a drawback of the P/E ratio:**
a. it only takes into account one year of earnings
b. earnings are subject to accounting entries that may not reflect the actual operations of the firm
c. earnings can be distorted by write-offs
d. the price is difficult to assess

476. **A valuation method that looks at that portion of earnings that is paid out to shareholders, and that seeks to calculate a present value for these future payments to shareholders, is known as the:**
a. Discounted Cash Flow Method
b. Dividend Discount Model
c. Discounted Earnings Model
d. Cash Flow Valuation

477. **True or False: The Price-to-Book ratio is more useful when a company has tangible assets on its balance sheet which have a value that is more easily determined.**

478. **Which of the following is likely have the highest dividend yield:**
a. fast growing companies

b. technology companies
c. biotech companies
d. utility companies

479. The percentage of earnings paid out as dividends to shareholders, is known as:
a. the dividend yield
b. the earnings ratio
c. the debt/equity ratio
d. the payout ratio

480. Which of the following ratios tries to adjust or normalize for growth differences between stocks/companies:
a. price to sales ratio
b. P/E ratio
c. price to book ratio
d. P/E to growth ratio

481. A market operator that buys and sells securities with a view to taking a spread between the purchase price and the sale price, and that holds the securities for short periods, also to facilitate the operation of a market in the securities, is best described as:
a. a mutual fund
b. a long-term investor
c. a corporate raider
d. a trader

482. True or False: In order to determine how currency movements will impact a company, it is necessary to look at where a company is generating its revenues and where it is incurring its costs.

483. True or False: Many of the stock market valuation measures including the P/E ratio can also be calculated for a stock market index.

484. Which of the following metrics can be used to look at the valuation of a company:
I. the P/E ratio
II. the P/Sales ratio
III. the dividend yield
IV. the discounted cash flow value
V. the price to book value

a. I only
b. I and II only
c. I, II and III only
d. I, II, III and IV only
e. I, II, III, IV and V

485. Which of the following valuation methods looks at more than one year of data:
a. the P/E ratio
b. the P/Sales ratio
c. the dividend yield
d. the discounted cash flow method

486. The discounted cash flow method of valuing stocks is complicated by the fact that:
I. we need cash flows for a long time into the future
II. it is difficult to know exactly what the discount factor should be
III. it requires a lot of assumptions, forecasting, and modeling
IV. it only looks at one year of data
V. it only looks at earnings

a. I only
b. I and II only
c. I, II and III only
d. I, II, III and IV only
e. I, II, III, IV and V

487. In the EV/EBITDA ratio, the EV is:
a. the excess value
b. the enterprise value
c. the entrepreneur value
d. the excess vortex

488. Which of the following is the main drawback of the EV/EBITDA ratio:
a. the EBITDA is affected by depreciation
b. the EBITDA is affected by the tax rate
c. the EV is difficult to calculate
d. it only looks at one year of EBITDA

489. To calculate the EPS of a company, an analyst would need:
a. the revenues of the company and the number of shares outstanding
b. the earnings of the company and the debt/equity ratio
c. the net income or profit of the company and the number of shares outstanding
d. the sales of the company and the number of investors in the company

QUESTIONS 490 - 507 ARE LINKED.

Use the following data for a company to answer the next series of questions:

Revenues	**$10,000,000**
Net Income	**$1,000,000**
Number of Shares Outstanding	**1,000,000**
Share Price on Stock Exchange	**$8.00**
Average Number of Share traded per day	**100,000**
Dividend	**$0.40**

490. The earnings for this company are:
a. $10,000,000
b. $1,000,000
c. $8.00
d. $125,000

491. The turnover for this company is:
a. $10,000,000
b. $1,000,000
c. $8.00
d. $125,000

492. The top line for the company is:
a. $10,000,000
b. $1,000,000
c. $8.00
d. $125,000

493. The bottom line for the company is:
a. $10,000,000
b. $1,000,000
c. $8.00
d. $125,000

494. The market capitalization for the company is:
a. $10,000,000
b. $1,000,000
c. $8,000,000
d. $2,000,000

495. The company is:
a. profitable
b. loss-making
c. bankrupt
d. not enough information has been provided to be able to tell

496. The equity of this company is:
a. private
b. public
c. both
d. neither

497. The earnings per share for this company are:
a. $8.00
b. $10.00
c. $1.00
d. $4.00

498. The dividend (per share) for this company is:
a. $1.00
b. $10.00
c. $4.00
d. $0.40

499. The dividend yield for this company is:
a. 10%
b. 8%
c. 7%
d. 5%

500. The total earnings that are paid out by the company in the form of a dividend are:
a. $1,000,000
b. $8,000,000
c. $10,000,000
d. $400,000

501. The earnings that are not paid out are referred to as, and total:
a. blown earnings and they total $1,000,000
b. spent earnings and they total $1,000,000
c. lost earnings and they total $600,000
d. retained earnings and they total $600,000

502. The sum of retained earnings and the dividend for the entire company are referred to as:

a. the earnings and they total $1,000,000
b. the revenues and they total $10,000,000
c. the number of shares and they total $1,000,000
d. the number of shares traded and this totals $100,000

503. **On the income statement, this company would have total costs, including cost of goods sold, operating expenses, interest expense and taxes of:**
a. $10,000,000
b. $9,000,000
c. $5,000,000
d. Difficult to tell from the data provided

504. **The P/E ratio for this company is:**
a. 10
b. 12
c. 8
d. 5

505. **The Price-to-Sales ratio for this company is:**
a. 1.0
b. 2.0
c. 0.5
d. 0.8

506. **If the earnings next year were a lot higher, then the P/E ratio on next year's earnings would be:**
a. a lot higher
b. the same
c. a lot lower
d. 0

507. **This company is:**
a. paying out 50% of its earnings and retaining 60%
b. paying out 50% of its earnings and retaining 50%
c. paying out 40% of its earnings and retaining 60%
d. paying out 60% of its earnings and retaining 40%

508. **A valid argument/Valid arguments for a company to retain more of its earnings would be:**
I. the company is generating very high returns on investment
II. the company is able to do more with each dollar of earnings than an investor can elsewhere
III. each dollar that is paid out is not likely to be invested as profitably elsewhere
IV. the company is growing (profitably) and needs the cash
V. the company will need capital in the next two years and retaining earnings reduces the need to sell new shares in the future

a. I only
b. I and II only
c. I, II and III only
d. I, II, III and IV only
e. I, II, III, IV and V

509. **True or False: With investments, risks always need to be thought about - in order to qualify the source and nature of the risk, specific terms are sometimes used.**

510. **Which of the following are considered risks depending on the type of investment:**
I. interest rate risk
II. reinvestment risk

III. default risk
IV. exchange rate risk
V. market risk

a. I only
b. I and II only
c. I, II and III only
d. I, II, III and IV only
e. I, II, III, IV and V

511. **The maximum loss for a bondholder is:**
a. the amount invested in the bonds
b. the total value of the bonds outstanding
c. the net worth of the provider of capital
d. infinite

512. **The maximum loss for a shareholder is:**
a. the amount invested in the stocks
b. the total value of the outstanding bonds
c. the net worth of the provider of capital
d. infinite

513. **A company or an individual are most likely to go bankrupt when which of the following single events occurs:**
a. income drops a lot
b. assets become worth a lot less
c. they can not meet their obligations to creditors
d. revenues drop a lot

TOTAL: 177 QUESTIONS

Mutual Funds and Index Funds

514. The idea behind a mutual fund is:
   a. to pool the money of many smaller investors and invest this larger sum on their behalf
   b. to have many investors each with completely different returns
   c. to give each investor an investment in one stock
   d. to avoid diversification

515. An investor that wants to buy a diversified portfolio of stocks, but does not want to manage the portfolio themselves would most likely invest in:
   a. a bond
   b. a stock
   c. a mutual fund
   d. gold

516. Which of the following statements regarding funds is true:
   I. funds typically pool the money of many investors
   II. funds often benefit from size and scale benefits over any individual investor
   III. funds will have documentation that details the characteristics of the fund
   IV. every fund is associated with a fund management or asset management company
   V. the investments of a fund could be difficult to replicate for the average investor because of the number of securities that would be required

   a. I only
   b. I and II only
   c. I, II and III only
   d. I, II, III and IV only
   e. I, II, III, IV and V

517. True or False: For a lot of investors, mutual funds make sense over buying individual stocks or bonds.

518. True or False: Each mutual fund has investment guidelines that define what the fund focuses on.

519. Advantages of mutual funds can include:
   I. diversification
   II. a professional making the investment decisions
   III. professional risk management
   IV. exposure to a large number of securities through one purchase
   V. they never go down

   a. I only
   b. I and II only
   c. I, II and III only
   d. I, II, III and IV only
   e. I, II, III, IV and V

520. Which of the following statements regarding mutual funds is true:
   a. the guidelines and the documentation define what the fund should invest in and determine a benchmark against which the performance of the fund can be measured
   b. mutual funds can typically invest in anything they like and they do not have a benchmark
   c. a mutual fund that is managed by a portfolio manager is said to be passively managed
   d. portfolio managers can be sure that every decision that they make is correct

521. **True or False: Mutual Funds are one of the main investment vehicles for private savers and investors.**

522. **True or False: Mutual funds exist in various forms in many countries and they are a widespread investing vehicle. In the UK they are referred to as unit trusts.**

523. **Mutual funds would typically be available through:**
   I. banks
   II. asset management companies
   III. mutual fund management companies
   IV. public companies that the mutual fund has invested in
   V. the government

   a. I only
   b. I and II only
   c. I, II and III only
   d. I, II, III and IV only
   e. I, II, III, IV and V

524. **Which of the following statements with respect to investment regulation is true:**
   a. if an investment firm is regulated, their investments never go down
   b. if an investment firm is regulated, everything they say will turn out to be true
   c. if an investment firm is regulated, there is no need for diversification
   d. regulation means that the investment firm has met certain criteria - it does not mean that we should not look around, inform ourselves, diversify and perform reference checks

525. **Which of the following statement(s) about mutual funds is/are true:**
   I. some mutual funds invest in US stocks
   II. some mutual funds invest in European stocks
   III. some mutual funds invest in Asian stocks
   IV. some mutual funds invest in US government bonds
   V. some mutual funds invest in the equity of the largest companies in the world

   a. I only
   b. I and II only
   c. I, II and III only
   d. I, II, III and IV only
   e. I, II, III, IV and V

526. **True or False: The benchmark of a mutual fund is typically a relevant index - for example a stock market index.**

527. **True or False: Mutual funds can either be actively or passively managed.**

528. **The manager of an actively managed mutual fund is known as:**
   a. the CEO
   b. the bondholder
   c. the portfolio manager
   d. the lender

529. **When a mutual fund is managed by a portfolio manager who is trying to beat a benchmark, the fund is said to be:**
   a. an index fund
   b. actively managed
   c. passively managed
   d. an exchange traded fund

530. **All of the following are typical responsibilities of the portfolio manager except:**
  a. selecting the investments for the fund
  b. managing the risk of the fund
  c. selecting stocks or bonds to overweight versus the benchmark
  d. managing the day-to-day operations of the companies that the fund has invested in

531. **An active portfolio manager is typically measured against a benchmark that he or she is trying to beat. This benchmark would usually be:**
  a. a stock
  b. a bond
  c. a commodity
  d. an index

532. **True to False: The performance of a mutual fund should be compared to an index or benchmark that is relevant for what that fund invests in.**

533. **True or False: Each stock in the S&P 500 index will have a certain percentage weight in the index.**

534. **True or False: One of the main activities of a portfolio manager is to overweight securities versus the benchmark that the portfolio manager thinks will do better than the benchmark, and to underweight securities versus the benchmark that he or she does not think will do as well as the benchmark.**

535. **Strategies that active managers might advertise as using to try and beat the performance of an index include all of the following except:**
  a. security selection
  b. sector selection
  c. market timing
  d. spin-the-bottle

536. **Skeptics of active management argue that:**
  a. markets are efficient
  b. markets are inefficient
  c. portfolio managers can successfully pick stocks that outperform the market
  d. timing the market is easy - just buy low and sell high

537. **Why might actively managed mutual funds have difficulty delivering performance that is better than the benchmark:**
  I. there are too many people trying to do the same thing
  II. the costs of active management outweigh the benefits
  III. markets are efficient
  IV. it is very difficult to time markets
  V. any single investor can not find the inefficiencies in the market consistently

  a. I only
  b. I and II only
  c. I, II and III only
  d. I, II, III and IV only
  e. I, II, III, IV and V

538. **Which of the following statements is false with respect to active management:**
  a. active management is usually significantly higher cost than passive management
  b. very few portfolio managers beat their benchmark over longer periods of time
  c. because of fees, it is harder for actively managed funds to beat their benchmark
  d. all portfolio managers beat their benchmark in developed markets

539. **Investors that argue that picking stocks is not a great way of beating the market are arguing for:**
  a. market inefficiency
  b. market irrelevance
  c. market efficiency
  d. market relevance

540. **People that argue that stock-picking based on publicly available information is a waste of time, might be arguing this because they believe:**
  I. markets are efficient (or specifically semi-strong form efficient)
  II. publicly available information is already reflected in stock prices
  III. too many people are trying to do the same thing
  IV. it is unlikely that any investor finds enough mispricings to outperform given the number of investors and the number of mispricings; and how many mispricings are needed to to outperform when mistakes and fees are included
  V. that you can not make money by investing in stocks

  a. I only
  b. I and II only
  c. I, II and III only
  d. I, II, III and IV only
  e. I, II, III, IV and V

541. **True or False: The performance of an actively managed fund is negatively affected by trading and management costs.**

542. **True or False: The alternative to having a fund actively managed is to have it passively managed.**

543. **A passively managed fund is most likely to offer which of the following benefits:**
  I. lower fees
  II. performance that is close to the benchmark or index
  III. a professional portfolio manager that makes the investment decisions
  IV. capital protection
  V. twice the return of other funds

  a. I only
  b. I and II only
  c. I, II and III only
  d. I, II, III and IV only
  e. I, II, III, IV and V

544. **Which of the following is an example of a passively managed fund:**
  a. a hedge fund
  b. an index fund
  c. a mutual fund with a star portfolio manager
  d. an actively managed fund

545. **True or False: Funds that are passively managed aim to replicate an index and re-weight securities to stay as close to the index as possible, in a fairly automatic manner.**

546. **Which of the following is generally a low-cost manner of investing in the largest publicly listed companies in a developed country:**
  a. a fixed income mutual fund
  b. a commodities fund
  c. a large-cap stock index fund
  d. an art fund

547. The reason that index funds make sense for so many investors is because:

I. it would be hard for an individual investor to buy enough securities to achieve similar diversification
II. they typically have lower fees than actively managed funds
III. they are a low-cost way of outsourcing the portfolio management process
IV. they always go up
V. they are a way of getting active management into the portfolio

a. I only
b. I and II only
c. I, II and III only
d. I, II, III and IV only
e. I, II, III, IV and V

548. Advantages of index funds include:

I. typically lower cost
II. outperformance of most active managers in developed markets over longer periods
III. performance is relatively easy to track - they tend to follow the index
IV. they are risk-free
V. a professional uses his or her judgment to take investment decisions

a. I only
b. I and II only
c. I, II and III only
d. I, II, III and IV only
e. I, II, III, IV and V

549. True or False: The concept of market efficiency relates to whether information that we can get or analyze is already reflected in the prices of securities.

550. An investor that believes that markets are efficient is most likely to own:

a. a single stock
b. a single bond
c. an index fund
d. a single commodity

551. True or False: It was probably easier for a single professional investor to outperform the benchmark when a larger percentage of investors was non-professional and a smaller percentage was professional.

552. In the US market, stocks have been observed to rise somewhat more consistently in January than in other months. If this 'January effect' was occurring consistently, it would be an example of an observable event that could be used as an example to refute efficient market theory because:

a. stocks should rise all year long
b. stocks should drop in January every year
c. everyone knows January is coming so the price rise should have taken place - it should be priced in
d. stocks should not go up

553. If one wanted to have exposure to stock markets through a low-cost index fund that is very liquid, one should look at:

a. hedge funds
b. actively managed funds
c. gold
d. exchange traded funds

554. Most exchange traded funds or ETFs are:

a. hedge funds
b. actively managed
c. passively managed
d. destined to go to zero

555. **True or False: Exchange traded funds allow investors to get exposure to a particular asset class very quickly.**

556. **Which of the following are advantages of exchange traded funds (ETFs):**
I. they trade like stocks
II. they can be bought and sold more quickly than regular mutual funds
III. they usually have lower fees than actively managed mutual funds
IV. they can allow an investor to get exposure to an asset class in one quick transaction
V. they can never go down

a. I only
b. I and II only
c. I, II and III only
d. I, II, III and IV only
e. I, II, III, IV and V

557. **An exchange traded fund is best described a:**
a. an illiquid fund that is sold with an operating memorandum
b. an unregulated fund often based in the Cayman Islands
c. a fund that only buys the stocks of stock exchanges
d. a fund that trades on an exchange

558. **A large part of the risk of buying an ETF is associated with:**
a. the skills of the investment manager
b. whether it can be sold again
c. whether the exchange will go out of business
d. the risk associated with the index or benchmark that the ETF is tracking

559. **A money-market mutual fund is a fund that invests in:**
a. equities
b. corporate bonds
c. highly rated short-term debt instruments
d. long-term debt

560. **A 'growth' oriented mutual fund would likely invest in:**
I. technology companies
II. growing companies
III. mature companies
IV. bankrupt companies
V. bonds

a. I only
b. I and II only
c. I, II and III only
d. I, II, III and IV only
e. I, II, III, IV and V

561. **An 'income' oriented mutual fund would most likely invest in which of the following:**
I. growth stocks
II. technology stocks
III. high dividend paying stocks

IV. bonds
V. commodities

a. I only
b. I and II only
c. I, II and III only
d. III and IV only
e. I, II, III, IV and V

562. The term 'bond fund' refers to:
a. a mutual fund that invests in bonds
b. a bond of a particular company
c. a bond of a particular government
d. a fund that does not invest in bonds

563. A 'sector fund' refers to a mutual fund that:
a. invests only in stocks
b. invests only in bonds
c. invests in the stocks of a certain sector - for example technology
d. can not go down

564. The term 'stock fund' refers to:
a. a mutual fund that invests in stocks
b. the stock of a particular company
c. the stock in a particular region
d. a fund that does not invest in stocks

565. A fund that invests in both stocks and bonds is known as a:
a. stock and bond fund
b. balanced fund
c. private equity fund
d. bond fund

566. True or False: The name of the mutual fund will typically give some idea as to how it is managed and what its benchmark is - to get the full picture one should look at the fund documents, and in particular the prospectus.

567. A mutual fund that can raise money continuously is known as:
a. a hedge fund
b. a closed-ended fund
c. an open-ended fund
d. a private equity fund

568. A mutual fund that can raises money only for a certain period of time or to a certain amount, and that is aimed at a majority of investors as opposed to only very sophisticated investors is:
a. a hedge fund
b. a closed-ended fund
c. an open-ended fund
d. a private equity fund

569. A typical mutual fund that grows in assets as money comes into the fund from investors, and that gets smaller if assets leave the fund can also specifically be referred to as:
a. an open-ended mutual fund
b. a closed-ended mutual fund
c. a short-selling fund
d. a bond fund

570. **A less common mutual fund that raises money for a specific amount of time, often to invest in less liquid assets is known as:**
   a. an open-ended mutual fund
   b. a closed-ended mutual fund
   c. a short-selling fund
   d. a bond fund

571. **The value of the investments in a mutual fund is known as the:**
   a. Management Fee
   b. Front-Load
   c. Performance Fee
   d. Net Asset Value or NAV

572. **Differences between a closed-ended and an open-ended fund include:**
   I. open-ended mutual funds can always take in money - closed-ended ones do not
   II. open-ended mutual funds typically contain liquid investments like US stocks and bonds, closed-ended funds might be justified for much less liquid investments
   III. a closed-ended fund typically takes in money for a limited time; an open-ended fund is usually continuously open for the life of the fund
   IV. an investor in an open-ended fund should be able to redeem from the fund at or very close to the NAV - this might not be the case with a closed-ended fund
   V. open-ended funds go up, closed-end funds always go down

   a. I only
   b. I and II only
   c. I, II and III only
   d. I, II, III and IV only
   e. I, II, III, IV and V

573. **True or False: Most mutual funds are open-ended.**

574. **An open-ended mutual fund should be able to take in assets continuously, and conversely return assets to investors if they want to get out of the fund. This is typically possible because the fund invests in:**
   a. liquid investments
   b. illiquid investments
   c. real estate
   d. art

575. **The manager/creator of a closed ended mutual fund would have a valid reason to consider this structure when:**
   a. it makes sense to restrict inflows and outflows to the fund because the investments are less liquid
   b. there is a desire to restrict outflows from the fund even though the investments are very liquid
   c. there is a desire to allow assets to come in and out of the fund continuously
   d. performance is likely to be very bad

576. **True or False: Because it is more difficult to take money out of, or to put money in to, a closed-ended mutual fund, closed-ended mutual funds are sometimes bought and sold at prices that are very different from the fund's NAV - in the case of open-ended funds this is not the case - transactions always take place at or near NAV.**

QUESTIONS 577 - 582 ARE LINKED.

In a given year, the following performances were observed (all of the numbers are net/after fees):

S&P 500: +20.07%
FTSE 100: +10.78%
Nikkei: -5.73%

Actively managed US mutual fund with benchmark S&P 500: +18%
Actively managed UK mutual fund with benchmark FTSE 100: +9%
Actively managed Japanese mutual fund with benchmark Nikkei: -4%

The total annual fees on index funds in the three regions are: 0.3%/year

577. The investor that would have had the best absolute performance over that year would have been the investor that had been invested in the:
  a. actively managed US mutual fund
  b. actively managed UK mutual fund
  c. actively managed Japanese mutual fund
  d. passively managed US index fund

578. The investor that would have had the worst performance in that year would have been invested solely in the:
  a. actively managed US mutual fund
  b. actively managed UK mutual fund
  c. passively managed Japanese mutual fund
  d. passively managed US index fund

579. Which of the following statements is true:
  a. the US mutual fund manager beat the benchmark
  b. the UK mutual fund manager beat the benchmark after fees
  c. the Japanese mutual fund manager beat the benchmark after fees
  d. none of the mutual fund managers beat their benchmarks

580. Which of the following managers has shown some skill or luck in beating their benchmark this year:
  a. the US mutual fund manager
  b. the UK mutual fund manager
  c. the Japanese mutual fund manager
  d. all of the managers

581. If an investor were to invest today (just after the above noted performance), he or she should:
  a. buy the actively managed US fund - it is the best performer
  b. buy the Japanese mutual fund - it is cheap
  c. buy the UK mutual fund - it seems like a steady performer
  d. consider a diversified portfolio of funds using dollar cost averaging knowing that past performance is not a good indicator of future performance

582. When looking at a table of actively managed mutual funds for the year in question, which of the following would definitely be the wrong conclusion(s), or based on insufficient information:
  I. the US mutual fund looks good
  II. the UK mutual fund looks good
  III. the Japanese mutual fund looks terrible
  IV. the Japanese market looks unattractive
  V. the US market looks expensive

  a. I only
  b. I and II only

c. I, II and III only
d. I, II, III and IV only
e. I, II, III, IV and V

583. Which of the following statements is true:

I. what the fund invests in is a very large determinant of the fund's performance
II. comparing mutual funds that invest in different regions or that have different indices does not provide a lot of information regarding manager skill
III. the most recent year of performance for a mutual fund is not enough information to conclude whether this is a good or bad fund
IV. historical performance is not an indicator of future performance
V. in order to assess the quality of a mutual fund company, one should look at more than one year of data as well as the investment management firm

a. I only
b. I and II only
c. I, II and III only
d. I, II, III and IV only
e. I, II, III, IV and V

584. True or False: The guidelines of a fund, and the performance of the benchmark, are very important factors in determining the overall performance of the fund.

585. True or False: Switching between mutual funds after periods of poor performance to invest in funds that have recently done well will always lead to better overall results.

586. True or False: Comparing the performance over the last year of different mutual funds that invest in different markets does not provide useful information.

587. True or False: A mutual fund or index fund should be bought from a reputable asset management/ fund company.

588. Before purchasing a mutual fund it is worth enquiring about:

I. the size and quality of the fund management firm
II. all of the fees associated with the fund
III. the performance of the fund(s)
IV. the amount of assets in the fund
V. the strategy of the fund and the benchmark for the fund

a. I only
b. I and II only
c. I, II and III only
d. I, II, III and IV only
e. I, II, III, IV and V

589. Two reasons that the amount of assets in a fund should be above a certain minimum is that:

I. we can be sure that others have done their homework and just invest alongside them
II. mutual fund expense ratios tend to go down as assets increase
III. we do not want to represent a large percentage of a fund ideally
IV. larger funds always outperform
V. larger funds do not charge management fees

a. I and II
b. I and III
c. II and III
d. II and IV

e. I. II and V

590. **True or False: Index funds often represent a great option for mutual fund investors.**

TOTAL: 77 QUESTIONS

HEDGE FUNDS

591. **True or False: Hedge funds share with mutual funds the characteristic that an investment manager invests a pool of money, typically on behalf of a number of investors in the fund.**

592. **Which of the following statements is typically true:**
   I. hedge funds are often less regulated than mutual funds
   II. one of the keys to evaluating hedge funds is to assess the investment manager
   III. hedge funds can employ more leverage than mutual funds
   IV. hedge funds are typically less restricted in what they can buy or sell than mutual funds
   V. a hedge fund can be invested in with very small sums of money by all investors

   a. I only
   b. I and II only
   c. I, II and III only
   d. I, II, III and IV only
   e. I, II, III, IV and V

593. **Which of the following statements is false:**
   a. hedge funds traditionally targeted sophisticated investors and/or high net worth individuals
   b. mutual funds are distributed widely - most banks will offer them
   c. mutual funds have no risk
   d. different mutual funds invest in different markets - there is a very wide range of them

594. **Which of the following statements apply to hedge funds:**
   I. hedge funds are more flexible in what they invest in and often do not have a benchmark
   II. instead of aiming to beat a benchmark, hedge funds often focus on absolute returns
   III. hedge funds often employ strategies that hedge risks
   IV. many hedge funds are theoretically in a position to make money whatever the market is doing
   V. hedge funds often employ leverage to increase their returns

   a. I only
   b. I and II only
   c. I, II and III only
   d. I, II, III and IV only
   e. I, II, III, IV and V

595. **Differences between mutual funds and hedge funds include:**
   I. mutual funds have a more clearly defined benchmark
   II. hedge funds are less regulated
   III. hedge funds often employ leverage
   IV. mutual funds typically do not short-sell securities
   V. hedge funds are often reserved for more sophisticated and/or high net worth investors

   a. I only
   b. I and II only
   c. I, II and III only
   d. I, II, III and IV only
   e. I, II, III, IV and V

596. **Which of the following statement(s) with respect to hedge funds and mutual funds is/are true:**
   I. hedge funds tend not to have a benchmark against which they are held
   II. hedge funds are usually reserved for sophisticated or high net worth investors
   III. hedge funds are often less regulated, so assessing the fund management institution is crucial

IV. mutual funds track the performance of an index more closely and the performance of the benchmark or index can be a very important driver of overall absolute performance
V. hedge funds never go down

a. I only
b. I and II only
c. I, II and III only
d. I, II, III and IV only
e. I, II, III, IV and V

597. **True or False: The risk of a particular hedge fund can be more difficult to assess than the risk of investing in a particular mutual fund.**

598. **When an investor claims to be able to 'generate alpha', this refers to an ability to:**
a. pick the right markets to be in
b. pick stocks that will outperform the broader market
c. never lose money
d. get out of the market at the right time

599. **True or False: The 'beta' of a stock compares the historical volatility of that stock to that of the index. A beta greater than one means that the stock is more volatile than the index.**

600. **Selling a stock without actually owning it is referred to as:**
a. long-selling
b. short-selling
c. same-selling
d. selling at a loss

601. **Short-selling is often associated with hedge funds. If a hedge fund sold a stock short, the hedge fund would:**
a. benefit from a rise in the share price
b. would not benefit whether the share fell or rose
c. benefit from a fall in the share price
d. lend the stock that it owned

602. **True or False: Selling securities short requires a party that holds the stock to be prepared to lend it to the short-seller.**

603. **Short-selling allows hedge funds to:**
a. make money from investments that rise in value
b. make money from securities that fall in value
c. sell investments that they own
d. guarantee strong performance to investors

604. **Mutual funds might be prepared to lend their stocks out because they:**
a. want the stocks to go down
b. want to be nice to short-sellers
c. get paid for lending them
d. don't want to hold them

605. **A mutual fund has made its portfolio of stocks available to an investment bank that will then use some of their stocks for lending to short-sellers. One of these stocks was lent to hedge fund that then sold the stock short. Which of the following could happen after that:**
I. the stock could go down
II. the stock could go up
III. the mutual fund is compensated for lending it

IV. the hedge fund pays a borrowing cost
V. the hedge fund decides to buy back the stock and it is ultimately returned to the mutual fund

a. I only
b. I and II only
c. I, II and III only
d. I, II, III and IV only
e. I, II, III, IV and V

606. Short-selling allows a hedge fund to benefit from:
a. a rise in the share price
b. an unchanged share price
c. a fall in the share price
d. shares just existing

607. In order for a hedge fund to be able to short-sell a stock, the following has to be true:
a. someone has to be willing to lend the stock
b. the stock has to be that of a US company
c. the stock must be of an oil company
d. the stock price has to be high

608. A fund holds a very liquid stock that they believe will rise in value. If they make the stock available for short-selling they could be considered:
a. foolish, because it is only going down and we can be sure about that
b. smart, because they are getting paid for lending it
c. foolish, because selling-short and lending stocks is always illegal
d. smart, because the lender will benefit from a fall in the share price

609. A certain hedge fund might:
I. buy a stock
II. short-sell a stock
III. buy a bond
IV. short-sell a bond
V. use leverage

a. I only
b. I and II only
c. I, II and III only
d. I, II, III and IV only
e. I, II, III, IV and V

610. A hedge fund that believed a certain stock would do very well, certainly versus the S&P 500 index, but that was worried about the broader market, should:
a. buy the S& P 500 index
b. sell the stock
c. buy the stock
d. buy the stock and sell (sell-short) the S&P 500 index

611. Which of the following, in relation to short-selling, would be of greatest concern to stock market regulators if it were to happen:
a. stocks declining in price gradually in light of deteriorating operating conditions
b. a number of large hedge funds short-selling a single company's stock very aggressively at the same time to the point that it begins to impact the company's operations
c. mutual fund companies making money through stock lending
d. stocks declining on poor earnings

612. The 'uptick rule' when in effect relates to:
a. selling a stock that is held by a mutual fund (a long position)
b. buying stocks
c. that a short-sale can only take place at a stock price higher than the last trade, or if the last trade was higher than the preceding trade
d. investment banking rules regarding mergers and acquisitions

613. Which of the following is not a hedge fund strategy or type:
a. opportunistic hedge funds
b. event-driven funds
c. relative value funds
d. mutual funds

614. A fund that invests in other hedge funds is knows as a:
a. mutual fund
b. an index fund
c. a fund of fund of funds
d. a fund of funds

615. A fund of hedge funds can be best described as a fund that:
a. invests in a number of hedge funds to diversify the risk
b. buys stocks and bonds
c. invests in money
d. buys corporate and government bonds

616. Funds of hedge funds are often tailored to private investors and typically have lower minimum investment requirements than single hedge funds. Which other advantages might a fund of funds offer:
I. diversification
II. a professional selecting the individual hedge fund managers
III. outsourcing of the due diligence
IV. easier to access than certain hedge funds
V. lower fees

a. I only
b. I and II only
c. I, II and III only
d. I, II, III and IV only
e. I, II, III, IV and V

TOTAL: 26 QUESTIONS

REAL ESTATE

617. Which of the following can be considered real estate:

I. undeveloped land
II. single family homes
III. office buildings
IV. condominiums
V. warehouses

a. I only
b. I and II only
c. I, II and III only
d. I, II, III and IV only
e. I, II, III, IV and V

618. True or False: One way of splitting the overall real estate market is into residential real estate and commercial real estate.

619. Which of the following statements with respect to real estate investing is true:

a. real estate never goes down
b. real estate markets are less liquid than the securities markets of developed countries
c. real estate cycles are very short
d. buying real estate property outright is known as indirect real estate investing

620. Which factor(s) is/are likely to have an impact on the price of real estate in a particular area:

I. the economy
II. interest rates
III. demographic/employment factors
IV. transportation related factors
V. supply

a. I only
b. I and II only
c. I, II and III only
d. I, II, III and IV only
e. I, II, III, IV and V

621. True or False: A mortgage is in effect a form of leverage, in that the buyer's money is augmented with borrowed money to make an investment that is larger than the equity capital contributed.

622. True or False: Mortgage interest rates are lower than many other interest rates especially credit card rates, because the money is being borrowed against an asset (a house) that can be sold, that can be repossessed, and that typically does not depreciate as quickly as consumable items.

623. True or False: There is often a difference in the way that we are taxed on our primary residence versus how we might be taxed on an investment property.

624. Real estate tax incentives for private individuals would most likely focus on:

I. home ownership
II. redevelopment or improvement of run-down areas
III. environmentally friendly initiatives
IV. speculation on luxury apartments
V. rental of commercial property

a. I only

b. I and II only
c. I, II and III only
d. I, II, III and IV only
e. I, II, III, IV and V

625. **The value of a property minus the debts including mortgages on the property is known as:**
a. the equity in the property
b. the debt of the property
c. the value of the property
d. the commission

626. **Sometimes the value of a property falls below the amount of the mortgage or the amount borrowed to purchase it. This is referred to as:**
a. positive equity
b. positive reinforcement
c. negative reinforcement
d. negative equity

627. **Which of the following statements is false:**
a. two main sources of return for a real estate investor are rental income and capital appreciation
b. real estate investing requires analysis, as does all investing
c. real estate never goes down
d. governments often incentivize home ownership - they typically do not incentivize speculation

628. **Professional real estate investors often do more than buy properties and wait. Professional real estate investing can involve which of the following:**
I. renovating run-down properties
II. splitting properties into multiple units
III. making use of government programs
IV. financial engineering
V. understanding local regulations and planning permissions

a. I only
b. I and II only
c. I, II and III only
d. I, II, III and IV only
e. I, II, III, IV and V

629. **Buying real estate though a fund is also known as:**
a. direct real estate investment
b. indirect real estate investment
c. real real estate investment
d. upside down real estate investment

630. **True or False: In the United States, the UK, and Canada, real estate funds tend to invest in residential real estate - in particular single family homes.**

631. **Real estate cycles are typically:**
a. very short
b. long
c. not something that has been observed over history
d. too short to notice

632. **Real estate should be thought of as:**
a. a long-term investment
b. a short-term investment

c. a permanently good investment
d. a permanently bad investment

633. **Advantages of a professionally managed real estate fund can include:**
I. each investor only needs to contribute a fraction of the overall sum or price of any property
II. a professional makes the investment decisions
III. some of the costs can be allocated across multiple projects
IV. a property fund can in some cases be more easily sold than a property
V. these funds can provide access real estate that would otherwise be difficult for an individual investor to purchase

a. I only
b. I and II only
c. I, II and III only
d. I, II, III and IV only
e. I, II, III, IV and V

634. **Which of the following would be an example of an indirect real estate investment:**
a. buying a principal residence
b. buying a real estate investment property
c. investing in a stock mutual fund
d. investing in a REIT

635. **Governments generally provide incentives to promote:**
a. real estate speculation
b. home ownership
c. flipping of real estate properties
d. renting real estate

636. **Which of the following statements about real estate is true:**
I. residential real estate refers to housing and apartments that people live in
II. commercial real estate includes office buildings
III. real estate always goes up
IV. real estate speculation is something that the government wants to encourage
V. real estate cycles are typically very short

a. I only
b. I and II only
c. I, II and III only
d. I, II, III and IV only
e. I, II, III, IV and V

637. **Which of the following costs would be relevant to the analysis of a real estate investment and the potential for making a return:**
I. property taxes
II. interest expense
III. maintenance fees
IV. capital gains taxes
V. taxes on rental income

a. I only
b. I and II only
c. I, II and III only
d. I, II, III and IV only
e. I, II, III, IV and V

638. **Which of the following statements makes the most sense:**
   a. real estate tends to perform well when the economy is weak therefore it is a great diversifier
   b. real estate tend to perform poorly when the economy is weak therefore it is a great diversifier
   c. real estate tends to perform great when the economy is weak therefore it is a poor diversifier
   d. real estate tends to perform poorly when the economy is weak and this makes it an ok diversifier

639. **True or False: An investment in real estate, unlike an investment in stocks in developed markets, can have significant carrying costs associated with it.**

640. **True or False: Transaction costs associated with buying and selling real estate are lower than those associated with stocks in developed markets.**

641. **The rental yield is defined as:**
   a. the annual rent on a property divided by the number of months
   b. the annual rent on a property divided by the value of the real estate object
   c. the price of a property divided by the number of months
   d. the price of a property divided by the annual rent

642. **If an investor wanted to know the annual percentage return based on the rent received and less any expenses, the appropriate single measure to look at would be the:**
   a. occupancy rate
   b. maintenance costs
   c. gross rental yield
   d. net rental yield

643. **The annual rent received divided by the current market value is known as the:**
   a. net rental yield
   b. annual bond yield
   c. dividend yield
   d. gross rental yield

TOTAL: 27 QUESTIONS

INVESTMENTS - COMMODITIES

644. **True or False: The word 'commoditization' is very closely linked to commodities - it refers to a loss of differentiation as a product for example becomes more generic.**

645. **The best definition for a commodity is:**
    a. something that comes out of the ground
    b. a product for which there is no qualitative differentiation across a market
    c. a product that is based on something living
    d. a stock

646. **True or False: Cars, phones or clothes from different manufacturers typically differ quite a bit from one another. With commodities, many producers produce an effectively identical product.**

647. **Which of the following are typically considered commodities:**
    I. gold
    II. wheat
    III. corn
    IV. coffee
    V. oil

    a. I only
    b. I and II only
    c. I, II and III only
    d. I, II, III and IV only
    e. I, II, III, IV and V

648. **Which of the following are typically considered commodities:**
    I. corn
    II. oil stocks
    III. gold stocks
    IV. mining companies
    V. farming companies

    a. I only
    b. I and II only
    c. I, II and III only
    d. I, II, III and IV only
    e. I, II, III, IV and V

649. **True or False: Supply and demand play a very large role in determining commodity prices.**

650. **True or False: Commodity prices tend to rise during periods of strong economic growth.**

651. **True or False: When there are concerns about the value of money potentially because monetary policy is very loose and/or investors are looking for safety, investors often look to gold to preserve investment values.**

652. **True or False: Trading commodities is easy - just buy low and sell high.**

653. **True or False: Commodities can provide diversification because they often perform well when inflation is high - stocks and bonds often do not perform well in a high-inflation environment.**

654. **True or False: Agricultural commodity prices can be affected by weather which is difficult to predict.**

655. **True or False: There is a difference between investing in the equity of companies that are involved in the commodities business, and investing in the commodities themselves.**

656. **The ownership of commodities among institutional and private investors has become more widespread over the last ten years. What would this mean in terms of the diversification benefits of adding commodities to a traditional portfolio of stocks and bonds:**
   a. the diversification benefits would be unchanged
   b. the diversification benefits would increase
   c. the diversification benefits would decrease
   d. the diversification benefits would greatly increase

657. **True or False: Many investors trade in the commodity markets through funds, exchange traded funds or derivatives such as futures, as opposed to trading the physical commodities themselves.**

658. **True or False: As many different types of commodities become easier to access for many investors, through ETFs and other derivatives, their diversification benefits would be expected to decrease.**

659. **Which of the following would typically drive the demand for certain commodities higher:**
   I. strong demand for products that use a particular commodity in their manufacture
   II. strong economic growth
   III. increased use of a commodity in the manufacture of certain products
   IV. fear about the value of money
   V. less use of the commodity in manufacturing

   a. I only
   b. I and II only
   c. I, II and III only
   d. I. II, III and IV only
   e. V only

660. **True or False: Commodity producers might sell their production forward in order to lock in a price in the future - on the other side of this trade, there could be a speculator who is betting on a higher price in the future.**

661. **Which of the following sectors have a close commodities link:**
   I. agriculture
   II. energy
   III. mining
   IV. technology
   V. telecommunications

   a. I only
   b. I and II only
   c. I, II and III only
   d. I. II, III and IV only
   e. I. II, III, IV and V

662. **Higher oil prices will most likely lead to:**
   I. higher costs for oil producers
   II. higher revenues for oil producers
   III. higher costs for companies that use oil
   IV. higher revenues for companies that use oil
   V. lower revenues for oil producers

   a. I only
   b. I and II

c. III only
d. II and III
e. V only

663. True or False: Commodities are a major input cost for many other industries including most manufacturing and transportation. That is why commodity price rises can be a concern.

664. True or False: Soft commodities are commodities like coffee, sugar and soybean - they share the characteristic that they are grown and not mined.

665. True or False: Hard commodities include metals and coal - they share the characteristic that they are mined and not grown.

666. Gold has tended to perform well as an investment when:
I. investors were seeking a safe haven
II. there were concerns about the value of money perhaps due to very loose fiscal or monetary policy
III. there are inflation concerns
IV. the cost of extracting gold drops
V. a number of very large gold discoveries have recently been made

a. I only
b. I and II only
c. I, II and III only
d. I. II, III and IV only
e. I. II, III, IV and V

TOTAL: 23 QUESTIONS

Other Investments & Terminology

667. <u>If an investment certificate provides a large percentage of the upside of a stock index, and protects capital on the downside, why might this not be a no-brainer:</u>

I. it could involve credit risk with the counter-party that is issuing the certificates
II. the investment might not provide the dividend yield
III. there might be hidden costs associated with the capital protection
IV. anything that sounds too good to be true should be looked at very carefully
V. there is no such thing as a good investment

a. I only
b. I and II only
c. I, II and III only
d. I, II, III and IV only
e. I, II, III, IV and V

668. <u>True of False: Futures allow speculators to take a view on price movements and they allow hedgers to protect themselves from price movements.</u>

669. <u>Who might be a user of futures contracts to protect from price movements:</u>

I. an oil company that sells oil
II. a car company that buys large quantities of steel
III. a multinational company that has a lot of earnings in foreign currencies
IV. a coffee company that sells coffee
V. a chain of cafés that buys a lot of coffee

a. I only
b. I and II only
c. I, II and III only
d. I, II, III and IV only
e. I, II, III, IV and V

670. <u>True or False: Forward contracts and futures contracts have a very similar function - both allow the contract-holder to buy or sell an asset at a specific price and at a specific time in the future. The main difference between them is that futures contracts are standardized and trade on an exchange.</u>

671. <u>One of the main differences between futures and options is that:</u>

a. futures are about things in the future, options are about things in the past
b. futures are bought, options are sold
c. futures are for speculation, options for hedging
d. the buyer of a futures contract has an obligation, the buyer of an option has an option

672. <u>The primary function of lotteries is to:</u>

a. provide a viable saving and investing alternative
b. allow many people to get wealthy
c. distribute the government's wealth
d. raise money for various agencies including governments in many cases

673. <u>Casinos are most likely to go bankrupt when:</u>

a. too many people go to the casino
b. too many people win at the casino
c. too few people go and therefore less wealth is transferred to the casino
d. people realize that this is the best way to build wealth

674. **The reason that casinos are often housed in very elegant buildings and in some cases can even provide free drinks is because:**
   a. they are like charities - they want to make people happy
   b. they are always running at a loss to provide a service
   c. in aggregate the people that go there lose significant sums of money to the casino
   d. they can afford to because the government supports them - people need to gamble

675. **It is not sensible to rely on the lottery to achieve our saving and investing goals because:**
   I. the odds are against us
   II. the outcome is too much out of our control
   III. we are likely to end up too rich
   IV. it is too easy
   V. it is sensible to rely on the lottery

   a. I only
   b. I and II only
   c. I, II and III only
   d. I, II, III and IV only
   e. I, II, III, IV and V

676. **True or False: Credit card companies can securitize the loans they have made to individual credit card holders by packaging the loans, describing them and parcelling them into securities that can be sold to other investors who then own credit card loans. This is referred to as securitization.**

677. **True or False: Securitization is best described as pooling and repackaging future cash flows to convert the cash flows into tradable securities.**

678. **Which of the following are often securitized:**
   a. credit card loans
   b. auto loans
   c. mortgages
   d. all of the above

679. **A financing company might securitize some of its loans for which of the following reasons:**
   I. it removes them from the asset side of the balance sheet
   II. it raises cash for the financing company
   III. it can make it easier to issue more loans
   IV. it transfers the risk of owning the loans to someone else
   V. it makes their loans assets more liquid

   a. I only
   b. I and II only
   c. I, II and III only
   d. I, II, III and IV only
   e. I, II, III, IV and V

680. **Many financial firms had large losses related to sub-prime mortgages in 2008. How could securitization have played a role in this situation:**
   I. the companies making the loans wanted to make as many as possible
   II. the companies issuing the loans were not the ones that would get hurt if there were a lot of defaults
   III. the loans were restructured and repackaged - this makes analysis even more difficult
   IV. the loans were not securitized
   V. securitization turned out to be illegal

   a. I only
   b. I and II only

c. I, II and III only
d. I, II, III and IV only
e. I, II, III, IV and V

681. **True or False: Securitization, or the process of creating a security out of something, refers to taking a certain set of future cash flows and creating a tradable instrument out of them that can be sold (and bought).**

682. **True or False: A collateralized debt obligation (CDO) is a type of asset backed security where different ratings are assigned to the different tranches based on their seniority.**

683. **Investments that appear too good to be true:**
   a. should be bought immediately
   b. probably are, and need to be looked at very carefully
   c. are never a scam
   d. will never go down

684. **A bank that assists companies in making mergers and acquisitions, that trades in stocks and bonds, and that helps users of capital issue stocks and bonds, would be best describes as:**
   a. a private bank
   b. a commercial bank
   c. a retail bank
   d. an investment bank

685. **Which of the following would most likely have a large network of branches to deal with some wealthy clients, but also many other types of customers:**
   a. an investment bank
   b. a retail bank
   c. private bank
   d. a central bank

686. **Underwriting of securities refers to:**
   a. a process of creating insurance that a stock will never go down
   b. making sure that investors have a diversified portfolio
   c. a way of raising capital for companies and governments with investors
   d. a way of taking the risk out of a portfolio

TOTAL: 20 QUESTIONS

THE ECONOMY

687. **The system that relates to the production, distribution and consumption of goods and services in a nation is broadly referred to as the:**
    a. bond market
    b. stock market
    c. economy
    d. trade deficit

688. **The size of an economy can be measured through the:**
    a. Gross Domestic Product (GDP)
    b. Great Domestic Product (GDP)
    c. Gross Dominion Product (GDP)
    d. Gross Domestic Produce (GDP)

689. **True or False: Labour and capital are two main inputs into the economy.**

690. **True or False: There are many surveys that are carried out to assess the state of the economy.**

691. **Which of the following groups might care about the state of the economy:**
    I. news agencies
    II. investors
    III. companies
    IV. governments
    V. central banks

    a. I only
    b. I and II only
    c. I, II and III only
    d. I, II, III and IV only
    e. I, II, III, IV and V

692. **Which of the following statements about economic data is/are true:**
    I. economic data typically captures data about the past
    II. economic forecasts can be wrong
    III. economic surveys depend on the views of those reporting to the surveys
    IV. GDP growth can slow down
    V. one can never be certain about the future

    a. I only
    b. I and II only
    c. I, II and III only
    d. I, II, III and IV only
    e. I, II, III, IV and V

693. **True or False: There are different ways of looking at certain parts of the economy - for example, one could look at the manufacturing sector, or exports, or employment, specifically - with each area being a part of the overall picture and helping form a view on the overall picture.**

694. **Which of the following statistics could be important to assessing the state of the economy:**
    I. GDP growth
    II. unemployment
    III. industrial production
    IV. retail sales
    V. manufacturing surveys

a. I only
b. I and II only
c. I, II and III only
d. I, II, III and IV only
e. I, II, III, IV and V

695. The increase in prices of goods and services in an economy is known as:
a. inflation
b. deflation
c. recession
d. depression

696. Which of the following would typically not lead to an increase in the prices of goods and services:
a. stronger growth
b. a disruption in the supply of goods and services
c. weaker growth
d. a lack of goods and services

697. Inflation is an area that governments and central banks care about because it:
a. causes growth
b. raises prices and therefore reduces purchasing power
c. reduces the cost of goods and services
d. can lead to deflation

698. Inflationary pressure is most likely to occur when:
a. the economy is slowing
b. the economy is in recession
c. banks are tightening their lending practices
d. growth is high and/or when banks are loosening their lending practices

699. When setting interest rate policy, the central bank of any particular country faces numerous challenges. These challenges include:
a. how other countries/the global economic environment will affect that country can be difficult to predict
b. there is always uncertainty when it comes to the future
c. economic data is generally historical and therefore there can be delays in perceiving changes in the state of the economy
d. all of the above

700. True or False: The real return is defined as the nominal return (which is the return by name and that we see on paper) minus inflation.

701. True or False: Central banks in the US, the UK and Europe play a major role in ensuring that inflation does not become too much of a concern.

702. Central banks control the availability of money and the cost of money in an economy. This is known as:
a. fiscal policy
b. monetary policy
c. trade policy
d. defense policy

703. The main tool for controlling inflation and stimulating the economy under normal circumstances is:
a. fiscal policy
b. foreign policy
c. defense policy

d. monetary policy

704. **As the economy slows and inflation drops, which of the following would be likely to happen:**

I. company revenues would be likely to go down
II. earnings would likely go down for many companies
III. unemployment might rise
IV. interest rates might be cut
V. interest rates might be raised

a. I only
b. I and II only
c. I, II and III only
d. I, II, III and IV only
e. I, II, III, IV and V

705. **Excessive inflation is considered undesirable because it:**

I. reduces purchasing power
II. means that our existing savings will buy less
III. can lead to price instability
IV. reduces prices
V. leads to interest rate cuts

a. I only
b. I and II only
c. I, II and III only
d. I, II, III and IV only
e. I, II, III, IV and V

706. **Inflation can also be thought of as:**

a. a price level
b. an old price level
c. a new price level
d. a change in price levels

707. **The return that an investor achieves after adjusting for the effect of inflation is known as the:**

a. nominal return
b. real return
c. inflation rate
d. interest rate

708. **Higher interest rates:**

a. make borrowing cheaper and stimulate the economy
b. make borrowing more expensive and slow the economy
c. mean higher taxes
d. are aimed at raising inflation

709. **If the Central Bank lowered interest rates by a 'quarter point', interest rates would be reduced by:**

a. 25%
b. 2.5%
c. .25%
d. .025%

710. **If the central bank lowered interest rates by 50 basis points, interest rates would be reduced by:**

a. 50%
b. 5.0%
c. .50%

d. .050%

711. **A basis point can be best described as:**
a. a percentage point
b. ten percentage points
c. a tenth of a percentage point
d. one hundredth of a percentage point

712. **Central banks, when they change interest rates, directly change:**
a. very short-term interest rates that will first affect banks and credit institutions
b. the dividend companies pay
c. long-term government bond yields
d. the return for long-term bond investors

713. **Which of the following is not a central bank:**
a. the European Central Bank
b. the Fed (The Federal Reserve System) in the US
c. the Bank of Japan
d. a bank that provides saving and deposit accounts

714. **A central bank can be described as:**
a. banks that provide investment banking services
b. banks that individual consumers would use
c. a bank for other banks and for the government
d. a bank that provides commercial mortgages

715. **True or False: When the central bank changes interest rates, it affects short-term interest rates for banks and credit institutions first, who then pass the changes in their situation on to their customers.**

716. **Interest rates for longer periods such as a year or even multiple years are to a large extent set by:**
a. central banks
b. investment banks
c. commercial banks
d. fixed income markets

717. **True or False: The key goal of most central banks today is price stability, which is another way of saying that they focus on keeping inflation (and deflation) under control.**

718. **Central banks can ultimately affect which of the following through their actions:**
I. inflation
II. deflation
III. growth
IV. employment
V. currency exchange rates

a. I only
b. I and II only
c. I, II and III only
d. I, II, III and IV only
e. I, II, III, IV and V

719. **Falling prices for goods and services is also known as:**
a. inflation
b. deflation
c. leverage

d. normal

720. **The agency that is responsible for setting interest rates in Europe is the:**
   a. Fed
   b. European Government
   c. European Central Bank
   d. French Government

721. **The agency that is responsible for setting interest rates in the USA is the:**
   a. Fed
   b. European Government
   c. European Central Bank
   d. French Government

722. **Government spending on public projects and taxation are elements of:**
   a. monetary policy
   b. fiscal policy
   c. trade policy
   d. defense policy

723. **Changing short-term interest rates that banks pay is a part of:**
   a. monetary policy
   b. fiscal policy
   c. trade policy
   d. defense policy

724. **Putting a tariff or charge on imported goods to protect domestic industries is a part of:**
   a. monetary policy
   b. fiscal policy
   c. trade policy
   d. defense policy

725. **True or False: Both monetary and fiscal policies impact the economy.**

726. **Which of the following policies would not stimulate the economy in the near term:**
   a. lowering interest rates
   b. increased government spending
   c. increased taxes
   d. a looser monetary policy

727. **True or False: A government can spend more than it receives in tax revenue - it can make up for the shortfall by borrowing.**

728. **Which of the following statements is false:**
   a. a government that spends more than it takes in is said to be running a deficit
   b. a budget surplus exists when the government takes in more than it spends
   c. when the government needs to borrow, it typically issues government bonds
   d. governments borrow through corporate bonds

729. **All of the following make setting monetary policy in a particular country a challenge except:**
   a. what is going on in other countries affects growth and that can be difficult to predict
   b. the central bank is trying to target the future and that is never an exact science
   c. economic surveys are never 100% exact
   d. there is too much corruption in the central bank and they never do what they say

730. **Central banks cut interest rates with an ultimate view to:**

I. making borrowing cheaper
II. making borrowing feasible for more companies
III. stimulating the economy
IV. making debt cheaper
V. decreasing the cost of money

a. I only
b. I and II only
c. I, II and III only
d. I, II, III and IV only
e. I, II, III, IV and V

731. **Sectors that are generally considered to be very sensitive to the economy include the:**
I. automotive sector
II. retail sector
III. biotech sector
IV. defense sector
V. utility sector

a. I only
b. I and II only
c. I, II and III only
d. I, II, III and IV only
e. I, II, III, IV and V

732. **A sector that is considered defensive would be the:**
a. automotive sector
b. retail sector
c. utility sector
d. technology sector

733. **An significant and sustained increase in the price of oil will most likely:**
I. increase the revenues of companies that sell oil
II. increase the cost of goods sold of companies that use oil to manufacture something else
III. lead to an increase in the price of gasoline
IV. lead to a transfer of wealth to nations or states that produce the world's oil
V. be good for the average consumer

a. I only
b. I and II only
c. I, II and III only
d. I, II, III and IV only
e. I, II, III, IV and V

734. **Countries that export more than they import have a:**
a. budget surplus
b. budget deficit
c. trade surplus
d. trade deficit

735. **Governments that spend more than they take in have a:**
a. budget surplus
b. budget deficit
c. trade surplus
d. trade deficit

736. Countries that import more than they export have a:
a. budget surplus
b. budget deficit
c. trade surplus
d. trade deficit

737. Governments that spend less than they take in have a:
a. budget surplus
b. budget deficit
c. trade surplus
d. trade deficit

738. True or False: Governments that spend more than they take in will often borrow. This borrowing ultimately has to be repaid, and in order to repay it they may have to raise taxes or cut spending.

739. Which of the following statements is true when the central bank is independent of the government:
a. monetary policy always takes fiscal policy into account because they are both the responsibility of the government
b. monetary policy always takes fiscal policy into account because they are both the responsibility of the central bank
c. monetary policy should take fiscal policy into account because they both impact the economy
d. monetary and fiscal policy never take one another into account

740. True or False: Governments create tax incentives to encourage behavior that they feel is in society's best interest.

741. True or False: Governments as elected entities, should have society's well-being as one of their main considerations.

742. Which of the following are elements of government fiscal policy:
I. government spending
II. taxation
III. the government budget
IV. interest rates
V. currency exchange rates

a. I only
b. I and II only
c. I, II and III only
d. I, II, III and V only
e. I, II, III, IV and V

743. A government entity might issue bonds for which of the following reasons:
I. they have a budget deficit
II. they need capital for a major project
III. tax revenues are falling short of their spending requirements
IV. they are looking to start a major investment period
V. they want to sell an equity stake in themselves

a. I only
b. I and II only
c. I, II and III only
d. I, II, III and IV only
e. I, II, III, IV and V

744. **True or False: A slowing economy can decrease the revenues of companies that are economically sensitive.**

745. **Which of the following is most likely to lead to higher asset prices:**
   a. lower interest rates and easier borrowing
   b. higher interest rates and more difficult borrowing
   c. a recession
   d. high unemployment and lower spending

746. **An industry where there is only one provider of a good or service is known as:**
   a. competition
   b. an oligopoly
   c. a monopoly
   d. a duopoly

747. **An industry where there are only two providers of a good or service is known as:**
   a. competition
   b. an oligopoly
   c. a monopoly
   d. a duopoly

748. **An industry where there are a small number of providers of a good or service is known as:**
   a. competition
   b. an oligopoly
   c. a monopoly
   d. a duopoly

749. **Money can be thought of all of the following except a:**
   a. medium of exchange
   b. means of storing value - a store of value
   c. unit of account
   d. a stock in a company

750. **True or False: Economists argue that some goods and services should be provided by the government because private companies can not deliver these goods and services at prices that consumers would buy them at, because only a part of the the value associated with them goes to the purchaser, while the rest goes to society as a whole, including to many consumers that are not paying for the good or service. These types of goods are often referred to as 'public goods'.**

751. **A discussion of public goods and externalities would be most likely to start in the context of:**
   a. pollution and lighthouses
   b. cars
   c. food
   d. clothing

752. **True or False: All other things being equal, investors would be more likely to want to hold a certain currency when deposits in that currency earn a higher interest rate.**

753. **High levels of unemployment could lead to the following:**
   I. lower tax revenues for the government
   II. higher social security and welfare benefit payments by the government
   III. a rise in the levels of crime
   IV. lower consumption
   V. higher levels of homelessness

   a. I only

b. I and II only
c. I, II and III only
d. I, II, III and IV only
e. I, II, III, IV and V

754. A government that cuts taxes and spends heavily is likely to:
I. stimulate the economy
II. reduce its budget surplus or even run a budget deficit
III. need to increase its tax revenues and/or reduce spending at some point in the future
IV. be able to continue to do this forever
V. cause a recession immediately

a. I only
b. I and II only
c. I, II and III only
d. I, II, III and IV only
e. I, II, III, IV and V

755. The 'public sector' refers to:
a. companies
b. the government
c. schools that are not private
d. the insurance industry

756. The 'private sector' refers to:
a. companies
b. the government
c. schools that are not private
d. the insurance industry

757. A capitalist system versus a communist system is intended to achieve which of the following:
I. meritocracy
II. a more efficient allocation of resources
III. competition
IV. a government that allocates resources on behalf of society
V. similar benefits for everyone

a. I only
b. I and II only
c. I, II and III only
d. I, II, III and IV only
e. I, II, III, IV and V

758. The idea that a capitalist system is preferable to a communist or socialist system is consistent with which of the following ideas:
a. the government is best placed to allocate resources
b. everyone should receive similar rewards irrespective of effort or ability
c. financial markets are the best allocator of capital, the private sector is the best provider of most goods and services
d. stock markets are bad

759. In many Western European countries during the second half of the 1990s, the country's government-owned telephone and telecommunications company was privatized, and the ownership of the company was in each case transferred from the government or its agencies (the public

sector), to investors that purchased shares/stocks in the company as the company was in each case listed on the stock market. This was done with a view to achieving which of the following:

I. decreasing government debt
II. stimulating competition
III. reducing the cost of telephone and telecommunications services for companies and individuals
IV. promoting an equity culture
V. reducing the quality of these services

a. I only
b. I and II only
c. I, II and III only
d. I, II, III and IV only
e. I, II, III, IV and V

760. **True or False: Governments tax certain items very heavily to receive tax revenues, and to discourage their consumption - examples of this include taxes on cigarettes, alcohol and gasoline.**

761. **True or False: Governments play a role in the allocation of capital alongside financial markets - they do this via their fiscal policy initiatives.**

762. **The reason that the US government does not just print dollars to pay off all of its debt and then secondly share some of the money with all US passport-holders is because it would:**
a. be too easy
b. eliminate a lot of jobs in the accounting and financial services profession
c. decrease the value of the dollar greatly and lead to very high inflation
d. not be possible to print money

763. **Stagflation refers to an environment in which growth is:**
a. strong and prices are dropping
b. weak and prices are dropping
c. strong and prices are rising
d. weak and prices are rising

764. **Stagflation has historically been very rare although some inflation is very common. The fundamental reason that stagflation is a very worrying scenario is because prices are:**
a. rising with strong growth, cutting interest rates will not work
b. rising with weak growth, the normal policy measures can not be implemented as easily
c. falling with weak growth, cutting interest rates will not work
d. falling with strong growth, raising interest rates does not make sense

765. **True or False: The most common technical definition of a recession is a period of decline in economic activity as measured by negative GDP growth lasting at least two quarters.**

766. **The government can be said to have balanced the budget when:**
a. interest rates are 0
b. when imports equal exports
c. when net tax revenues equal government expenditure
d. when growth is constant

767. **The phrase 'economies of scale' refers to:**
a. the economies of large countries
b. the budget surplus of large governments
c. producing something more cheaply on a per unit basis when many units are made
d. cost cutting at a company

768. **When a company is nationalized:**

I. the company is being listed on the stock market
II. the company will be held by shareholders
III. the company is going public
IV. the company is no longer controlled as other listed companies typically are
V. the government is taking over ownership of the company

a. I only
b. I and II only
c. I, II and III only
d. I, II, III and IV only
e. IV and V only

769. When a company is privatized:

I. the company is being listed on the stock market
II. the company will be held by shareholders
III. the company is going public
IV. the company is no longer controlled as other listed companies typically are
V. the government is taking over ownership of the company

a. I only
b. I and II only
c. I, II and III only
d. I, II, III and IV only
e. IV and V only

770. Which of the following could play a role when a company is nationalized:

I. the company is on the brink of failure
II. the company is strategically important
III. the government does not want the company to fail
IV. the government believes it should play a role in the management of this company
V. the failure of this company could cause problems for other significant firms

a. I only
b. I and II only
c. I, II and III only
d. I, II, III and IV only
e. I, II, III, IV and V

771. Proponents of widespread nationalization of businesses typically believe that:

a. companies are better held by outside shareholders
b. private control is better for companies
c. the government is a better allocator of resources and manager of goods and services
d. only a capitalist system will allow a proper allocation of capital and companies to prosper and fail as required

TOTAL: 85 QUESTIONS

SAVING AND INVESTING IN PRACTICE - INTRODUCTION

772. **Thinking about financial matters is something we should do:**
    a. once in a while
    b. naturally as part of everyday life
    c. never do
    d. only when forced to by a lack of money

773. **An often quoted Wall Street saying is:**
    a. there is always a free lunch
    b. there is no such thing as a free lunch
    c. dinner is on me
    d. breakfast is the most important meal of the day

774. **Saving can be best described as:**
    a. earning more than spending
    b. spending more than earning
    c. earning more than investing
    d. investing

775. **Investing can be best described as:**
    a. following the latest fashion
    b. going with the crowd
    c. gambling
    d. allocating capital based on analysis, bearing in mind diversification, risk-management, tax considerations, time horizons among other fundamental saving and investing principles

776. **One of the byproducts of knowing about saving and investing is that:**
    I. we can understand what is being spoken about in the press
    II. we have a better chance of not falling victim to bad financial ideas
    III. we can have a dialogue with a financial adviser and it will not seem like a foreign language
    IV. we can think for ourselves and not always follow the crowd blindly
    V. every investment we are involved in will be fantastic

    a. I only
    b. I and II only
    c. I, II and III only
    d. I, II, III and IV only
    e. I, II, III, IV and V

777. **Which of the following statements with respect to saving and investing in practice is true:**
    I. having an understanding of this subject can improve our understanding of available alternatives
    II. ideally saving and investing is not a process of high-risk trial and error
    III. making use of things we can be sure about is a good start
    IV. managing risk has to be a key element of any saving and investing plan
    V. this subject is to a large extent based on fairly simple concepts

    a. I only
    b. I and II only
    c. I, II and III only
    d. I, II, III and IV only
    e. I, II, III, IV and V

778. **To save and invest intelligently, we need to:**
    a. dedicate a lot of time to the project

b. just let someone else do it
c. develop an understanding and automate what we can
d. give up before we start

779. **Investing is mostly about:**
a. being right all of the time - one less than satisfactory investment will always wipe us out
b. never making mistakes - why bother
c. taking huge bets - otherwise it is not worth it
d. making informed decisions, taking thought-out action and managing risk

780. **True or False: When it comes to investing, there are some things we can be certain about, and others that are inherently filled with uncertainty. Good investors will make use of all of the things they feel certain about and try to minimize the risk with things that they feel uncertain about.**

781. **In investing, things that we can be certain about include:**
I. saving tax on the annual returns helps improve the return over the long term significantly
II. the effect of compounding at 5% every year is affected dramatically by the length of time that the compounding takes place
III. when any single investment has some risk, diversification is a good idea
IV. for an asset that moves up and down on a monthly basis, but up over the long-term, dollar cost averaging can decrease the purchase price
V. some people argue that developed markets are efficient and this makes market timing and stock picking very difficult

a. I only
b. I and II only
c. I, II and III only
d. I, II, III and IV only
e. I, II, III, IV and V

782. **Things that we can not be certain about include:**
I. next year's stock market performance
II. the performance of a single stock
III. the exact growth of the economy
IV. where interest rates will be exactly in 12 months
V. what exchange rates will be for certain currencies

a. I only
b. I and II only
c. I, II and III only
d. I, II, III and IV only
e. I, II, III, IV and V

783. **Successful investors are:**
a. never wrong
b. never right
c. never investing
d. right more often than wrong and managing risk

TOTAL: 12 QUESTIONS

THE IMPACT OF TIME

784. **Which of the following statements is true with respect to stocks, bonds and cash:**
   a. investments that have historically had higher returns have tended to have higher volatility
   b. investments with higher returns have tended to have lower volatility
   c. the volatility of all investments is the same
   d. volatility is higher when our time horizon is higher

785. **Which of the following statements about the US stock market is false:**
   a. the stock market has tended to go up over long time periods
   b. the stock market is very volatile over any one-year period, less so over the longer term
   c. the return of the stock market has been more steady over longer periods
   d. the stock market return is very predictable if investing for a shorter period

786. **True or False: The day-to-day, or even the year-to-year, fluctuations become less relevant if our time horizon is longer (as long as the investment is solid etc.).**

787. **True or False: One of the implications of short-term stock market volatility is that investors with longer time horizons would be the ones with more stock market investments typically.**

788. **True or False: If we felt that we could be more certain that an investment was going to rise in the long-term, but we were less certain that it would do so in the short-term, it would make sense to think of this as a potential long-term investment.**

789. **True or False: The time horizon that we have for our investments is one of the most important considerations when it comes to thinking about saving and investing.**

790. **Rank the following investments in terms of expected volatility:**
   I. short-term US government debt (Treasury Bills)
   II. 5-year US government notes (Treasury Notes)
   III. 5-year corporate bonds
   IV. US stocks

   a. IV. III, II, I
   b. IV, II, III, I
   c. II, IV, III, I
   d. I, II, III, IV

791. **Past performance is most likely to be:**
   a. a very good guide to future performance
   b. a great indicator of future performance
   c. the best indicator of future performance
   d. a poor indicator of future performance

792. **A 'five-bagger' is a investment that:**
   a. trades at $5
   b. has a yield of 5%
   c. whose price has gone up five-fold
   d. has dropped 50%

793. **An investor that had a long time horizon would typically hold more:**
   a. bonds
   b. cash
   c. stocks
   d. commodities

794. **True or False: As we get older, it makes more sense to have money that we need for retirement in stocks.**

795. **True or False: An investor that has a longer time horizon would typically have more stocks than one who has a very short time horizon.**

796. **Which of the following should have some impact on the time horizon for our investments, or the time horizon for some of our investments, and correspondingly how we think about asset allocation:**
   I. our age
   II. when we expect to retire
   III. when our kids go off to college
   IV. upcoming major expenditures
   V. our market outlook for the next week

   a. I only
   b. I and II only
   c. I, II and III only
   d. I, II, III and IV only
   e. I, II, III, IV and V

797. **A 20-year old college graduate and a 65-year old retiree are most likely to:**
   a. have the same investment objectives and the same investments
   b. have different investment objectives but should invest in the same way
   c. have the same investment objectives but very different investment approaches
   d. have different investment objectives and potentially very different investment approaches

798. **Someone that is 64 years old and one year away from retirement, compared to a 23-year old college graduate starting a first job, is likely to have have more of which of the following assets in his or her portfolio:**
   a. cash and other very low-risk investments
   b. emerging market stock mutual funds
   c. passively managed Asian stock mutual funds
   d. MSCI World ETFs

799. **True or False: An investor that wants to invest for the long term should put all of his or her money into the US stock market.**

TOTAL: 16 QUESTIONS

Timing Investments and Dollar Cost Averaging

800. Following the crowd blindly is not a good strategy because:
a. everyone is an idiot
b. prices often already reflect the expectations of the crowd
c. crowds can trample you
d. it is guaranteed to make money - but investing is not about making money

801. Human psychology - especially greed and fear are most likely to:
a. help us with our investments
b. be a hindrance - we might buy for fear of missing something and/or sell at the bottom
c. help us with our relationships
d. make us be great investors

802. True or False: Human nature can lead to poor investment decisions.

803. Buying an investment that everyone is buying:
a. ensures a lower price
b. can lead to too high a price
c. means not following the crowd
d. always leads to excellent returns

804. True or False: Emotions and what we hear can influence our investment decisions.

805. Selling when everyone else is selling is potentially a bad idea because:
a. prices will be higher
b. prices will be lower
c. it is all about being different
d. it will be too easy to sell

806. Which of the following investments is most likely to fall a lot in the short term:
a. a much loved investment with good news that were expected
b. a much loved investment with slightly disappointing news
c. an unloved investment with news that were expected
d. an unloved investment with good news

807. When good news is priced into an investment and everyone loves it, the biggest risk is that:
a. the investment disappoints slightly versus these very high expectations
b. more investors start to like the investment and the price rises
c. even expected news makes the investment rise strongly
d. the investment is not really there

808. Which of the following investments is most likely to rise a lot in the short term:
a. a much loved investment with news that were expected
b. a much loved investment with good news
c. an unloved investment with news that were expected
d. an unloved investment with better than expected news

809. Anchoring is a mental process by which we fix our minds on the price that something traded at in the past - for example a higher price than where we bought it, and a price that is higher than where we could sell it now. Knowing this, anchoring is most likely to:
a. stop us from selling an investment even though we should
b. make us sell investments that have not gone down
c. help us deal with our investments without any emotion whatsoever
d. help us with our other emotional problems

810. In order to be effective, saving and investing should be:
a. fun, not too time consuming, and sensible
b. stressful and high risk
c. a bloodbath
d. risky - to the point of risking our entire existence

811. Smart professional investors:
I. always follow the crowd
II. believe everything they read
III. think for themselves
IV. try to figure out things that are not priced into investments or generally recognized
V. believe in doing their homework before investing

a. I only
b. I and II only
c. III and IV only
d. III, IV and V only
e. I, II, III, IV and V

812. True or False: The less people are following a potential investment or asset, and the less people there are rigorously analyzing the data, the higher the likelihood of mispricings.

813. The greater fool theory incorporates the concept of:
a. fundamental value
b. buying sound companies at the right price
c. short-term market timing
a. being able to find someone that will pay more irrespective of value

814. When everyone loves a certain investment, and everyone is speaking about it, and it is on the front page of the newspapers, we should be most concerned about:
a. buying the investment too cheaply
b. whether we might be overpaying for the investment and what the impact of a small change in perception might be
c. not following the crowd
d. interest rates

815. One way to avoid letting emotions drive our investment decisions is to:
a. day-trade like a maniac
b. go with what we feel like
c. automate the investment process
d. give up, start again, give up, start again etc.

816. Prices that get completely out of line with reality and fundamentals are a feature of:
a. troubles
b. bubbles
c. soaps
d. hills

817. Bubbles are most likely to be the result of:
a. sellers asking too high prices
b. buyers wanting too low prices
c. individual thinking by investors based on their own analysis
d. a herd mentality - everyone doing the same thing and often ignoring fundamentals

818. Timing the stock market can be best described as:

a. straightforward, just buy low and sell high
b. straightforward, that is why most traders make money in all market conditions
c. difficult, too many people are doing the same thing and markets are fairly efficient
d. neither straightforward nor difficult - time is just an illusion

819. Which of the following statements about timing the markets is true:

I. buying after the market has gone down ensures that it will go up again
II. buying after the market has started going up ensures that the trend will continue
III. selling after the market has risen by at least 10% is a good strategy
IV. most long-term investors rely on timing the market for a majority of their returns
V. we can be sure about the past, but not so certain about the future, and timing buys and sells is a waste of time for most investors

a. I only
b. I and II only
c. I, II and III only
d. I, II, III and IV only
e. V only

820. True or False: An alternative to trying to time the market is to automate regular investments thereby avoiding timing decisions and ensuring that the savings are set aside and that the investments are made consistently and not skipped based on a feeling regarding the market. This also gives us more time to focus on other things.

821. Day-traders are most likely to get involved in the stock market and make money:

a. when the market is falling
b. all of the time - they will make money under all conditions typically
c. during a bull market
d. during a bear market

822. Dollar cost averaging refers to:

a. buying the same number of shares periodically (for example every month)
b. buying the same number of bonds every month
c. buying different investments every month - each time with a similar amount of money
d. investing the same sum of money periodically (for example every month) in the same investment

823. The best way of describing why dollar cost averaging works is by saying that buying:

a. the same amount periodically ensures that the average price is lower
b. less when the price is low ensures a lower average price
c. more when the price if high, ensures a lower average price
d. more when the price is low, and less when the price is high, leads to a lower average price

824. Dollar cost averaging implicitly recognizes that:

a. timing markets is difficult, and a waste of time for most investors
b. timing markets is highly profitable
c. timing markets is difficult but by automating the timing we have a shot
d. we can time markets as long as we remember to buy high and sell low

825. An advantage of dollar cost averaging is that it:

a. requires very little attention once an automated process is set up
b. allows us to become full-time day-traders
c. ensures higher purchase prices
d. ensures investments never go down

826. A method that can be used to make contributions of equal sums periodically is known as:

a. anchoring

b. dollar cost averaging
c. timing investments
d. active mutual fund management

827. **Dollar cost averaging can:**

I. avoid market timing
II. bring the average cost of investments down
III. automate a part of the investment process
IV. allow a part of saving and investing plan run itself
V. avoid all losses

a. I only
b. I and II only
c. I, II and III only
d. I, II, III and IV only
e. I, II, III, IV and V

TOTAL: 28 QUESTIONS

TAXES AND COMPOUNDING

828. **True or False: Governments often put in place policies that are aimed at improving the quality of lives for voters and the public in a country. The government can use the budget to achieve this.**

829. **Tax incentives are best described as:**
   a. higher taxes for good ideas
   b. lower taxes for behavior that the government is trying to discourage
   c. lower taxes for behavior that the government wants to encourage
   d. higher taxes for behaviors that governments want to encourage

830. **Governments often provide tax incentives that relate to saving and investing for which of the following reasons:**
   I. having retirees with adequate savings is in the government's best interest
   II. savers and investors play a role in providing capital to companies and governments
   III. the government wants to encourage saving and investing
   IV. the government wants to discourage saving and investing
   V. governments want people to be poor

   a. I only
   b. I and II only
   c. I, II and III only
   d. IV only
   e. III, IV and V only

831. **Government tax incentives to promote saving and investing are:**
   a. illegal
   b. worth investigating
   c. unheard of
   d. never available

832. **The government is least likely to incentivize:**
   a. spending on a home purchase
   b. spending on education
   c. credit card spending on clothes
   d. charitable giving

833. **Saving the on the annual return each year would lead to savings that end up growing:**
   a. similarly
   b. less
   c. slightly more
   d. much more

834. **True or False: Tax considerations are a legitimate consideration when it comes to investing. Total returns are the final objective - minimizing taxes can play a role in this. Minimizing taxes should not be the only or main concern as this by itself does not necessarily ensure the best return.**

835. **True or False: Many countries have created a system whereby money can be set aside on a tax-free basis and is allowed to grow on a tax-free basis to provide savings for retirement.**

836. **True or False: The idea behind most pension plans and retirement plans is to provide savings and/or an income for when someone is no longer working.**

837. **True or False: Having a robust pension and retirement planning system is in the best interests of society, and therefore ultimately of government, typically, as well.**

838. **Which of the following might be benefits of a well-functioning pension or retirement system:**

I. adequate savings for more retirees
II. large pools of capital that are invested in the financial markets to fund companies and governments
III. a lower percentage of retirees living in poverty
IV. governments do not have to provide welfare benefits to retirees to the same extent
V. guaranteed returns each year for all investors

a. I only
b. I and II only
c. I, II and III only
d. I, II, III and IV only
e. I, II, III, IV and V

839. **True or False: The two main types of pension plans are known as defined benefit and defined contribution (plans).**

840. **The vast majority of company pension plans that employees can join today in the United States are:**

a. defined contribution plans
b. defined benefit plans
c. defined return plans
d. none of the above

841. **When the media speaks about pension plans that are 'underfunded' they are speaking about:**

a. defined contribution plans
b. defined benefit plans
c. defined return plans
d. none of the above

842. **True or False: With a defined benefit pension plan, the worker - also known as the plan participant - does not play a role in choosing the investments.**

843. **True or False: In the United States, the UK and Canada (among many others), defined benefit pension plans were common in the past - today, almost all new company pension plans are defined contribution plans. Defined benefit plans are still common in the public sector (government.**

844. **Which of the following statements is/are true and is/are illustrative of some of the differences between defined benefit and defined contribution plans:**

I. defined benefit plans 'define the benefit', often based on a multiplier of final years' salaries
II. defined contribution plans focus on the contribution - the benefit is then determined by the amount contributed and the performance of the assets invested in
III. in a defined benefit plan the investment decisions are not made by the employee - they involve complicated calculations (made by actuaries) regarding future potential liabilities
IV. in a defined contribution plan, the plan member (the employee) decides to a large extent how much to contribute and how the funds are to be invested
V. a defined contribution plan typically requires a bit more initiative on the part of the employee, but it also provides more control and will not end up 'underfunded' (because there is no promised benefit) if the employer gets into trouble or does not set aside sufficient contributions

a. I only
b. I and II only
c. I, II and III only
d. I, II, III and IV only
e. I, II, III, IV and V

845. **A 401k in the United States is a:**

a. mutual fund
b. stock fund
c. bond fund
d. retirement savings plan

846. A pension plan that pays the retiree based on their earnings in the years preceding retirement is a type of:
a. defined benefit plan
b. defined contribution plan
c. savings plan
d. mutual fund plan

847. A pension plan that pays retirement benefits based on what the retiree contributed and the returns that were achieved is known as a:
a. defined benefit plan
b. defined contribution plan
c. savings plan
d. mutual fund plan

848. A 401k plan is a type of:
a. defined benefit plan
b. defined contribution plan
c. chequing account
d. mutual fund

849. Stories of companies that are unable to meet the pension plan obligations of plans that were often set up some time ago, usually relate to:
a. defined benefit plans
b. defined contribution plans
c. savings plans
d. mutual fund plans

850. Which of the following statements is true:
a. a 401k plan is the same thing as a stock
b. a mutual fund is by definition a tax efficient wrapper and we can buy lot of 401k plans
c. a 401k plan is a mutual fund by definition
d. a 401k plan can be considered a tax efficient wrapper which can invest in mutual funds

851. True or False: A defined benefit plan is a liability of the plan 'sponsor' - the company or government offering the plan - if the sponsor runs into financial difficulties, the benefits for retirees could be impacted.

852. A company might opt for a defined contribution plan over a defined benefit plan because:
I. it does not want to have a liability for retirees in the future
II. it does not want to have the burden of predicting how much needs to be set aside
III. it is difficult to predict how the number of employees paying into the plan will develop
IV. it wants the employees to have more say in how the money is managed
V. it wants to make use of the 401k structure

a. I only
b. I and II only
c. I, II and III only
d. I, II, III and IV only
e. I, II, III, IV and V

853. **True or False: The assets of some long-established defined benefit plans are insufficient to cover the defined benefits partly because the number of retirees has gone up a lot, while the number of people paying in to the plan has decreased greatly.**

854. **True or False: A defined benefit plan involves assumptions regarding lifespans and investment returns, as well as detailed calculations to try to assess how much money needs to be in the plan.**

855. **A defined benefit plan with insufficient assets to cover the defined benefits is:**
    a. overfunded
    b. underfunded
    c. funded
    d. not funded

856. **In the UK, a government sponsored structure that allows after-tax money to be set aside in order to grow tax-free, is known as a:**
    a. defined benefit pension plan
    b. 401k
    c. an ISA - an Individual Savings Account
    d. a checking account

857. **True or False: A money purchase plan is a type of defined contribution pension plan.**

858. **True or False: Pension laws and contribution rules vary between countries and can change over time, but the generic structures, the plans, and their characteristics can be understood by knowing a few key concepts, and then looking at the plans in more detail.**

TOTAL: 31 QUESTIONS

DIVERSIFICATION

859. **True or False: Diversification can be described as mixing different investments that do not move perfectly together in order to spread risk.**

860. **Diversification can be best thought of as:**
   a. a leveraging of returns
   b. a means of guaranteeing returns
   c. a way of borrowing against future returns
   d. a risk management technique

861. **Diversification is achieved by:**
   a. adding more of the same investments to a portfolio
   b. adding leverage to a portfolio
   c. mixing different investments within a portfolio
   d. selling the entire portfolio

862. **Which of the following statements with respect to diversification is/are true:**
   I. diversification is an important part of a successful saving and investing plan
   II. diversification can also be referred to as 'not putting all your eggs in one basket'
   III. diversification aims to ensure that some investments go up while others are going down
   IV. diversification relies on all investments moving together
   V. diversification depends on some investments going to zero

   a. I only
   b. I and II only
   c. I, II and III only
   d. I, II, III and IV only
   e. I, II, III, IV and V

863. **Diversification when properly executed can theoretically do all of the following except:**
   a. obtain a higher return for a similar level of risk
   b. reduce the level of risk for a given expected return
   c. limit the impact of a single investment going down a lot
   d. ensure we never lose money

864. **Investing in international stocks is:**
   a. a crazy idea - most other countries are uncivilized
   b. a potentially good way to diversify and get access to some market-leading companies
   c. a bad idea - we should always put all of our eggs in one basket
   d. not even worth considering

865. **True or False: Sometimes investments that appear to have nothing to do with each other might move together nonetheless because they are owned by the same investors.**

866. **The more two different investments move together, the more they can be said to be:**
   a. coordinated
   b. correlated
   c. concentrated
   d. cultivated

867. **True or False: Diversification makes a case for combining investments that do not move perfectly together.**

868. **True or False: Investments that do not appear to move together under normal market conditions, might move together more under extreme market conditions when all investors are selling them as a group.**

869. **In extreme market conditions, for example major market corrections, the following would be most likely to happen:**
   a. diversification benefits would increase and investments would move more independently
   b. diversification benefits would decrease and investments are at risk of going down together
   c. investments would go up in value
   d. investments would not move in value

870. **Which pairs below are more diversified than either item in each pair alone:**
   I. stocks and bonds
   II. US stocks and International stocks
   III. international stocks and US government bonds
   IV. bonds and commodities
   V. a US portfolio containing the 500 largest US companies and an S&P 500 index fund

   a. I only
   b. I and II only
   c. I, II and III only
   d. I, II, III and IV only
   e. I, II, III, IV and V

871. **Which of the following investments can help achieve diversification:**
   I. stocks
   II. bonds
   III. commodities
   IV. real estate
   V. international stocks

   a. I only
   b. I and II only
   c. I, II and III only
   d. I, II, III and IV only
   e. I, II, III, IV and V

872. **True or False: Funds (mutual, index, exchange traded) provide an increased level of diversification over holding a small number of securities. In fact, often funds hold more securities than it would be possible for a single individual to own - this has contributed to the popularity of funds.**

873. **True or False: Cash should also be considered an asset class for diversification purposes.**

874. **True or False: Diversification can take place across securities, across asset classes and across geographic regions.**

875. **Which of the following would be considered an asset class:**
   I. stocks
   II. bonds
   III. commodities
   IV. cash
   V. real estate

   a. I only
   b. I and II only
   c. I, II and III only

d. I, II, III and IV only
e. I, II, III, IV and V

876. Diversification often has something to do with which of the following:
a. leverage
b. fees
c. asset allocation
d. accounting

877. Which of the following statements is true:
I. professional investors will use diversification
II. there are solid mathematical principles behind the theory of diversification
III. diversification is a part of prudent portfolio management
IV. the level of diversification varies amongst investors, however some level of diversification is present with almost all investors
V. diversification is only for very risk-averse investors

a. I only
b. I and II only
c. I, II and III only
d. I, II, III and IV only
e. I, II, III, IV and V

878. Two stock markets on two continents have very different fundamentals in terms of country growth, demographics, exports versus imports, dominant industries, government policy and earnings. As investors in these two continents diversify their investments and become investors in both countries (as do investors from other countries), the correlation (the amount by which these two countries' markets move together) would be expected to:
a. go down
b. stay the same
c. increase
d. stay the same or go down

879. Two different stocks might move together or be correlated because:
I. they are in the same industry
II. they sell the same products
III. they buy the same raw materials
IV. they are in the same index
V. they are owned by similar groups of investors

a. I only
b. I and II only
c. I, II and III only
d. I, II, III and IV only
e. I, II, III, IV and V

TOTAL: 21 QUESTIONS

TRANSACTION COSTS

880. **An investment firm or bank typically gets paid:**
   a. when we get rich
   b. if we have a great saving and investing plan
   c. on the products they sell, per transaction and as a percentage of assets they manage
   d. only if we end up 100% satisfied over the very long term

881. **True or False: Investment products can have explicit fees or hidden fees.**

882. **True or False: An annual fee that reduces our percentage return by a few percent each year can have a large impact over the long term.**

883. **When it comes to fees and transaction costs on investments, a reasonable philosophy might be summarized as:**
   a. never pay transaction costs
   b. pay the highest fees possible
   c. always go for the lowest cost service
   d. try to understand what the fees relate to and pay those that make sense - avoid others

884. **True or False: Unnecessary fees and transaction costs can hurt our return over the long-term significantly.**

885. **In order to save on fees, fund investors would be least likely to focus on:**
   a. index funds
   b. ETFs
   c. passively managed funds
   d. actively managed funds

886. **True or False: An investor should understand all transaction fees, management fees and other potential fees associated with an investment prior to making the investment.**

887. **Mutual fund fees could include:**
   I. sales loads, sales charges on purchases and deferred sales charges
   II. redemption fees, account fees and purchase fees
   III. management fees
   IV. distribution fees
   V. other expenses

   a. I only
   b. I and II only
   c. I, II and III only
   d. I, II, III and IV only
   e. I, II, III, IV and V

888. **True or False: A no-load mutual fund will not have any expenses.**

889. **When it comes to mutual funds, which fees should we care about:**
   a. sales fees
   b. sales loads
   c. annual operating expenses including the management fee
   d. all of the fees as they all reduce return

890. **True or False: In the US, a good source of unbiased consumer information regarding mutual fund charges and fees is the US Securities and Exchange Commission (SEC).**

891. **<u>If a mutual fund is described as a no-load fund, which of the following statements is true:</u>**
   a. it will certainly have no fees associated with it
   b. it has a sales load
   c. it has a redemption load
   d. it will not have a sales or redemption load but could have many other charges

892. **<u>A fund is a no-load fund. This fund might have the following other fees or charges:</u>**
   I. redemption fees
   II. purchase fees
   III. account fees
   IV. annual operating expenses
   V. sales load fees

   a. I only
   b. I and II only
   c. I, II and III only
   d. I, II, III and IV only
   e. I, II, III, IV and V

893. **<u>Which of the following statements regarding expense ratios is/are true:</u>**
   I. they are the operating expenses as a % of assets
   II. they are also sometimes referred to as the management expense ratio or MER
   III. they do not include sales loads or redemption fees
   IV. they include all expenses and fees
   V. a higher expense ratio is always better

   a. I only
   b. I and II only
   c. I, II and III only
   d. I, II, III and IV only
   e. I, II, III, IV and V

894. **<u>True or False: A great place to find detailed information regarding a funds fees and characteristics is in the prospectus.</u>**

895. **<u>True or False: A 1% difference in the annual return over 10 or 20 years or more can have a very large impact on the amount that we end up with.</u>**

896. **<u>True or False: Index funds tend to have the lowest fees and can be an excellent alternative for investors in developed markets.</u>**

897. **<u>True or False: Load fees typically go to a selling broker and not to the fund management firm.</u>**

898. **<u>True or False: Some fees are avoidable - on that basis we can often increase returns without compromising quality.</u>**

899. **<u>In the context of mutual funds, a front-end load is:</u>**
   a. an annual management fee for the fund
   b. a fee that the investor pays when the fund is purchased
   c. a fee that the investor pays when the fund is sold
   d. a fee that the investor never has to pay

900. **<u>In the context of mutual funds, a back-end load is:</u>**
   a. an annual management fee for the fund
   b. a fee that the investor pays when the fund is purchased
   c. a fee that the investor pays when the fund is sold

d. a fee that the investor never has to pay

901. Front-end loads and back-end loads typically go to:
a. the fund
b. the fund manager's private bank account
c. the fund management company
d. the broker or introducer

902. A no-load fund, does not charge:
a. any fees
b. load fees
c. management fees
d. account fees

903. True or False: Even though a mutual fund might not have load fees, it could still have a number of other fees.

904. True or False: The business of mutual funds has become a fairly mature and competitive business - correspondingly there might be opportunities to reduce fees in some cases without compromising quality.

905. True or False: Smart investors look at fees and try to assess which ones are justified and which ones are not.

906. Performance after fees is referred to as:
a. gross performance
b. levered performance
c. future performance
d. net performance

907. True or False: Structured products including capital-guaranteed products are prime targets for hidden fees because of their complexity.

TOTAL: 28 QUESTIONS

Getting Started

908. If we were to start thinking about implementing a saving and investing plan, the best first two things to do would be to:

a. start investing and take big bets
b. start investing and monitor investments
c. monitor investments and take big bets
d. take stock of our finances and gather information

909. Which of the following can be objectives of a financial plan:

I. capital preservation
II. capital appreciation
III. current income
IV. total return
V. interest rates

a. I only
b. I and II only
c. I, II and III only
d. I, II, III and IV only
e. I, II, III, IV and V

910. True or False: The objectives of a financial plan should be defined before starting any thought on investment selection.

911. An investment plan might operate within certain constraints. Constraints of this type could include:

I. liquidity issues
II. time horizon
III. tax issues
IV. legal and regulatory factors
V. unique needs and preferences

a. I only
b. I and II only
c. I, II and III only
d. I, II, III and IV only
e. I, II, III, IV and V

912. A financial plan begins with:

a. an analysis of investments
b. selection of investments
c. purchase of investments
d. an understanding of risk tolerance, goals, time horizon etc.

913. A good saving and investing plan:

I. can run itself to a large extent
II. makes use of things we can be sure about
III. is tax efficient
IV. takes huge risks and gambles
V. pays out a lot of fees

a. I only
b. I and II only
c. I, II and III only
d. I, II, III and IV only

e. I, II, III, IV and V

914. **The decision to invest in stocks versus bonds versus cash versus commodities and real estate is known as:**
a. stock picking
b. asset allocation
c. liability management
d. capital structure

915. **True or False: Asset allocation is more important than stock selection to an investor over a long period of time and in varying market conditions.**

916. **True or False: Preparing a balance sheet for ourselves or for our families is a good way of taking stock and seeing where we are.**

917. **Which of the following items would be included on our personal or on our family balance sheet:**
I. cash in bank account
II. our investments
III. any debts
IV. property investments
V. mutual funds

a. I only
b. I and II only
c. I, II and III only
d. I, II, III and IV only
e. I, II, III, IV and V

918. **On our personal balance sheet, the assets minus the liabilities would be:**
a. what we owe, our debts or our liabilities
b. what we make, our income or our revenues
c. what we own, our equity or our net worth
d. what we paid, our cost or our total expenditure

919. **On a personal balance sheet, liabilities would include which of the following:**
I. mortgages
II. credit card debts
III. a loan to a friend
IV. a school loan
V. our investments

a. I only
b. I and II only
c. I, II and III only
d. I, II, III and IV only
e. I, II, III, IV and V

920. **True or False: It is possible to prepare a personal income statement for ourselves.**

921. **Which of the following items would be included on our personal or on our family income statement:**
I. our income
II. property taxes
III. gasoline expenses
IV. dividends we receive
V. the value of our investments

a. I only
b. I and II only
c. I, II and III only
d. I, II, III and IV only
e. I, II, III, IV and V

922. With our personal income statement, we could figure out:
a. how we are invested
b. how much money we owe
c. whether our investments are going up
d. how we are spending our money

923. The purpose of preparing our personal balance sheet would be to figure out:
a. how much we make
b. how much we spend
c. how much we are saving
d. our net worth

924. True or False: A balance sheet is a snapshot at a point in time, whereas an income statement is a summary of events over a period of time.

925. True or False: In a personal income statement, revenues would include:
a. a salary received
b. expenses
c. investments owned
d. debt/liabilities

926. Which of the following are good reasons to set money for savings aside first:
I. it ensures that the money is saved
II. it effectively simulates a lower income
III. it can be a part of automating the process
IV. it can be a part of using dollar cost averaging
V. it ensures that the investments never go down

a. I only
b. I and II only
c. I, II and III only
d. I, II, III and IV only
e. I, II, III, IV and V

927. True or False: An cash fund for emergencies is a good idea.

928. In order to track spending, which of the following prepared in detailed form would be most useful:
a. a balance sheet
b. an income statement
c. a credit card statement
d. a bank statement

929. In order to track net worth, investments and liabilities, which of the following prepared in detailed form would be most useful:
a. a balance sheet
b. an income statement
c. a credit card statement
d. a bank statement

930. A budget for a family showing expenses on a monthly basis would most resemble:

a. a balance sheet
b. an income statement
c. a credit card statement
d. a bank statement

931. **After an analysis of our own finances, a likely first step would be:**
a. paying down high interest credit card debt
b. investing in stocks immediately
c. increasing our debt levels
d. quitting our jobs

932. **True or False: In a fairly priced market, a large part of investing refers to selecting appropriate investments and managing risk. It is not that stocks are necessarily better investments than bonds or vice versa in all circumstances - a large part of investing is about making sensible investments based on individual time horizons, risk tolerances and preferences.**

933. **True or False: The solidity and integrity of the counter-party is one of the most important considerations before considering any financial transaction.**

934. **Of the following alternatives, which is likely to be the most sensible saving and investing program:**
a. buying a single stock periodically using dollar cost averaging
b. buying an S&P 500 ETF in one lump sum
c. investing in stocks globally, bonds, commodities, cash and real estate with small contributions over the long-term using dollar cost averaging, tax savings and diversification
d. buying a lottery ticket and hoping

935. **An investor buys the stock of a single company as a complement to a diversified portfolio of index funds and other investments. He or she would theoretically be most likely to be successful with this investment in a stock when he or she:**
a. is buying it because everyone says it is a great idea
b. is buying it with no knowledge of the company
c. knows the company well and has good reason to believe that the company will deliver better results than investors in general expect
d. knows the company well and believes that the company will disappoint the market

936. **A financial scheme that promises to triple our money with no risk is likely to be:**
a. a great idea
b. a very good idea
c. a scam
d. an idea worth putting all of our money into

937. **When looking at investments, it might be useful to think about:**
I. why the investment might make sense
II. whether we are we dealing with a trustworthy counter-party
III. how the counter-party being paid
IV. why everyone isn't doing this
V. what the worst-case outcome could be (the absolute worst case)

a. I only
b. I and II only
c. I, II and III only
d. I, II, III and IV only
e. I, II, III, IV and V

TOTAL: 30 QUESTIONS

Answers

The correct answers are marked in bold, and where appropriate a further explanation is provided, also in bold. In some cases, the question and answer together form a complete statement of a fact or provide a complete definition of a term, or the topic is addressed elsewhere - in these limited cases there might not be a further explanation or the further explanation might be shorter.

Saving and Investing Introduction

1. **Over the past decades, we have become:**
   a. less responsible for our finances - governments have become more responsible
   b. more responsible for our finances - governments and employers less so
   c. we are equally responsible - nothing has changed
   d. totally irresponsible - in fact no one should be responsible for our finances

   This is partly because employers are moving from defined benefit to defined contribution plans (discussed in detail later), and also because government welfare programs are being cut not increased in many countries, and also perhaps because of a larger trend to bring accountability and choice back to the employees and the savers and investors who ultimately have to live with their saving and investing outcome, and who are ultimately responsible for the subject as it applies to themselves.

2. **Money usually becomes an issue when:**
   a. there is not enough of it
   b. we have been saving and investing diligently
   c. we have been planning properly
   d. we make a lot of it and save intelligently

   That is unfortunately when it will get the most attention - and cause the most stress.

3. **Understanding finance and money is important because:**
   a. it can improve the quality of our lives
   b. it is a very important part of the world around us
   c. if we do not understand it, we are much more likely to make financial mistakes
   d. of all of the above

   All of these factors are good reasons to work on our financial literacy.

4. **Which of the following are good reasons for learning about saving and investing:**
   I. it is a big part of the world around us
   II. it is spoken about in the press all day long
   III. we are putting ourselves at a disadvantage without some knowledge of this material
   IV. we can have a better understanding of our financial options
   V. we can have better dialogue with financial advisers

   a. I only
   b. I and II only
   c. I, II and III only
   d. I, II, III and IV only
   e. I, II, III, IV and V

   Saving and investing matters are in the press and other media on an ongoing basis - without some knowledge of the material, all of this discussion just passes us by. With an understanding of the subject, we are better positioned to understand our options whether related to employer pension plans or bank products. It also makes it more possible to ensure that we understand what financial advisers might be suggesting, that we can express our preferences and also reduce the risk of falling for scams.

5. **Which of the following are good reasons to save some money:**
   I. to have an emergency fund
   II. for a house
   III. for education

IV. for retirement
V. for unforeseen circumstances

a. I only
b. I and II only
c. I, II and III only
d. I, II, III and IV only
e. I, II, III, IV and V

All of these are good reasons to save - saving greatly assists in allowing larger sums to accumulate and without it, it is very possible to end up living paycheck to paycheck without being set up for any major expenditures.

6. **The best time to save money is:**
a. in retirement
b. during high earning years
c. never
d. as a student

In retirement, most people are more likely to be living off the savings that they had accumulated during their working years. It is difficult for many students to save, although it is not a bad idea, due to the cost of studies. During high earning years is the best answer - and if we can automate a part of the process, we might not even notice the amounts that we are not spending on a monthly basis as our savings accumulate.

7. **When it comes to understanding finance and the world around us, one of the keys is to get:**
a. just the sound-bites
b. a few interesting facts for use at social events
c. the complete picture - to be able to interpret new information and potentially have a view
d. none of the facts - because the subject is not important

This seems obvious but so much of the information on the subject is incomplete or is more focused on making a decision, over understanding the actual working parts.

8. **Saving and investing can be best described as:**
a. putting money aside and putting in place structures with a view to letting it grow slowly
b. taking large risks and hoping for the best
c. following other people's advice blindly
d. speculation

Like many things, saving and investing takes time, and short-cuts that promise unrealistic results can often be scams. It takes time to save a lot of money and to make it grow - having said that, once it is started and if we automate as much as we can and monitor the investments, it can largely run itself - time will pass inevitably - the key is not to have lost the opportunity to have done something positive during that time.

9. **Which of the following is not a result of being financially literate:**
a. it can help assess which investments could not possibly be a good idea
b. it can assist in understanding financial advice
c. it will ensure that we never have a risk of a loss in any investment
d. it can reduce risk, partly by ensuring that all of our eggs are not in one basket

Not understanding investment choices, and then making choices, is not a recipe for consistently great results. Many investments come with some risk of loss - the key is to understand the risk - to manage the risk - to bet on things that we can be sure about like tax savings, dollar cost averaging etc. and to diversify.

10. <u>We should think of saving and investing as:</u>
    a. the main way of generating wealth
    b. a way of retaining and accumulating funds that can complement an income
    c. a way of winning the lottery with more work
    d. a waste of time

    Taking big bets only with a view to replacing our income in the short-term and entirely can be a recipe for disaster. We should have a baseline plan in place that allows assets to grow without too much manual intervention, and that will replace our income at the latest by when know we will no longer have an income for sure - in retirement (and with larger amounts saved and better returns hopefully well before). If we want to set aside some additional sums to be more aggressive with as well (and that we would be prepared to lose more of as well) then that would be a complement to a baseline plan.

11. <u>Saving, investing and financial markets can be thought of as:</u>
    a. a fad that is not going to last
    b. things that affect only a small part of the population
    c. things that only bankers need to think about
    d. one of the backbones of developed civilization that affect almost everyone

    This subject and many of the concepts like providers and users of capital, equity and debt etc. has been around for hundreds of years in many different countries and regions. Where and how companies are funded, the stock market, the economy, interest rates etc. play such an important role - that is why they are spoken about so much.

12. <u>Potentially the worst time to start thinking about saving and investing matters is when:</u>
    a. we have money to save and invest
    b. we are in a very bad financial situation
    c. everything is going well with our jobs
    d. we are planning for the future

    The other answers are all very good times to think about - and to take action with respect to - the subject of saving and investing. When in a bad financial situation, our options are often more limited, and we will have lost the opportunity to have had time working for us in terms of the amounts saved and the growth of capital, and therefore have less room for maneuver. It will also be a lot more stressful.

13. <u>When people start talking about stocks and bonds we should:</u>
    a. shut off completely as matter of principle
    b. at least have some clue as to what these two things are
    c. scream and leave the room
    d. tell them that stocks and bonds don't exist

    Stocks and bonds are spoken about a lot including in the press and amongst people and friends - this is another reason why why it is worth having some idea of what these things are.

14. <u>True: Our financial system is built on a few very fundamental concepts and most products and ideas follow from these concepts.</u>

    These are very key concepts like providers and users of capital, equity and debt, compounding - the good thing is that they are fundamental and not that complicated - and that they are covered throughout the remainder of this book.

15. <u>False: Learning about saving and investing can only be justified by greed.</u>

Definitely false - It can be justified by simply wanting to take care of ourselves and our families, and wanting to be aware of the world around us.

16. **False: Saving and investing is so complicated that we are better off not knowing anything about it.**

    First of all it is not that complicated, and secondly we are certainly not better off not knowing anything about it.

17. **True: Saving and investing is a long-term project.**

    True - the long-term allows more money to be saved, it allows dollar cost averaging to play a role and it allows the effects of compounding to be most beneficial. The long-term is also where we will end up by definition.

18. **True: Knowing about saving and investing will help us understand what is being spoken about in the media.**

    True - so much of what is written in the press, and on TV relates to finance, money, saving and investing.

19. **Which of the following is the best definition of investing:**
    a. saving money
    b. trial and error
    c. gambling
    d. committing money with a view to gaining a financial return

    Investing is slightly different to saving - saving is getting the money aside and not spending it, investing involves doing something with it to try and make it grow.

20. **Which of the following is most closely tied to the study and science of money, the management of money and financial markets:**
    a. accounting
    b. finance
    c. bookkeeping
    d. administration

    The other areas are also linked but they are not as closely linked to whole area. If we ever wanted to get more detail on any subject, then finance books are a great source of academic information - sometimes more so than 'personal finance' books because the latter often give advice which may or may not be good, or relevant, for everyone given diverse situations.

21. **The topics of saving and investing and finance are frequently discussed:**
    I. in the money or financial section of the newspaper
    II. on the evening news
    III. on the front page of the newspaper
    IV. at the bank
    V. amongst friends and in relationships

    a. I only
    b. I and II only
    c. I, II and III only
    d. I, II, III and IV only
    e. I, II, III, IV and V

    They are discussed in a lot of places.

22. **Saving money can be best described as:**
   a. investing money
   b. buying mutual funds
   c. putting money in a pension plan
   d. spending less than one is earning

   It is not complicated but really worth focusing on to make sure it actually takes place.

23. **A difference between saving and investing is:**
   a. there is none
   b. saving is higher risk than investing
   c. saving money is not a good idea - investing is
   d. saving relates to keeping money, investing relates trying to get a return

   As noted in question 19 as well.

24. **Which of the following statements is true:**
   I. saving money can form the basis for subsequent investments
   II. investing is higher risk than saving
   III. not saving can lead to financial problems
   IV. not saving can lead to excess leverage
   V. saving is an easy first step, investing can require a bit more thought

   a. I only
   b. I and II only
   c. I, II and III only
   d. I, II, III and IV only
   e. I, II, III, IV and V

   Investing is where we are faced with choices and where financial literacy really helps.

25. **Potential problems that could arise if we do not play a role in our finances and investments are:**
   I. it leaves room for abuse
   II. we are not well positioned to monitor how things are going
   III. we would not be well-placed to have a dialogue regarding our investments
   IV. we would not be able to assess what financial advisers are saying
   V. we would not be well-positioned to understand investment alternatives presented to us

   a. I only
   b. I and II only
   c. I, II and III only
   d. I, II, III and IV only
   e. I, II, III, IV and V

   Having some knowledge ourselves can help reduce the risk of falling for financial scams and can help us have a better dialogue with financial advisors if we choose to use them.

26. **Victims of investment scams are most likely going to be:**
   a. informed investors
   b. professional investors
   c. gullible and uniformed individuals
   d. no one - there are no investment scams

   Unfortunately it can happen to a lot of people, but it is most likely to happen when we can not assess or discuss what we are presented with.

Total: 26 Answers

Compounding

27. <u>Compounding money can be best described as:</u>
   a. adding return to a sum of money, getting return on new larger sum - repeating again, again and again
   b. repeatedly earning a return on sums of money that grow with each incremental return
   c. gaining an increasingly larger return as prior returns are added to the existing amount
   d. all of the above

   These are all very similar and rewordings of what compounding is.

28. <u>The most important single concept behind compounding is:</u>
   a. getting a very large return once
   b. repeatedly getting a return
   c. removing the return each time it is earned
   d. being very active in moving the money around

   Compounding involves getting larger returns after prior returns have been added to the amount we started with. It only works if we repeatedly earn returns and add them to the original amount.

29. <u>Compounding, by definition, can only take place if:</u>
   a. the return each year is very high
   b. the return is added to the existing amount and future returns added to consequently larger amounts
   c. the return of any given year is removed each year
   d. the returns are the same each year

   If we remove the return each year, the amount will not grow faster and faster each year because the amount that we are earning the return on is not growing.

30. <u>True: Compounding can take place in a bank account as well as with many other investments.</u>

   As long as there is a return that is increasing the original amount, compounding can take place.

31. <u>Compounding is a powerful concept, because it can:</u>
   a. allow large sums to be saved with relatively small regular contributions
   b. allow small sums to be saved with large regular contributions
   c. multiply our savings many times almost overnight
   d. result in lottery like winnings that have no basis in any financial reasoning

   That is the beauty of it - that small amounts (that we might not even miss) over a long period of time can grow to very large sums (that we would really benefit from having).

32. <u>True: With compounding, the amount that we can compound our money to over the long term can be much larger than the sum of the amounts contributed.</u>

   True - because we are earning a return not only on the amounts contributed, but also on all of the prior returns.

33. <u>Earning a 5% annual return on $100, after one year will mean a new sum of:</u>
   a. $105.00
   b. $150.00
   c. $100.50
   d. $500.00

   $100 x (1 + 5%) = $100 x 1.05 = $105.00

34. **If we add this first-year return to the $100, and let this new amount grow at 5% for a second year, the dollar amount by which the new sum grows by in the second year will be:**
   a. less than in the first year
   b. more than in the first year
   c. same as the first year
   d. either more or less than in the first year

   After the first year, we will have $105 - in the second year, 5% of $105 is $5.25, so it is already growing by a larger dollar amount (since we are earning a 5% return on the $5 return earned in the first year, in addition to the $100).

35. **Compounding has been described as the 8th wonder of the world. Why is this likely to be the case?**
   a. no one can understand it
   b. it can not be analyzed on a simple spreadsheet
   c. it ensures that no investment can ever fall
   d. it can make savings grow so much over the long term

   It can definitely be understood and we could do a lot of examples of how it could look on a spreadsheet. What makes it a wonder is the power of earning a return on prior returns.

36. **Compounding is sometimes described as, or can be thought of as:**
   a. a snowball rolling down a hill and getting bigger and bigger
   b. a snowball being thrown against a wall
   c. snowflakes melting on the ground
   d. a snowman that is being built

   That is one analogy for the process.

37. **Because compounding with a positive return means that money grows by a larger amount with each year that it is being done, we should be aware that:**
   a. starting late is fine because we can always catch up at the end
   b. someone that starts early will not save more than someone that starts late
   c. it does not matter when we start
   d. starting early is theoretically best because it allows more returns to be added, the sum to be larger, and the returns each year to be larger

   This is one of the implications of how compounding works - if we do not have those prior returns, the result is very very different.

38. **When it comes to compounding, which of the following will we be least likely have control over, and/or where should we be most aware of the risk:**
   a. the amount we contribute
   b. the length of time that save for
   c. when we start
   d. the return that we get in any given year

   We can control when we start and how much we contribute, and to some extent for how long we contribute. The return is often set by other entities - for example, the bank, or it might be determined by the stock market - in general, it is determined more by the nature of the investment (and it is more difficult to predict).

39. **Which of the following is/are important factor(s) affecting how much our money grows to:**
   a. the amount we save
   b. the return we get
   c. the length of time that the money compounds for
   d. all of the above

All of them play a role certainly.

40. **True: Getting a slightly higher return without taking more risks, is sometimes possible at the bank by committing to leaving the money on deposit for a longer period of time.**

This is obviously very much worth looking into. It can happen because it gives the bank more options to do more with our money. By making longer-term commitments for example and earning a higher return themselves, they are then able to pay us a higher return as well.

41. **The saying 'pay yourself first' refers to:**
   a. spending money on luxury items for yourself first
   b. setting some money aside for saving and investing before we do anything else
   c. going to the bar for a good time with every paycheck
   d. an illegal activity

This is a phrase that is sometimes used in personal finance books to refer to saving money before we do anything else, so we do not miss the money and simulate a lower income effectively.

42. **The interest rates that we pay on debt, versus the interest rate we get on savings are usually:**
   a. higher
   b. lower
   c. the same
   d. none of the above

This is one of the ways in which banks and credit card companies make money - they make money on the difference between what they pay to have access to the money, and what they charge others to borrow it. The higher interest rate also reflects the risk of making the loan - when we lend money to a bank by depositing money the risk is low (large banks are typically stable institutions and in many countries at least a portion of our deposit is guaranteed (for example by the FDIC in the US)). When a credit card company or bank lends to an individual, the risk is clearly much higher.

43. **Which of the following statements is true:**
   I. a borrower borrows money
   II. a lender lends money
   III. lenders and borrowers can transact with one another
   IV. a borrower lends money
   V. a lender borrows money

   a. I only
   b. II only
   c. I, II, III only
   d. I, II, IV and V only
   e. I, II, III, IV and V

A lender can lend money to a borrower. The lender can earn a return for lending it and the borrower can have access to capital (and pays for it). This is one of the foundations of finance - the interaction between providers and users of capital.

44. **Interest rates on borrowed money are typically higher, when:**
   a. the likelihood of getting the money back is lower for the lender
   b. the likelihood of getting the money back is higher
   c. when the loan is risk free
   d. the borrower is buying a house

The higher interest can be thought of as a higher cost for the risky loan.

45. <u>**Which of the following do lenders typically consider to be the least risky type of borrowing, and where correspondingly interest rates are usually lowest:**</u>
a. when we borrow to make high risk investments
b. when we borrow for something we do not need
c. when we borrow to purchase a house to live in
d. for property speculation

The interest rate for borrowing for a house is usually lower than a lot of other interest rates, since the house is an asset that holds value better than a lot of consumable items, and that can be found and repossessed if necessary.

46. <u>**Borrowing at high interest rates, means that the money we owe grows:**</u>
a. more slowly
b. more quickly
c. at the same speed
d. none of the above

For example, $100 with a 20% interest rate becomes $120 in one year (grows by $20), $144 in two years (grows by $24 in the second year) and $172.80 in three years (grows by $28.80 in third year).

47. <u>**A company might believe that it is justified in borrowing because:**</u>
a. the return that it can get on the borrowed money is higher than the cost of borrowing
b. the return that it gets is lower than the cost of borrowing
c. it is never done - companies never borrow money
d. it is bad for the company

Companies often borrow money, and they do it because they hope to earn a return on the money they are receiving. For companies, interest payments are typically tax-deductible as well.

48. <u>**Which of the following could be used to calculate how money compounds:**</u>
a. a spreadsheet program like Excel
b. a compound interest calculator on the web
c. a financial calculator
d. all of the above

A spreadsheet is probably most illustrative - the others can be looked at as well.

49. <u>**The nature of compounding makes a strong case for:**</u>
I. starting early
II. getting a reasonable return
III. trying to get a consistent return
IV. trying to save taxes on the returns
V. taking huge bets

a. I only
b. I and II only
c. I, II and III only
d. I, II, III and IV only
e. I, II, III, IV and V

Compounding is all about getting repeated returns and the money growing more quickly as the returns are added to the existing sum. Taking huge bets can cause huge losses which really hurts returns and is not part of a core compounding plan - one that uses dollar cost averaging (to be discussed), and one that also makes use of any available tax savings.

50. **Unpaid credit card debt often compounds like savings, but differs in that:**
   a. this debt usually grows more slowly
   b. this debt usually does not grow
   c. this debt usually grows much more quickly
   d. they both grow randomly

   Credit card debt typically has very high interest rates and can be very damaging to consumers.

51. **A valid reason that might partly explain the extremely high typical interest rates on credit card debt might be:**
   a. the loans are low-risk
   b. the loans are risk-free
   c. the loans are always against solid assets
   d. the loans are very risky and the risk of default is higher - they are often against assets that can not be resold easily and that will typically be worth much less as soon as purchased

   I-III are not true - in fact in most cases the opposite is true. Credit card companies (like most businesses) want to make money - in this case they are making a lot money off consumers who do not pay down their balances and pay interest - having said that, the loans are much more risky, and some will just not be repaid - the credit card companies have to price this in as well.

52. **Having an outstanding credit card balance is most often:**
   a. a good idea
   b. a bad idea
   c. a terrible idea
   d. an excellent idea

   The amount that we owe simply grows too fast if we leave it outstanding.

53. **Making only the minimum payment on a credit card is:**
   a. going to pay off the card very quickly
   b. still going to cost us a lot in interest on the debt
   c. a good idea because we are letting our money grow
   d. a bad idea because it will decrease our outstanding balance

   Keeping any balance means paying a lot of interest at such high interest rates. Making the minimum payment usually does not reduce the principal significantly and will definitely mean a lot of interest.

54. **Buying consumables on a credit card and not paying the interest or principal is:**
   a. a good idea because it will make the money that we owe grow very quickly
   b. a bad idea because it will mean that we don't owe any money
   c. a bad idea because the amount that we owe will grow quickly, effectively making the purchased items much more expensive
   d. a good idea because we want the credit card companies to make a return at our expense

   Any item that we purchase, where we pay the corresponding balance on a credit card much later, will mean a much higher amount paid in the end.

55. **In 2005, bank regulators and advocacy groups in the United Stated proposed a revised set of guidelines to raise the minimum payment on a credit card from 2% of the outstanding balance to 4% of the outstanding balance. These guidelines were most likely put forward in order to:**
   a. help credit card companies
   b. help retailers
   c. help the government
   d. protect consumers

The smaller the minimum payment, the larger the outstanding balance and the greater the interest. Consumers that pay the minimum payment and keep paying with an outstanding balance for years and years are the most profitable customers credit card companies can have.

56. Paying as much as possible, or ideally the total balance each month, on a credit card means:
 a. higher costs over the life of the credit card because monthly payments have risen
 b. higher payments over the life of the card because more interest would have to be paid
 c. the same level of payments over the life of the card
 d. significantly lower payments over the life of the card because of lower accumulated interest

 The interest - the interest on the balance and the interest on interest are much larger if the balance is kept outstanding.

57. Credit card companies are likely to make the most money when:
 a. consumers pay off their balances each month
 b. consumers keep an outstanding balance for a long period
 c. consumers default on their credit card debt
 d. consumers do not use their credit card

 As per the previous examples.

58. True: A credit card charges 26% interest on any outstanding balance from month end - this is a guaranteed after-tax cost. Since the likelihood of finding an investment that will provide a guaranteed after-tax return of over 26% is virtually zero, paying down the credit card first is always the best investment option.

 We can think about not paying this high interest as an investment that provides a 26% after tax return. With a 26% rate of interest an outstanding amount doubles in 3 years (1.26^3).

59. If a sum of money was left to compound for 20 years at 10% compounding annually, the amount the saver would have at the end, when compared to the sum he or she started with would be:
 a. about twice as much
 b. about five times as much
 c. almost seven times as much
 d. about ten times as much

 We can see this with a simple spreadsheet starting with $1,000, for example. The compounding would look as follows:

Year	Beginning of Year	End of Year
1	1,000.00	1,100.00
2	1,100.00	1,210.00
3	1,210.00	1,331.00
4	1,331.00	1,464.10
5	1,464.10	1,610.51
6	1,610.51	1,771.56
7	1,771.56	1,948.72
8	1,948.72	2,143.59
9	2,143.59	2,357.95
10	2,357.95	2,593.74
11	2,593.74	2,853.12
12	2,853.12	3,138.43
13	3,138.43	3,452.27

14	3,452.27	3,797.50
15	3,797.50	4,177.25
16	4,177.25	4,594.97
17	4,594.97	5,054.47
18	5,054.47	5,559.92
19	5,559.92	6,115.91
20	6,115.91	6,727.50

We can also calculate this follows:

1,000 x (1 +10%)^{20} or 1,000 x 1.1^{20} = 6,727.50

60. **Which if the following would result in a higher amount saved:**
   a. $1,000 compounding for 5 years at 10% annually
   b. $1,000 compounding for 10 years at 5% annually
   c. $100 compounding for 50 year at 10% annually
   d. $100 compounding for 100 years at 5% annually

We could get to the answer by constructing the same table as in the previous question, or use a compound interest calculator on the web with the current principal, number of years, and the interest rate entered for each of the four scenarios to arrive at the answer. We could also perform the simple calculation:

= 100 x 1.05^{100} for d. and a similar one for all of the other ones, and we would get:

a. $1,610.50
b. $1,628.89
c. $11,739.08
d. $13,150.13

This example is designed to show how important the length of time is - in a. and b. we start with 10 times as much initial capital ($1,000 vs. $100) and despite this we end up with much less. And in d. we have half the interest rate/return (5% vs. 10%) but end up with quite a bit more.

61. **Saving $5.00 every day for 10 years, with the money compounding at 8% every year (annually) will result in overall savings closest to:**
   a. $5,000
   b. $10,000
   c. $20,000
   d. $30,000

Saving $5 every year equates to saving 365.25 x $5 = $1,826.25 every year. We can compound this amount annually to get the following result.

Year	At Start of Yr	Interest (8%)	Amt Saved in Yr	End of Yr
1	0.00	0.00	1,826.25	1,826.25
2	1,826.25	146.10	1,826.25	3,798.60
3	3,798.60	303.89	1,826.25	5,928.74
4	5,928.74	474.30	1,826.25	8,229.29
5	8,229.29	658.34	1,826.25	10,713.88
6	10,713.88	857.11	1,826.25	13,397.24
7	13,397.24	1,071.78	1,826.25	16,295.27
8	16,295.27	1,303.62	1,826.25	19,425.14

9	19,425.14	1,554.01	1,826.25	22,805.40
10	22,805.40	1,824.43	1,826.25	**26,456.08**
TOTAL:		**8,193.58**	**18,262.50**	

So at the end of Year 10, total savings are $26,456.08 whereas the total amount contributed was only $18.262.50.

62. **True: The Rule of 72 can be used to calculate how long approximately it would take for money to double with a given return. For example - with a return of 6%, it would take roughly 72/6=12 years for the money to double.**

This is a handy little rule of thumb that can give very quick compounding approximations of how long it would take to double your money. We can check if this is true in this case by calculating:

1.06^{12} = 2.01 - in other words the amount doubled in 12 years with 6% compound interest.

63. **Someone with $1,000 is able to grow their money at 4%. Which of the following statements is true:**
I. the return in the first year will be $40
II. the return in the second year, if the first-year return is removed will be $40
III. the return in the second year if the first-year return is added to the $1,000 will be higher than $40
IV. if the money were left to compound at the same rate, it would double in approximately 18 years
V. if each year's return is added to the existing sum, the money will grow by the same percentage each year, but by a larger dollar amount each year

a. I only
b. I and II only
c. I, II and III only
d. I, II, III and IV only
e. I, II, III, IV and V

I. $1,000 x 4% = $40
II. $1,000 + $40 - $40 = $1,000. $1,000 x 4% = $40
III. $1,040 x 4% = $41.60 > $40
IV. Rule of 72: 72/4 = 18. Can also be checked with a spreadsheet or calculator
V. Yes, it will compound at 4%. We can see (also from III.) that this amount will grow by a larger dollar amount each year

64. **What is the interest per year on an outstanding credit card balance of $5,000 if the credit card company charges interest of 20%:**
a. $100
b. $500
c. $600
d. $1,000

20% x $5,000 = $1,000

65. **An investor expects the stock market to return 12% on average. She is paying 20% on her $5,000 credit card balance. She has $4,000 of cash that she does not need right now and would like to invest, or use to pay down debt. Which decision would make sense:**
a. invest the money in the stock market to get the 12% return
b. spend the money and increase the credit card debt
c. repay credit card debt - the effective 'return' at about 20% is much higher than the 12% (expected)
d. borrow more on the credit card and invest the $4,000 as well as the additional borrowing

Not only is the stock market return lower - it is also not risk-free (it is expected) and the return will probably be reduced by the taxes she will have to pay (so it will actually be a lower net return). The amount by which the credit card debt compounds at (or the amount she can save by paying down the credit card) is for certain.

66. True: Compounding, either on our debts or on our savings, often takes place automatically and without manual intervention from us.

Our credit card debt will definitely compound by itself if we do not do anything about it. Our savings can also compound - whether in a bank account or a brokerage account (as long as we are getting a return). We can even automate the regular contributions in many cases to make use of dollar cost averaging.

TOTAL: 40 ANSWERS

Debt, Equity and Financial Markets - Providers and Users of Capital

67. **True: When an individual, a company or a government borrow money and pay interest on this money, an entity on the other side of that transaction is likely to be getting a return for having made it available.**

    This is the underlying concept of 'providers and users of capital' and the interaction that allows savers to compound their money while companies and governments use the money to undertake projects/initiatives.

68. **True: Savers and investors can also be thought of as providers of capital in the context of financial markets.**

    Savers and investors fulfill the role of providers of capital.

69. **Which of the following can be considered key principles of our capitalist saving and investing system:**
    I. goods that are economically viable are provided; they are purchased by those able to pay
    II. companies that can deliver returns should have access to capital
    III. generally companies that are not economically viable will fail
    IV. all goods are provided to all consumers
    V. the government should and will usually compete with companies in most industries

    a. I only
    b. I and II only
    c. I, II and III only
    d. I, II, III and IV only
    e. I, II, III, IV and V

    Choices I-III are fundamental principles of our capitalist system. All goods are not provided to all consumers - consumers can buy what they can afford. In a capitalist system, the government only gets involved in areas where the service can not be met (or should not be met) by the private sector effectively, such as a policing for example.

70. **In which of the following situations could we consider ourselves a provider of capital in the context of debt, either directly or indirectly:**
    a. buying a car
    b. keeping a balance in a bank account
    c. borrowing on a credit card
    d. buying a stock

    This provides capital to the bank to make further loans to companies or individuals and is one of the sources of funding for a bank. When we buy a car we are just making a purchase - when we borrow on a credit card we are a user of debt capital - i.e. we are borrowing money (at a very high interest rate). When we buy a stock we are a provider of equity capital.

QUESTIONS 71 & 72 ARE LINKED.

71. **A provider of capital can compound their money by:**
    a. lending it
    b. buying it
    c. spending it
    d. renting it

Lending money means providing capital (through debt). We can not buy capital. Spending money does not provide capital for a return, and we can not rent capital.

72. True: The other way (other than way of previous question) for providers and users of capital to interact is through equity or ownership.

The two ways for providers and users of capital to interact are through debt and equity. The last question was focused on debt.

73. As a saver and an investor, our foremost consideration should be:
a. providing capital where it is needed
b. helping out
c. getting a positive return and managing risk
d. helping the needy

The other actions could certainly have merit in the context of charity - they are just not saving and investing strategies.

74. Providing capital in the interest of benevolence or goodwill, and without a desire or expectation of a financial return, is known as:
a. speculation
b. short-selling
c. investing
d. charity

As per question 73.

75. True: Investors are providers of capital in the context of users and providers of capital.

Investors in this context provide the capital and are looking for the return.

76. Which of the following are often considered major providers of capital:
I. private investors or high net worth individuals
II. investment funds
III. pension funds
IV. insurance companies
V. sovereign wealth funds

a. I only
b. I and II only
c. I, II and III only
d. I, II, III and IV only
e. I, II, III, IV and V

All of these are groups of investors that are very commonly spoken about:
I. who are looking for a return and for whom wealth preservation will likely be most important
II. who invest depending on their mandate on behalf of institutions and/or private clients
III. who are looking for a return for their retirees
IV. who for example manage the money that they take in though insurance premiums, and from which they have to pay out claims
V. who might manage the money of an oil-rich country, resulting from a trade surplus from oil exports for example

77. One of the core ideas behind debt, equity and financial markets relates to an interaction between:
a. providers and users of capital
b. speculators and gamblers

c. hedging companies and insurance companies
d. short-selling companies and newspapers

This is one of the basic principles of our financial system.

78. **Providers and users of capital can potentially interact, because**
I. the user of capital requires capital
II. the provider of capital is looking for a return
III. the user of capital may be able to offer a return
IV. one has money looking for a return, the other needs it
V. providers of capital rely on returns to compound their money

a. I only
b. II only
c. II, III only
d. I, II, IV and V only
e. I, II, III, IV and V

These are all reasons why providers and users of capital can interact in a way that benefits both sides - resulting in a mutually beneficial transaction.

79. **True: Whether an agency is a provider or user of capital relates to their role in a specific situation - they might fulfill a different role in a separate transaction.**

For example a bank has providers of capital - outside shareholders and bondholders (who have effectively provided the capital to the bank), yet it itself could be a provider of capital to a person that is borrowing in the form of a mortgage.

80. **Which of the following statement(s) relating to equity and debt is/are correct?**
I. one side of a debt transaction is lending money for a return
II. a user of capital in a debt-based transaction borrows money
III. a provider of capital that owns a part of a company is involved in an equity transaction
IV. debt and equity can be thought of as two main ways by which providers of capital (savers and investors) and users of capital (companies and governments) can interact
V. debt and equity are the same thing

a. I only
b. I and II only
c. I, II and III only
d. I, II, III and IV only
e. I, II, III, IV and V

Equity and debt are clearly not the same thing - all of the others are true.

81. **In which of the following situations could we consider ourselves a provider of capital in the context of equity, either directly or indirectly:**
a. buying a car with cash
b. keeping a balance in a bank account
c. borrowing on a credit card
d. buying a stock

a. No debt or equity
b. Providing capital to bank
c. Using capital in the form of debt from a credit card company
d. Provider of capital in the form of equity

82. Lending money involves:
   a. debt
   b. equity
   c. shares
   d. stocks

   It is a debt-type transaction (in contrast to an equity or ownership transaction).

83. A lender is:
   a. someone that lends money
   b. someone that borrows money
   c. someone that has no money
   d. someone that wants money

   Someone that borrows money is a borrower. Someone that lends money is a lender.

84. A borrower is:
   a. someone that lends money
   b. someone that borrows money
   c. someone that has no money
   d. someone that wants money

   Someone that borrows money is a borrower. Someone that lends money is a lender.

85. When we are talking about lending and borrowing money, we are talking about:
   a. debt
   b. equity
   c. options
   d. stocks

   Stocks are pieces of ownership or equity. Lending and borrowing have to do with debt.

86. A bank that lends money is seeking a return through:
   a. an equity investment
   b. a debt investment
   c. a stock investment
   d. a commodity investment

   Lending and borrowing have to do with debt. Equity and stock have to do with ownership - the other main way that providers and users of capital interact.

87. When we are talking about ownership, we are talking about:
   a. debt
   b. bonds
   c. equity
   d. lending

   Bonds are slices of debt, and debt is all about lending and borrowing (a bondholder is a lender). Ownership is about having equity.

88. Anyone that owns a piece of a company, owns a piece of the:
   a. debt
   b. equity
   c. bonds
   d. liabilities

When we own a piece of a company, for example by owning a share or a stock in the company, we own a piece of the equity of the company.

89. **Investors that buy the equity of a company, can also be referred to as:**

I. debtholders
II. equityholders
III. bondholders
IV. owners or part-owners of a company
V. lenders

a. I only
b. I and II only
c. I, II and III only
d. II and IV only
e. I, III and V only

Debtholders, bondholders and lenders have all provided capital in the form of debt. Equityholders are owners or part-owners of the company and they own the equity of the company.

90. **Two major distinct groups of providers of capital are:**

a. debtholders and equityholders
b. debtholders and bondholders
c. equityholders and shareholders
d. stockholders and shareholders

A bondholder is a debtholder; a shareholder is an equityholder; and stockholders and shareholders are the same thing.

91. **The equity of a large company is often split into smaller pieces. This statement is:**

a. true, and these pieces are known as stocks or shares
b. true, and these pieces are known as debt
c. true, and the pieces do not have a name
d. not true

That is what stocks (or shares) are - pieces or slices of the equity of a company.

92. **Someone that owns a share in a company, owns:**

a. a part of the equity of that company
b. a part of the debt of the company
c. bonds of the company
d. the liabilities of the company

When we own a piece of a company, for example by owning a share or a stock in the company, we own a piece of the equity of the company.

93. **An investor that buys a bond is effectively:**

a. lending money
b. borrowing money
c. taking an ownership stake
d. buying equity

A purchaser of a bond has bought a piece of the debt of a company or government or other group of borrowers, and has provided capital in the form of debt and lent money. On the other side is a company, government or other group of borrowers that has issued bonds (or securitized their debt) and borrowed money from many providers of capital/bondholders.

94. <u>True: The owner of a stock in a company is an equityholder in that company.</u>

When we own a piece of a company, for example by owning a share or a stock in the company, we own a piece of the equity of the company, and we are an equityholder.

95. <u>True: Shareholders are the owners of a business.</u>

Shareholders provide capital in the form of equity and own the business.

96. <u>True: Stockholders can also be referred to as shareholders in a company.</u>

Stocks and shares are terms that are typically used interchangeably, as are the terms stockholders and shareholders.

97. <u>True: When the amount of money that companies borrow gets very large, the way in which the providers of capital provide the money is often through bonds.</u>

Selling bonds (pieces or slices of debt) allows companies to borrow money from a large group of investors who when they buy a bond have made a loan to the company subject to the terms and conditions of the bond.

98. <u>Which of the following statements is/are true:</u>

I. the equity of a company can be split into stocks or shares for large companies
II. the equity of a company can be split into bonds for large companies
III. the debt of a company can be split into stocks or shares for large companies
IV. the debt of a company can be split into bonds for large companies
V. equity and debt are never parceled into smaller slices

a. I only
b. II only
c. I and III only
d. I and IV only
e. V only

Both equity and debt can be parceled into smaller slices known as stocks and bonds respectively.

99. <u>The owners of a company are seeking a return through:</u>

a. an equity investment
b. a debt investment
c. a bond investment
d. a commodity investment

An owner has equity in the company.

100. <u>Which of the following is not an advantage of having the equity of a company split into stocks or shares that can be bought and sold on a stock exchange:</u>

a. it makes owning a part of the company easier
b. it makes it easier for investors to sell an ownership stake
c. it allows companies to raise capital by selling more stocks/shares
d. it allows an investor to buy the whole company by buying a single stock

Having stocks trade on an exchange makes getting an ownership stake easier, it makes selling an ownership stake easier and companies can raise more capital by selling more shares more easily usually. The owner of a single stock owns only a small portion of the company. One would have to buy all of the stocks of the company in order to buy the whole company.

101. **Which of the following statements provides the same information as saying that a company is fully financed through equity:**
   I. the company has no debt outstanding
   II. the company only has equityholders
   III. the company has bondholders
   IV. the company has no bondholders or other debt
   V. the company has borrowed money

   a. I only
   b. II only
   c. I and II only
   d. I, II and IV only
   e. II and IV only

   The company only has equity financing so there is do debt outstanding and there are therefore also no bondholders (debt) and it has not borrowed money (debt).

102. **True: When a company goes public, equity that was held privately becomes more publicly available.**

   The equity is then available on the stock exchange and the company is said to be public.

103. **If a company raises money by borrowing more, it will have:**
   a. more equity outstanding
   b. less equity outstanding
   c. more debt outstanding
   d. less debt outstanding

   Borrowing more means that the amount of outstanding debt increases.

104. **Which of the following is true:**
   a. a company can finance itself via equity and debt
   b. a company can only finance itself via debt
   c. a government can finance itself via equity and debt
   d. a government can only finance itself via equity

   Companies can finance themselves via equity and debt; governments can finance themselves via debt but not equity because the government can not sell ownership stakes in itself.

105. **True: The holder of a government bond has effectively lent money to the government.**

   Governments issue government bonds and other government debt to borrow money - the holder of government debt such as a bond has lent money to the government.

106. **False: Smaller slices of debt are known as stocks.**

   They are known as bonds.

107. **Two major, distinct ways in which providers and users of capital interact are:**
   a. stocks and shares
   b. equity and debt
   c. equity and stocks
   d. debt and bonds

   These are the two fundamental and distinct ways - all of the other choices represent ways of referring to one of these two ways.

108. False: Smaller slices of equity are known as bonds.

They are known as stocks.

109. False: The return to debtholders is generally more variable than the return to equityholders.

Bondholders typically get a fixed rate of interest, and are paid first from revenues as shown on the income statement; they also have a higher seniority in the capital structure in case of bankruptcy. The return to equityholders is generally more variable than the return to bondholders.

110. True: When we borrow money to purchase an asset, we are employing leverage.

Leverage refers to augmenting an amount of equity with debt to be able to have a greater financial impact (make a larger purchase).

111. Which statement(s) with respect to leverage is/are true:

I. leverage typically involves borrowing money to purchase an asset
II. leverage increases the riskiness for equityholders
III. leverage can mean that we lose our money (our equity) more quickly
IV. leverage is often used in home purchases
V. too much leverage is very dangerous

a. I only
b. I and II only
c. I, II and III only
d. I, II, III and IV only
e. I, II, III, IV and V

I. This is what leverage is.
II. With leverage, a smaller move in the asset price has a bigger impact on equity. For example, if we use $90 of debt to purchase asset for $100 (and we use $10 of equity), if the asset price moves very quickly to $90 (so we can ignore the interest cost), then we still owe $90 (debt), and equity is wiped out
III. See II
IV. This is called a mortgage - interest rates are typically lower, the asset is tangible and it can be found and repossessed by the bank - so they feel more comfortable. In other words: it is a relatively safe form of collateral, and interest rates tend to be lower than for other loans
V. See II

112. True: Debt and equity are the two main forms through which providers of capital and users of capital can interact.

These are two fundamental and distinct ways for providers of capital to provide capital, and for users of capital to access capital.

113. Which of the following statements is false:

a. the debt of a company is generally considered less risky than the equity of the same company
b. United States or United Kingdom government debt is considered very low risk, if not risk-free
c. if a company goes bankrupt, equityholders are considered first in terms of repayment
d. United States government bonds are lower risk than a US company's bonds since the company is more likely not to be able to make an interest or principal payment

The debt of a company is generally considered less risky than the equity of the same company because interest is paid first and because of seniority on balance sheet in case of bankruptcy. Government debt in the US and UK is considered risk-free - corporate debt is not and is higher risk.

114. **Which of the following is the best definition of a security:**
   a. an investment instrument issued by a government or corporation that offers evidence of equity or debt and that represents financial value
   b. a pool of money that is going to be managed by a portfolio manager
   c. a legal entity that is set up to conduct a certain business
   d. an unregulated investment pool that is typically set up to generate absolute returns for sophisticated investors

   This is the definition of a security; b. is a definition of a mutual fund; c. is the definition of a company and d. is the definition of a hedge fund.

115. **True: Stocks and bonds are sometimes more generally referred to as being examples of securities.**

   These are the two most common types of securities.

116. **Which of the following can not issue stocks:**
   a. a US company
   b. a UK company
   c. a German company
   d. a US government

   Governments can borrow money (and therefore issue bonds) but they can not sell ownership stakes in themselves (or issue stocks) as agencies that represent the interests of the public at large.

117. **Equity can also be thought of as:**
   a. the amount that an asset can be sold for
   b. the amount that remains when we sell an asset and have repaid all of the liabilities
   c. revenues
   d. net income

   The equity is the ownership interest - it is the amount that is left over if we sell something and repay all of the debt on the item. Revenues and net income are entries on an income statement and are not about value but about how money was made.

118. **The primary difference between stocks and bonds is:**
   a. stocks go up, bonds might go up
   b. stocks should be considered better investments
   c. stocks are issued by companies, bonds can not be issued by companies
   d. stocks represent ownership, bonds are typically lending instruments

   The first two are not differences between the two and are not inherently true. Companies can issue bonds. Stocks represent equity or ownership and bonds are lending/debt instruments.

119. **Which of the following can not be considered an equity or ownership instrument:**
   a. a stock
   b. a share
   c. private equity
   d. a corporate bond

   a., b., and c. are equity or ownership interests. A corporate bond is a bond issued by a company, and as a bond, it is a lending instrument and therefore not an equity or an ownership instrument.

120. **In order for a company to have its shares listed on a stock exchange, it has to:**
   a. go public

b. go private
c. go bankrupt
d. go insane

Listing your shares on the stock exchange is what going public refers to.

121. The more money an investor borrows to purchase an investment, the higher the:
a. equity
b. leverage
c. ownership
d. dividend

The more debt there is and the the greater the amount borrowed, the greater the leverage and the greater the possible purchase with a given amount of equity.

122. True: Stocks are considered equity or ownership securities.

That is what stocks or shares are - slices of the equity of a company.

123. A provider of debt capital can also be referred to as a:
a. borrower
b. lender
c. shareholder
d. revenues

A provider of debt capital lends money and is a lender - the user of debt capital is a borrower.

124. It would be correct to say that:
a. leverage has no impact on an investor's return
b. leverage magnifies returns for equityholders on the upside but not the downside
c. leverage magnifies returns for equityholders on the downside but not the upside
d. leverage magnifies returns/losses for equityholders both on the downside and the upside

Let's look at this through examples. If we use debt of 50, and equity of 50 to purchase an item for 100, if the price of the item goes up 20% to 120 very quickly and the debt remains at 50 - then the equity will have gone from 50 to 70 (Item: 120; Debt: 50, Equity: 70). The equity will have risen by 40% (from 50 to 70). With higher leverage, the situation might look as follows: with debt of 80, and equity of 20, if the item again rises by 20% to 120 very quickly; with the debt remaining unchanged at 80, the equity will have gone from 20 or 40. (Item: 120; Debt 80, Equity: 40). In this case the equity will have risen by 100% (from 20 to 40). We can see how with the higher leverage the change is more pronounced. We could do the same thing if the item fell in value to 80; in which case, in the first scenario, the equity would have fallen by 40% (50 to 30) and in the second scenario by 100% (20 to 0).

125. A common form of leverage for many people is:
a. paying for a car in full
b. paying for a house in full
c. a mortgage
d. paying for groceries with cash

Paying for something in full does not involve leverage (there is only equity and no debt). Mortgages are very common and are debt against the purchase of real estate.

126. It would be more sensible to argue for the use of leverage when:
a. we expect the value of the asset to drop
b. we have no idea where the asset will go

c. we expect the value of the asset to be stable and slowly rising (although we can always be wrong)
d. the asset is very risky

Leverage magnifies returns and therefore c. makes the most sense - the purchase of a house would generally be assumed to have these characteristics.

127. **An individual buys a home by putting down 20% of the purchase price and borrowing the rest. The cost of selling the house is 5% of the sales price. If the asset falls in value and she was forced to sell it 20% below the purchase price, which of the following statements would be true with respect to the investor after the sale:**
a. she would have made money
b. the investor would have broken even
c. the investor would have lost a small part of the down payment
d. she would have lost more than the entire 20% down payment

She would have lost the 20% down payment when the property fell in value by 20%. The additional 5% cost to sell the property would increase the loss.

128. **Leverage makes the equity of a company:**
a. less risky
b. more risky
c. more stable
d. more certain to go up

More risky in the sense that a smaller change in the value of the company or its assets will have a greater impact on the price of the equity.

129. **When the equity of a company is held by a small group of investors/founders and it is not traded on an exchange, it is known as:**
a. private equity
b. public equity
c. stocks
d. bonds

This is what private equity is. The equity is public when it trades in the form of stocks on an exchange - bonds are not equity.

130. **The equity of a company before the company has gone public and sold shares on a stock exchange is known as:**
a. public equity
b. negative equity
c. private equity
d. brand equity

This is the definition of private equity.

131. **Which of the following is not considered a characteristic of private equity:**
a. illiquidity
b. it can be difficult to value
c. it trades on the stock exchange
d. it is riskier than equity of larger companies

A., b., and d. are true. Public equity trades on a stock exchange. Private equity does not. It can be more difficult to value because the information is more difficult to get and because the company's prospects are often more uncertain since private companies are often smaller and less established.

132. **Which of the following would be the least likely investor in private equity:**
   a. the founders of the company
   b. family and friends of the founders
   c. a small circle of sophisticated high net worth individual investors
   d. an investor that invests in stocks only

When a company is founded, the founder(s) and perhaps some friends and family often own all of the equity. Quite often the company might then look for more capital from other private individuals who have money (which high net worth individuals do). As an aside, the advantage of raising money in the form of equity at the beginning (when the company is probably not making a lot of money), is that it does not require interest payments (unlike borrowing the money), although it does mean giving up some of the ownership of the company. An investor that only invests in stocks (public equity) would be the least likely investor in private equity.

133. **True: The most common way for most investors to have ownership stakes in large companies is through stocks on a stock exchange either directly, or indirectly though funds.**

Because stocks are publicly available and easier to acquire - also there are many stock mutual funds that allow private investors to get exposure to owning stocks via funds.

134. **True: We can become a part-owner in many of the largest companies in the world by buying stocks in these companies.**

The owner of a share or stock is a part owner in the company.

135. **True: Every investor that owns a share or stock in a company is a part-owner of that company.**

136. **The event that takes place when a company goes from having private equity, to having public equity, is known as:**
   a. the graduation
   b. the initial public offering (IPO)
   c. the bond issue
   d. the debt issue

Private equity goes from being private to public via the initial public offering.

137. **Which of the following refer to the same event:**
   I. going public
   II. the initial public offering (IPO)
   III. listing the shares
   IV. selling bonds
   V. selling shares to the public for the first time

   a. I only
   b. I and II only
   c. I, II and III only
   d. I, II, III and IV only
   e. I, II, III and V only

Going public, the IPO and listing the shares all refer to when shares are sold to the public for the first time, as the equity goes from private to public. Selling bonds is not related to this.

138. **Advantages of listing their shares on a stock exchange for a company typically include:**
   I. access to more investors
   II. increased exposure for the firm

III. consumers of their products can also be shareholders/owners of the firm
IV. increased ability to raise additional capital
V. a liquid ownership interest that could be used for acquisitions

a. I only
b. I and II only
c. I, II and III only
d. I, II, III and IV only
e. I, II, III, IV and V

These are the key advantages of having shares listed on an exchange.

139. True: Stock markets and exchanges exist around the world, and a public company will often have its shares listed on an exchange in its home country.

Companies often list their shares where they are incorporated - i.e. their home country.

140. True: Companies and governments need investors, and investors need profitable investment opportunities - hence the opportunity for a structure that benefits both sides.

This is the fundamental concept behind the interaction of providers and users of capital.

141. History has shown that:
a. the fastest growing companies or sectors will always be the fastest growing going forward
b. companies often go through different stages of growth, and because of innovation, the future is likely to be different than the past
c. nothing ever changes
d. a company that is growing quickly today, might slow when it gets larger but it is almost certain to be the fastest growing company again

This is by far the best answer - companies typically do go through cycles and often very fast growing companies will grow more slowly later in their lives as it is no longer possible to maintain the same percentage growth rates, in part due to size.

142. When a company goes bankrupt and it appears that they can only meet a small part of their debt obligation, which of the following is likely to happen:
I. the share price will go to zero, or very close to zero
II. the equity of the company will be worth nothing or very close to nothing
III. the very junior debt is going to be worth nothing or very close to nothing
IV. the most senior debt that is repaid first might still have some value
V. the company would restructure by selling assets or restructuring their financing

a. I only
b. I and II only
c. I, II and III only
d. I, II, III and IV only
e. I, II, III, IV and V

If the company is bankrupt and it appears that only a small part of the debt obligation can be met, then the left side of the balance sheet (assets) will be smaller than the debt on the right side which has priority over the equity. All equity will be wiped out (I and II) and only a part (the senior part) of the debt will have some value (III and IV). The company is also likely to restructure (V).

143. Which of the following are generally recognized as phases of a company's life cycle:
I. start-up
II. growth

III. maturity
IV. decline
V. fraud

a. I only
b. I and II only
c. I, II and III only
d. I, II, III and IV only
e. I, II, III, IV and V

I-IV are a list of some of the important phases for many companies. Fraud can happen but it is not considered a part of a typical company's life cycle.

144. Stocks can be described as:
a. slices of ownership in companies
b. slices of ownership in governments
c. slices of debt in companies
d. slices of debt in governments

Stocks are slices of the equity or ownership in companies.

145. Corporate bonds can be described as:
a. slices of ownership in companies
b. slices of ownership in governments
c. slices of debt in companies
d. slices of debt in governments

Corporate bonds are bonds of companies - pieces of the debt of companies.

146. Government bonds can be described as:
a. slices of ownership in companies
b. slices of ownership in governments
c. slices of debt in companies
d. slices of debt in governments

Government bonds are bonds of governments - pieces of the debt of governments.

147. When one company wants to buy another company and issues shares to finance the transaction, the services that it might draw on in this context are most likely to relate to:
a. commercial banking
b. investment banking
c. commodities trading
d. bond trading

These are typical investment banking activities.

TOTAL: 81 ANSWERS

FINANCIAL STATEMENTS

148. The analysis and study of a company's assets, liabilities, cash flows and income falls into an area of study known as:
   a. economics
   b. accounting
   c. biology
   d. derivatives

   This is what accounting involves.

149. Having some idea regarding financial statements is useful because:
   I. they are spoken about very frequently
   II. they provide a lot of insight into how stocks and bonds might behave
   III. it helps understand how companies make money
   IV. they help illustrate leverage
   V. an investor has to prepare them very regularly on behalf of the company

   a. I only
   b. I and II only
   c. I, II and III only
   d. I, II, III and IV only
   e. I, II, III, IV and V

   Financial statements and some of the items on them like revenues, net income etc. are spoken about very frequently. Furthermore, they provide a lot of insight into how companies make money, what their financial position is, what their assets are, what the leverage is, and how the stocks and bonds might be valued. Investors do not have to prepare them on behalf of the company regularly (although they might create their own statements as part of their analysis) - the company prepares them (or their accountants) and they are often checked by auditors.

150. True: The Annual Report for a company will provide a summary of what happened in a given year for a company and of the status of the company at the end of the reporting period - it will typically include the three most common financial statements - the balance sheet, the income statement and the cash flow statement.

151. True: The financial statements that are found in the Annual Report often come with footnotes that can be very important in understanding the company.

   These will provide more information on the items that are listed in the financial statements.

152. A company's annual report could be of interest to:
   I. investors
   II. employees
   III. mutual fund managers
   IV. hedge fund managers
   V. stock analysts

   a. I only
   b. I and II only
   c. I, II and III only
   d. I, II, III and IV only
   e. I, II, III, IV and V

They are clearly of interest to investors (I, III and IV) and stock analysts (V). Employees (II) can also learn a lot about their firms from the annual report.

153. The ________ checks a company's finances for accuracy in the annual report.
 a. stock trader
 b. bond trader
 c. auditor
 d. investment bank

The role of an auditor is to check a company's financial statements.

154. True: Stock analysts can calculate a large number of ratios based on the income statement, balance sheet and cash flow statement to gain further insights into a company's financial state.

This is often done and can include the P/E ratio, debt/equity ratios etc.

155. Which of the following is not a typical financial statement:
 a. the balance sheet
 b. the income statement
 c. the cash flow statement
 d. the overall statement

A., b. and c. are the three common financial statements. D. does not exist as a recognized financial statement.

156. True: The income statement provides a summary of a company's revenues, costs and expenses, leading to the income for the company.

The income statement provides this summary over a period of time, for example one year.

157. Which of the following are other words for a company's income or net income:
 I. net profit
 II. profit
 III. earnings
 IV. revenues
 V. sales

 a. I only
 b. I and II only
 c. I, II and III only
 d. I, II, III and IV only
 e. I, II, III, IV and V

The net profit is sometimes abbreviated as the profit for the company. The earnings for the company are the same thing as the net profit, and they are the revenues or sales with all costs subtracted to arrive at what the company earned over that period.

158. The sales of a company are also known as the company's:
 a. cash flow
 b. net income
 c. costs
 d. revenues

Sales and revenues are the same thing, and are typically the first line of the income statement.

159. The income statement from top to bottom typically contains:

a. revenues minus all expenses to give a figure for the net income
b. assets and liabilities
c. cash flows
d. stocks and bonds

This is the most common form of the income statement and it summarizes this information over a certain time period, such as a year.

160. The income statement could be summarized as:
a. stocks minus bonds
b. revenues minus cost of goods sold minus operating expenses minus non-operating expenses, such as interest and taxes, to arrive at the net income
c. revenues minus operating expenses minus taxes minus dividends minus cash flows
d. assets minus liabilities

This is the same are question 159 with more detail regarding all of the items subtracted to get from revenues to net income.

161. One of the key principles of the income statement is that it is intended to show the company as:
a. historical entity - it is intended to capture the distant past
b. a going concern - a company that is in business and will continue operations
c. a company in liquidation - a company that will finish operations with no need to reinvest
d. a dormant company - a company that is currently not active

This is one of the key principles behind how the items are considered on the income statement - more information on this is provided in question 182.

162. The terms 'top line' and 'bottom line' correspond to where the items appear on the:
a. balance sheet
b. income statement
c. cash flow statement
d. annual report

The 'top line' therefore refers to revenues or sales, and the 'bottom line' refers to net profit or earnings.

163. A company's 'top line' refers to:
a. its earnings
b. its revenues
c. its cash flows
d. its dividends

That is based on how the income statement looks typically.

164. A company's 'bottom line' refers to:
a. its earnings
b. its revenues
c. its cash flows
d. its dividends

That is based on how the income statement looks typically.

165. When a company makes a loss, which of the following is certain to be true:
a. the revenues are negative
b. cash flow will be negative
c. earnings will be negative

d. earnings will be up

A loss is when earning are negative, i.e. earnings or profits are less than zero.

166. **True: We can capture a company's sales over a given period and subtract all expenses including interest and taxes to find out how much profit the company is making.**

This is effectively what the income statement does.

167. **True: When a company has sales, the income statement illustrates that debtholders get paid interest before earnings are calculated.**

This is reflected in the order in which items typically appear on the income statement (interest appears as a non-operating expense in the income statement and the earnings are at the bottom after all expenses have been subtracted).

168. **True: The earnings of the company are more relevant for equityholders than they are for debtholders.**

Debtholders get paid interest before the earnings. The earnings are either paid to equityholders in the form of dividends or retained on the balance sheet where they form part of the shareholders' equity.

169. **True: The structure of the income statement typically gives a very clear indication as to whether bondholders or equityholders get paid first.**

170. **True: Whether debtholders or equityholders get paid first is relevant to the discussion of risk and returns.**

The fact that debtholders get paid first reduces risk - the profits and the appreciation of the company's value for a healthy company benefit mainly the equityholders who are compensated for the extra risk with a higher return if the company performs well.

171. **Companies can do all of the following with their earnings except:**
   a. retain them
   b. pay them as dividends
   c. show them on their income statements
   d. call them revenues

Companies either retain their earnings (keep them within the company and where they will grow the balance sheet) or pay them out to shareholders. Earnings are shown on the income statement. They can not call them revenues since these are different items clearly.

172. **The income statement is:**
   a. a snapshot at a point in time
   b. a summary of events over a period of time
   c. not usually in the annual report
   d. the same thing as a balance sheet

For example a year - such as an income statement in the annual report.

173. **Which one of the following terms is not like the other three:**
   a. net income
   b. earnings
   c. profits
   d. revenues

The other three all refer to the same thing.

174. **The income statement would contain the following entries:**
    I. revenues
    II. operating expenses
    III. earnings
    IV. assets
    V. liabilities

    a. I only
    b. I and II only
    c. I, II and III only
    d. I, II, III and IV only
    e. I, II, III, IV and V

The other two are items on the balance sheet.

175. **True: Companies can choose to pay out a part of their profits or net income in the form of a dividend.**

That is one of the choices - the other one is to retain the earnings within the company in which case they can be used to reinvest in the business.

176. **Which of the following could cause higher earnings, all other things being equal:**
    I. revenues were higher
    II. taxes were lower
    III. the company had a one-off gain
    IV. the interest expense was lower
    V. material costs/cost of goods sold were lower

    a. I only
    b. I and II only
    c. I, II and III only
    d. I, II, III and IV only
    e. I, II, III, IV and V

I and III would make revenues higher and with costs the same (all other things being equal), net profit would be higher. II, IV and V would mean lower costs and with revenues the same this would also lead to a higher net profit.

177. **False: The income statement balances.**

No, the balance sheet balances and it has two side that can balance. The income statement is a list from revenues to net income with all of the costs for the company shown.

178. **The net margin of a company is defined as the net income divided by the revenues. The net margin indicates which of the following for the period:**
    I. the earnings generated per dollar of revenues
    II. the company's profitability
    III. how much of every dollar of sales made it to earnings for that period
    IV. the company's balance sheet structure
    V. the number of shareholders in the company

    a. I only
    b. I and II only
    c. I, II and III only

d. I, II, III and IV only
e. I, II, III, IV and V

I. yes - as a percentage
II. yes - in that it provides a percentage of how much of revenues or sales become net profit
III. yes - in that it provides a percentage of how much of revenues or sales become net profit
IV. no - it does not provide any information on the balance sheet as both entries are income statement entries
V. no - it has nothing to do with the number of shareholders

179. **True: Earnings that are retained within the company (i.e. not paid out as dividends) would end up in the shareholders' equity portion of the balance sheet.**

That is where (cumulative) retained earnings are shown.

180. **True: The choice of depreciation method can affect a company's earnings.**

Faster (higher) depreciation leads to lower earnings, and slower (lower in any given year) depreciation would lead to higher earnings.

181. **Companies that have earnings of zero are:**
a. bankrupt
b. not making revenues
c. breaking even
d. having large losses

Breaking even is when the company is not making any money (just), so earnings or profits are zero, because all costs equal revenues and therefore revenues - costs = 0.

182. **True: The income statement is intended to show a company as a going concern.**

All of the financial statements are prepared on this basis unless there are reasons to believe that the company should no longer be considered as a going concern. What this means for example is that assets are recorded at historical or market value and depreciated, instead of considering what they would be worth in a liquidation where they might be worth much less/written off more aggressively.

QUESTIONS 183 & 184 ARE LINKED.

183. **True: When a company purchases a major piece of equipment to be used for a number of years, it might pay for it all at once or over time. In either case, the income statement would not show the entire cost in any one year, but instead show an annual expense to reflect the use of the item.**

The income statement would show an annual charge for depreciation. If the whole item was shown as a cost in one year, it would depress earnings significantly in that year and also not reflect that the item had a useful life over which it was used.

184. **The cost of this asset would typically be spread as annual expenses over the useful life of the item. This expense is known as:**
a. cost of goods sold
b. tax expense
c. depreciation
d. earnings

This is what deprecation is - more detail of why this is done is provided in question 183.

185. **The entry on the income statement that reflects the material costs of items sold is:**

a. operating expenses
b. cost of goods sold
c. interest expense
d. taxes

Cost of goods sold includes the material costs of the items sold - other main expense items on the income statement are 'selling, general and administrative expenses (S,G&A)', 'depreciation', 'research and development (R&D) expenses' and non-operating expenses such as interest and taxes.

186. Depreciation can also be described as:
a. the cost of employees
b. the cost of renting an office
c. an expense for wear and tear that is intended to capture the reduction in value of an item over its useful life
d. company sales

187. A company with costs that are fixed in the short term, sees its revenues decline very suddenly by 10% - the earnings of the company are likely to be down:
a. less than 10%
b. 10%
c. significantly more than 10%
d. not at all

For example, if a company has revenues of 100, costs of 90 and therefore net income of 10 (to simplify), if revenues fall by 10%, to 90, costs will still be close to 90 in the short term (for the sake of simplification) so net income would be close to 0 - in other words, it would drop significantly.

188. A sudden 10% rise in the revenues of a company is likely to cause:
a. earnings to rise by less than 10%
b. earnings to also rise by exactly 10% always
c. earnings to stay the same
d. earnings to rise by potentially much more than 10%

For example, if a company has revenues of 100, costs of 90 and therefore net income of 10 (to simplify). If revenues rise by 10%, to 110, some costs will change and some will not - costs will rise by less than 10% - for example costs could be 95, then net income would be 15 (up 50%).

189. Company 'RED' supplies paint to the car manufacturer 'WHEELS'. This paint would be recognized as follows:
I. revenues for the company RED
II. revenues for the company WHEELS
III. cost of goods sold for the company RED
IV. cost of goods sold for the company WHEELS
V. assets for both companies

a. I only
b. II only
c. II and III only
d. I and IV only
e. V only

Company RED sells the paint and would recognize the sales in the sales or revenue line. For company WHEELS this would be a material cost recorded in the cost of goods sold.

190. Which of the following would not impact the earnings of a company:

a. a decline in revenues due to a slowing economy
b. a rise in material costs
c. an increase in the tax rate the company has to pay
d. an increase in the company's dividend

Dividends are paid out of earnings, they do not alter the earnings and also are not shown on the income statement.

191. **True: The net margin is a measure of the profitability of a company and is intended to show how much each dollar of revenues or sales provides in terms of net income. It is calculated by dividing net income by revenues (in %).**

That is the definition of the net margin.

192. **True: We could prepare an income statement for our personal financial situation by summarizing a typical month or year. A detailed statement of this type could show where our money is going and how much is left over, and could be used to figure out how much more we could theoretically save.**

Yes, and this can be a very worthwhile exercise to show how much we are making and where our money is going over a given time period, and thereby potentially also provide some indication of where there might be opportunities for saving.

193. **True: We could schematically and logically represent a company by showing its assets on the left side, and the way that it has funded itself on the right side.**

This is the balance sheet.

194. **True: By showing a company's assets, liabilities and shareholders' equity, we can get a very good sense for the amount of leverage in the company.**

Leverage is reflected in the amount of debt a company has either as a percentage of equity (the debt/equity ratio) or as a percentage of assets.

195. **True: Showing the assets of a company on the left side, and how these assets are funded on the right side is known as a balance sheet.**

This is what a balance sheet is.

196. **If the assets are found on the left side, which of the following would typically be found on the right side of a balance sheet:**
a. cash
b. shareholders' equity and liabilities
c. revenues
d. cash flow

If the assets are on the left side (uses of funds) as they typically are, then the sources of funds (equity and debt) are shown on the right side so that the two sides balance.

197. **Companies are financed, in general terms, by:**
a. assets and liabilities
b. equity and debt
c. debt and bonds
d. assets and stocks

These are the two main sources of funds - providers of capital either provide capital to companies in the form of debt (lending) or equity (ownership).

198. On a balance sheet, the assets are shown typically on:
   a. the left side
   b. the right side
   c. the top
   d. the bottom

199. On a balance sheet, the right side typically shows:
   a. the assets
   b. shareholders' equity and liabilities
   c. the income
   d. the revenues

   With the assets being on the left side.

200. True: The assets on the left side of the balance sheet equal the value of the shareholders' equity and liabilities on the right side.

   These are the components of the left and right sides that balance.

201. The balance sheet is:
   a. a snapshot at a point in time
   b. a summary of events over a period of time
   c. not usually in the annual report
   d. the same thing as an income statement

   A balance sheet would capture how things looked for example at the end of the financial year or at the end of the reporting period.

202. Which items on the balance sheet balance:
   a. assets on one side and debt on the other
   b. assets on one side and equity on the other
   c. assets and debt on one side and equity on the other
   d. assets on one side and equity and debt on the other

   This is the underlying fundamental concept behind the balance sheet.

203. When the value of the assets of a healthy company go up greatly:
   a. the liabilities do not change that much - but the shareholders' equity goes up greatly
   b. neither shareholders' equity nor liabilities go up
   c. the liabilities go up greatly
   d. the cost of goods sold of the income statement reflects this increase

   When the left side of the balance sheet goes up (the assets), the liabilities (the debt) on the right side would not change that much (the company does not owe more money suddenly). It is the value of the equity that rises a lot in value to keep the balance sheet in balance. This just shows how an owner benefits when the value of an asset rises (in this case with leverage), just as it is the owner that would lose more value when the asset falls in price.

204. The main beneficiaries of a rise in the value of the assets of a healthy company are:
   a. lenders to the company
   b. bondholders of the company
   c. shareholders or owners of the company
   d. government bondholders

   As per the rise in equity and as discussed also in question 203.

205. **Bonds that a company has issued to finance itself would appear in:**
   a. the assets portion of the company's balance sheet
   b. the equity portion of the company's balance sheet
   c. the liabilities portion of the company's balance sheet
   d. they would not be shown

   Bonds that are issued are debt that is outstanding and a liability of the company.

206. **If a company buys a factory, that factory would appear on:**
   a. the asset portion of that company's balance sheet
   b. the equity portion of that company's balance sheet
   c. the liabilities portion of that company's balance sheet
   d. nowhere

   And depending on how it was paid for, other entries on the balance sheet would reflect the purchase to keep the balance sheet balanced (for example cash down on the left side where factory is or debt up on right side).

207. **Stocks that a company issues would appear where on the balance sheet:**
   a. the assets side (left side)
   b. as shareholders' equity (right side)
   c. the liabilities side (right side)
   d. as revenues (top of income statement)

   These would be a source of funds (equity funds) and would appear on the right side.

208. **If a company invested some of its surplus cash in government bonds, these bonds would appear where on the balance sheet:**
   a. the assets side (left side)
   b. as shareholders' equity (right side)
   c. the liabilities side (right side)
   d. as revenues (top of income statement)

   These would be assets of the company if it had bought them with cash and held them as investments (cash would go down on left side).

209. **True: When a company issues new shares to the market for cash, the right side of the balance sheet would show the equity getting larger and the left side would show the cash that was taken in from the sale.**

   This is one possible event that could cause a change in the balance sheet and is mainly intended to illustrate that there are specific places where these entries would go, and that the balance sheet would still be required to balance.

210. **If a company buys back its own shares with cash, the balance sheet will reflect:**
   a. a decrease in liabilities
   b. a decrease in liabilities on the right side and a decrease in inventory on the left side
   c. a decrease in equity on the right side and a decrease in debt on the right side
   d. a decrease in cash on the left side and a decrease in equity on the right side

   This is another possible event that could cause a change in the balance sheet - at the end the balance sheet would still be required to balance.

211. **True: After a new item is added to the balance sheet such as a new asset, the balance sheet will still be required to balance.**

By definition the balance sheet always balances. If the asset was bought with cash, the left side would show the decrease in cash, and the addition of the asset.

212. **Which of the following is true:**
    I. Assets = Equity + Liabilities
    II. Equity + Liabilities = Assets
    III. Equity = Assets - Liabilities
    IV. Liabilities = Assets - Equity
    V. Assets - Liabilities = Equity

    a. I only
    b. I and II only
    c. I, II and III only
    d. I, II, III and IV only
    e. I, II, III, IV and V

    These are all restatements of each other, but should all make sense also when read or thought about in the context of a balance sheet and how it balances.

213. **The value at which things are recorded on the balance sheet is known as:**
    a. the book value
    b. the market value
    c. the loss value
    d. the liquidation value

    The book value is the value at which the value of items are recorded in the 'books' - like the balance sheet. For assets the book value is based on the historical cost of the item.

214. **True: The balance sheet shows the capital provided by the owners the lenders.**

    Showing these sources of funding is what the right side of the balance sheet typically shows.

215. **True: If a company buys a piece of equipment using cash, cash on the left side of the balance sheet would go down and the item would be recorded on the left side of the balance sheet as an asset. The balance sheet would still balance.**

    In this case the cash (asset) would be replaced by the piece of equipment (asset) on the left side of the balance sheet - the right side would remain unchanged. The balance sheet is always required to balance.

216. **True: If a company buys a piece of equipment using debt, the item would be recorded on the left side of the balance sheet and the debt on the right side. The balance sheet would still balance.**

    The piece of equipment would be added to the left side, where assets go, and the right side would increase to reflect the addition of the piece of equipment - specifically if debt was used to buy the equipment, then the debt would increase. The balance sheet would still be required to balance.

217. **A company has financed itself through debt and equity (which also includes retained earnings). The ratio of debt to equity is a measure of:**
    a. the profitability of the company
    b. the leverage on the balance sheet
    c. the sales of the company
    d. the cash flow of the company

    The amount of debt, either with respect to the amount of equity, or with respect to the total value of the assets, is a measure of the leverage.

218. **In order to raise cash on its balance sheet, a company can do which of the following:**

I. sell new shares
II. sell new bonds
III. borrow money from a bank
IV. sell assets for cash
V. retain more of its earnings

a. I only
b. I and II only
c. I, II and III only
d. I, II, III and IV only
e. I, II, III, IV and V

All of these would raise cash or keep more cash on the balance sheet as follows:
I. Left Side: Cash up; Right Side: Shareholders' Equity up
II. Left Side: Cash up; Right Side: Debt up
III. Left Side: Cash up; Right Side: Debt up
IV. Left Side: Cash up, other assets down; Right Side: unchanged
V. Left Side: Cash up; Right side: equity/retained earnings: up

219. **In the above example, which of the actions that the company could take would not increase the size of the balance sheet (i.e. make the left side larger and the right side larger).**

I. sell new shares
II. sell new bonds
III. borrow money from a bank
IV. sell assets for cash
V. retain more of its earnings

a. I only
b. II only
c. III and V only
d. IV only
e. I, II, III, IV and V

In this case one part of the assets would decrease due to the sale, and another part (the cash) would increase due to the sale - the cash would go up but the other assets down, so it would be more of a transfer and the balance sheet would not grow.

220. **True: We can use the concept of a balance sheet to look at our own finances.**

We can summarize our assets and our liabilities - the difference between the two would be what we owned (our equity) or our net worth.

221. **True: We can prepare a balance sheet for our personal finances showing our assets, our debt and the equity. The equity in such a balance sheet would also be our net worth.**

222. **True: The concept of a balance sheet - the equity, the leverage, and their sensitivity to moves in the price of an asset can be used to think about many different investment situations.**

For example, an asset worth 100 which is purchased with 80 of debt would provide a return of 100% if the asset price rose 20% (to 120) or a loss of 100% if the asset price fell by 20% (to 80) (with no change in the debt over the short term).

223. **The equity in our homes can be calculated by taking:**

a. the value of the home less any debts or mortgages against the home

b. the value of the home plus any debts or mortgages against the home
c. the amount of the mortgages on the home
d. the amount of rent that we pay

Equity = Assets - Debt; in this case the only asset is the home.

QUESTIONS 224-230 ARE LINKED.

224. **An investor buys an asset using 50% equity (own money) and borrowing the rest. The interest rate on the borrowed money is 8%. The amount borrowed is closest to:**
a. 10% of the asset
b. 20% of the asset
c. 50% of the asset
d. 100% of the asset

50% is equity, and 50% is debt.

225. **The purchaser of the asset can also be referred to as:**
I. the owner
II. the provider of equity capital
III. the provider of debt capital
IV. the bondholder
V. the lender

a. I only
b. I and II only
c. I, II and III only
d. I, II, III and IV only
e. I, II, III, IV and V

226. **If the asset price rises by 20%, the return to the provider of the debt capital is closest to:**
a. 8%
b. 10%
c. 20%
d. 40%

The return to the debtholder is fixed at 8%.

227. **If the asset price falls by 20%, the return to the provider of the equity capital is closest to:**
a. 8%
b. -8%
c. -20%
d. -40%

For example, if the asset cost 100, and was financed with 50 of equity and 50 of debt, if the asset fell by 20% (to 80) then the debt would still be 50 and the equity would have dropped to 30. A drop from 50 to 30 represents a loss of 40%.

228. **If the asset price falls by 20%, the return to the provider of the debt capital is closest to:**
a. 8%
b. -8%
c. -20%
d. -40%

The return to the debtholder is fixed at 8%.

229. <u>If the value of the asset rises by 20%, the return for the owner will be:</u>
   a. 8%
   b. 10%
   c. 20%
   d. 40%

   For example, for an asset of 100 financed with 50 of equity and 50 of debt - if the asset rose by 20% (to 120), and if we assume that debt would still be 50, then the equity would have risen to 70. A rise from 50 to 70 represents a gain of 40%.

230. <u>By how much would the value of the asset have to fall for the owner to lose all of his or her money:</u>
   a. 10%
   b. 20%
   c. 50%
   d. 100%

   With 50 of equity and 50 of debt, for all of the equity to be wiped out the asset would have to fall from 100 to 50 or 50%, leaving only the 50 of debt.

231. <u>True: The capital structure of a company refers to the structure of the company's financing on the right side of the balance sheet. These sources of capital have different 'seniorities' in terms of which receive interest first, and which are paid off first in the event of a bankruptcy or liquidation.</u>

   The debtholders for example get paid before the equityholders - there can also be different seniorities to the debt with the most senior debt being repaid first.

232. <u>What is the correct order (from most senior to least senior) for the following sources of funding:</u>
   I. senior debt
   II. subordinated debt
   III. equity

   a. I, II, III
   b. III, II, I
   c. II, I, III
   d. III, I, II

   Debt is senior to equity as we know. Senior debt is senior to subordinated debt (as their names suggest) .

233. <u>True: One of the main objectives of the cash flow statement is to calculate the change in cash levels over a given year.</u>

   This is what the cash flow statement is used for.

234. <u>True: The cash flow statement typically starts with the net income from the income statement and then makes certain adjustments to calculate cash flow from operations. Cash flow from investing and financing are also looked at separately in the cash flow statement.</u>

   This is the general structure of a typical cash flow statement.

235. <u>True: Depreciation on the income statement is a non-cash charge.</u>

   True - it is a charge to recognize the wear and use of an item during the accounting period and is typically a percentage of the item's cost to reflect a decline in value during the accounting period. Because it is a non-cash charge it is added back to the net income on the cash flow statement in the course of calculating cash flow from operations.

236. **<u>True: A share issue would not be shown on the income statement but it impacts the company - in particular cash levels and the equity on the balance sheet. A share issue would be shown on the cash flow statement and the balance sheet.</u>**

Because a share issue is not be part of the operations of the company - it is not shown on the income statement. A share sale for cash clearly would change the level of cash in the company which is worth monitoring - it is the cash flow statement that records this in the financing section of the cash flow statement.

237. **<u>Cash flow statements are useful because:</u>**
I. there are non-cash entries on the income statement such as depreciation
II. income statements focus on operations and not financing or investing
III. the income statement might recognize revenues even though the cash has not been received
IV. monitoring the cash position of a company is very important to ensure survival
V. income statements show the company as a going concern but might not show all cash flows exactly as they take place

a. I only
b. I and II only
c. I, II and III only
d. I, II, III and IV only
e. I, II, III, IV and V

These statements are all true - and highlight why the cash flow statement is useful.

238. **<u>A cash flow statement is typically split into the following categories to reflect where the cash flows took place:</u>**
a. operating, investing and financing activities
b. buying and selling
c. assets and liabilities
d. revenues, costs and income entries

239. **<u>True: The net change in cash that is calculated from the cash flow statement would be reflected in the balance sheet over time.</u>**

The change in cash from the cash flow statement over a given year for example, would also be reflected in the difference in the cash on the balance sheet at the beginning of the year (or at the end of the prior year) and the end of this year.

240. **<u>True: Depreciation is reflected (and accumulated) on the balance sheet showing how assets are depreciating over time by allowing a net book value to be calculated.</u>**

The balance sheet typically records the initial value of the asset, the accumulated depreciation, and then the current/net book value (initial value - accumulated depreciation).

241. **<u>Earnings are more relevant for equityholders than debtholders because:</u>**
I. debtholders are paid interest before earnings are even calculated
II. earnings can be paid out as dividends which equityholders receive
III. if the earnings are retained they become a part of shareholders' equity
IV. equityholders own the company; whatever is left over after expenses and liabilities is effectively theirs
V. equityholders are always paid all earnings in cash every year in all cases

a. I only
b. I and II only
c. I, II and III only
d. I, II, III and IV only

e. I, II, III, IV and V

I-IV are correct - equityholders only receive the dividends that are paid out of earnings each year.

242. **<u>A company buys a major piece of equipment that has a useful life of 10 years using cash. Which of the following would be expected to happen:</u>**

I. the cash flow statement would show the outgoing cash flow
II. the balance sheet would reflect a decrease in cash and the acquisition of this equipment
III. the income statement would reflect a deprecation charge each year over the useful life
IV. the balance sheet would over time reflect the accumulated depreciation to show the reduction in book value since purchase
V. the full cost of the piece of equipment would be recorded as a cost in the income statement

a. I only
b. I and II only
c. I, II and III only
d. I, II, III and IV only
e. I, II, III, IV and V

V is not true given that the item is depreciated, and therefore only a charge to reflect the use of the item over its useful life is recognized each year. All of the others are true.

TOTAL: 95 ANSWERS

Financial Markets

243. <u>True: Stocks and bonds trade on financial markets.</u>

Stocks and bonds (and commodities) trade between many buyers and sellers on markets which are generically referred to as financial markets.

244. <u>True: One of the main benefits of a market is that it allows many different entities to come together to do business.</u>

245. <u>Financial markets exist to:</u>
   a. provide a place for gamblers
   b. allow governments to have an IPO
   c. allow providers and users of capital to interact
   d. allow private equity to trade

This is one of the main goals of the financial markets - to allow providers and users of capital to interact.

246. <u>True: Investors come to the financial markets seeking a return.</u>

247. <u>True: The return that financial markets provide can be a key element of how savers and investors compound their money.</u>

This relates back to the concept of providers and users of capital.

248. <u>Ideally, financial markets:</u>
   a. provide a place for investors to earn returns
   b. allow companies that need capital to raise it
   c. provide transparent and liquid trading in securities
   d. all of the above

These are some of the key reasons why financial markets are so important and so crucial to our economic system.

249. <u>True: Financial markets have been around for hundreds of years.</u>

250. <u>True: Financial markets offer advantages to both providers and users of capital.</u>

For providers of capital they offer better choice, liquidity and transparency - for users of capital they offer access to a greater number of potential investors for example.

251. <u>Advantages of financial markets for users of capital can include:</u>
   I. access to more investors
   II. a higher profile for firm
   III. an externally determined price for equity and debt
   IV. easier access to capital
   V. less reporting requirements

   a. I only
   b. II only
   c. I,III and V only
   d. II and IV only
   e. I, II, III and IV

I. because more investors will find the user of capital and because more investors go there

II. being listed (the IPO), share price performance, quarterly results all can mean that a listed company will be in the spotlight from the media much more
III. having an externally determined share price for example is often used to judge executive performance (and to set compensation)
IV. this can be the case due to the greater number of investors in one centralized market
V. listed companies typically have greater greater reporting requirements, set by the exchange, and therefore V is not true.

252. True: One of the key roles of the financial markets is to figure out to whom money should be provided based on the expected ability to provide a return.

That is what investors try to do through the financial markets - provide capital to users of capital, such as companies, that they think will provide a return.

253. The financial markets can provide which of the following advantages to providers of capital or savers and investors:

I. choice
II. centralization of transactions
III. improved transparency
IV. improved liquidity
V. no risk in any investment

a. I only
b. II only
c. I,III and V only
d. II and IV only
e. I, II, III and IV

I-IV are some of the key features of financial markets.
I. financial market offer investors seeking returns tremendous choice
II. buys and sells (and information) are centralized when for example in the case of a stock market, the companies could be located almost anywhere
III. both in terms of the price and volume with respect to the securities, and also w.r.t. the additional reporting requirements that often come with being on traded on a financial market
IV. it is typically easier to buy and sell investments without moving the price than would be the case in less liquid private markets
V. is not true

254. Which of the following is/are function(s) of the financial markets:

I. to make appropriate allocations of capital possible
II. to allow good firms to get access to funding
III. to provide a place for savers and investors to seek returns
IV. to allow buying and selling of stocks and bonds
V. to give investors choice

a. I only
b. I and II only
c. I, II and III only
d. I, II, III and IV only
e. I, II, III, IV and V

Again reasons why financial markets are so important.

255. Financial markets in principle allow all of the following except:

a. providers of capital the potential to compound their money
b. users of capital access to capital via investors that also participate there

c. investors to have access to a broad selection of investments
d. a guaranteed return for providers of capital or investors in all cases

An investor in a stock who then becomes a part-owner of that company certainly does not have a guaranteed return.

256. **Financial markets are intended to ensure that there is:**
a. capital for all companies
b. capital for bad companies
c. an efficient allocation of capital
d. a random allocation of capital

Meaning that good companies can get access to capital to provide goods and services that society values and is willing to pay for.

257. **Which of the following trade on financial markets:**
I. stocks
II. bonds
III. commodities
IV. derivatives
V. currencies

a. I only
b. I and II only
c. I, II and III only
d. I, II, III and IV only
e. I, II, III, IV and V

258. **Securities including stocks and bonds trade in the financial markets at:**
a. the book value
b. the market value
c. the loss value
d. the liquidation value

Items are are shown at book value on the balance sheet.

259. **True: There are many different types of financial markets that we can speak about - for example, the stock market, the bond market etc.**

260. **The market for government debt that has been split into smaller slices to facilitate trading is known as the:**
a. government bond market
b. government equity market
c. corporate bond market
d. stock market

b. does not exist
c. lending/debt market for corporations/companies
d. market for slices of ownership in companies

261. **The market for securities that represent ownership in companies is known as the:**
a. government bond market
b. government equity market
c. corporate bond market
d. stock market

a. this is a lending/debt market
b. does not exist
c. lending/debt market

262. **A large publicly traded company would most likely raise equity capital via the:**
a. commodities market
b. corporate bond market
c. government bond market
d. stock market

The stock market is a market for the publicly traded equity (or slices of equity) of companies.

263. **A large publicly traded company that has a large number of bonds outstanding, would most likely raise large amounts of additional debt capital via the:**
a. commodities market
b. corporate bond market
c. government bond market
d. stock market

The corporate bond market is where corporate bonds trade - slices of the debt of companies.

264. **Well-functioning financial markets benefit from:**
I. transparency - the ability to see prices and get information readily
II. liquidity - it is easy to buy and sell securities
III. many participants
IV. choice for investors in terms of investments
V. a regulatory structure - in terms of how information is disclosed, insider trading laws etc.

a. I only
b. I and II only
c. I, II and III only
d. I, II, III and IV only
e. I, II, III, IV and V

265. **The stock market has something in common with which of the following other markets:**
a. the government bond market - both are for debt
b. the corporate bond market - in both cases the users of capital/issuers are companies
c. the market for government debt - they both have the same users of capital
d. the market for government securities - in both the government is the user of capital

The stock market is for the equity of companies - not debt and not governments.

266. **True: In financial markets like major stock exchanges, large numbers of investors buy and sell large numbers of securities during market trading hours, and sometimes even after the market closes.**

267. **Financial markets are important because they facilitate:**
a. the interaction between governments and shareholders
b. the interaction between accountants and lawyers
c. the interaction between shareholders and bondholders
d. the interaction between providers and users of capital

That is one of the main functions of financial markets.

268. **A privately held company first sells stock to the public and lists itself on the stock exchange at the:**
a. company formation

b. first bond sale
c. initial public offering
d. private equity placement

The initial public offering (IPO) is when a private company sells stock to the public for the first time. After the IPO, the company is said to be public and the shares are listed on a stock exchange.

269. **A company that already has its shares trading on the stock market issuing more shares is referred to as a(n):**
a. initial public offering
b. IPO
c. secondary offering
d. bond sale

This is the definition of a secondary offering.

270. **True: The market that comprises initial public offerings is sometimes also referred to as the primary market. The market for stocks that have already been issued can also be referred to as the secondary market.**

By definition.

271. **An investor that buys a stock on a stock exchange is most likely to be buying it from:**
a. the government
b. the company that issued it
c. another investor
d. the tax authorities

The company selling stock happens much less frequently and this would be a part of a more formal process like a secondary, or primary stock issue, where there would be additional disclosure requirements.

272. **An investor might sell a stock for which of the following reasons:**
I. the investor believes the stock will go down
II. the investor needs cash
III. the stock has reached a price target
IV. the investor is unsure about the stock market
V. the investor owned the stock as part of a hedge against another position and is getting out of the overall position

a. I only
b. I and II only
c. I, II and III only
d. I, II, III and IV only
e. I, II, III, IV and V

273. **The expression a 'zero-sum game' refers to:**
a. a game where no one wins
b. a game where no one loses
c. a situation in which the gains of the winners equal the losses of the losers
d. a situation in which the same winners always win and the same losers always lose

Zero-sum game is a term for a situation in which there is no value created and where there is just a transfer of value from the losers to the winners.

274. **Which of the following is generally considered a zero-sum game or situation:**

a. communication and cooperation
b. gambling
c. saving and investing
d. the stock market

If one player wins, then another player or the casino would have lost the same amount.

275. **True: A market in which securities trade by phone or computer is known as an OTC (over-the-counter) market.**

By definition.

276. **True: Because of their importance to society, to investors and to companies and governments, securities markets are often regulated.**

277. **False: The fact that a securities market is regulated ensures that no investment can lose a significant amount of value.**

Regulations relate to transparency, reporting requirements, disclosure, fraud etc. - an investment can still lose a lot of value.

278. **Well-designed securities laws in developed countries are intended to:**
a. allow very few players to get rich
b. allow a small group to benefit from insider information
c. level the playing field between different investors and promote broad participation in saving and investing
d. turn securities markets into a place where no one can gain any benefit

This is done for example through disclosure requirements and insider trading laws.

TOTAL: 36 ANSWERS

INVESTMENTS - DEBT AND BONDS

279. **True: The issuer of a bond is typically borrowing money, the purchaser of a bond is typically lending money.**

    The issuer (seller) is providing the bond with certain terms and conditions in return for having access to the money (borrowing the money) - the purchaser of the bond is lending money.

280. **Debt investments and bonds relate to:**
    a. ownership
    b. lending
    c. equity
    d. shareholding

    By definition.

281. **True: When we keep money in a bank account, the bank typically pays interest because the money has value to the bank. They are able to pay interest because they can do something with the money that allows them to get interest (of which they pay us a part).**

282. **True: When we keep money in a bank account, we can think of ourselves as having lent money.**

    We have effectively lent the money to the bank - in order to ensure that this is safe for us, banks are regulated, and the deposits often insured - for example by the FDIC in the United States.

283. **True: We can think of bonds as loans that have been converted into securities.**

284. **Differences between stocks and bonds include:**
    I. stocks represent ownership, bonds do not
    II. stocks are typically more volatile than bonds
    III. there are more different bonds than stocks available
    IV. stocks trade on the stock market, bonds do not
    V. bonds often have a limited life or maturity, stocks do not

    a. I only
    b. I and II only
    c. I, II and III only
    d. I, II, III and IV only
    e. I, II, III, IV and V

    I. True - bonds are loans
    II. Stocks are typically more volatile because the outcome for a stock is less range-bound - it can go up a lot, and it goes to zero before a bond would for the same company
    III. the same company can issue many different bonds with different seniorities (order of repayment), different maturities (time to repayment) and different coupons
    IV. and V. are both true

285. **Which of the following could be an issuer of bonds:**
    I. a foreign car company
    II. a pharmaceutical company
    III. a technology company
    IV. a foreign government
    V. our government

    a. I only
    b. I and II only

c. I, II and III only
d. I, II, III and IV only
e. I, II, III, IV and V

Governments can issue bonds and so can companies.

286. Debt investments like bonds are also generically often referred to as:
a. equities
b. fixed income investments
c. commodities
d. convertibles

Because they often pay a fixed coupon or interest.

287. True: Most governments are very large issuers of bonds.

Governments raise money for major projects and when they are running a deficit for example. They can pay interest from tax revenues.

288. Which of the following is not a typical characteristic of bonds:
a. maturity
b. coupon
c. dividend
d. face value or par value or principal

A dividend is a characteristic of a stock - it is a payment that shareholders receive - all of the others are characteristics of bonds.

289. Which of the following can not be considered a form of debt, or a debt instrument:
a. a bank loan
b. a savings account
c. a stock
d. a government bond

A stock is a form of equity.

290. The payment to bondholders by the issuer made periodically (for example twice a year) is:
a. the dividend
b. the liability
c. the coupon
d. the revenues

That is the definition of a coupon.

291. True: Bonds can be thought of as a series of cash flows.

A bond will specify a maturity date, a par value, and the coupons that the bondholder would expect to receive and their timing. A stock could also be thought of as a series of cash flows, but a stock does not have a defined life (the maturity of the bond), and the cash flows (dividends) and the final value depend a lot on how the company is doing, therefore it is more difficult to think of a stock just as a series of cash flows.

292. True: Governments borrow money through the bond markets for major expenditures that they might have in one year. They are in a position to pay interest in large part as a result of the money they take in through taxes.

Taxes are the main source of revenues for governments. Governments often borrow money either because they are running a deficit (spending more than taking it) or to borrow for large expenditures.

293. Investors that hold bonds are going to get a cash return while holding the bonds from:
a. the coupon
b. the dividend
c. capital gains
d. depreciation

That is the definition of a coupon.

294. The amount of money that an investor would receive on maturity of a bond is known as the:
a. depreciation
b. face value or par value
c. coupon
d. price

295. The periodic payments that bonds make, which represent a form of interest, are known as:
a. the maturity
b. coupons
c. principal
d. duration

That is the definition of a coupon.

296. The time to repayment of the principal of the bond is known as the bond's:
a. maturity
b. coupon
c. principal
d. duration

The time to maturity of the bond is the time to the date on which the bond will repay the principal or par value.

297. Which of the following terms is not like the other three:
a. maturity value
b. face value
c. par value
d. coupon

a., b. and c. have to do with the amount that is repaid on maturity of the bond. Coupons are periodic interim payments made to the bondholder while holding the bond.

298. A measure of the time it takes an investor to receive payments both through coupons and the principal payment is known as the:
a. coupon
b. duration
c. maturity
d. face value

The maturity is a measure of the time that it takes to receive the principal payment. The duration is defined as the weighted average term to payment of the cash flows on a bond and includes both the coupons and the principal/par value payment. It is a term that is sometimes spoken about in the context of bonds and this is what it is.

299. **True: One definition of duration is that it is the cash-weighted average time to maturity of a bond.**

300. **True: Most bonds in the United States make semi-annual payments.**

Both government and corporate bonds in the United States typically make semi-annual payments. The same is true in the UK and in Europe. Zero-coupon bonds as the name suggests do not pay coupons and only repay a par value.

301. **If a bond makes semi-annual payments, it would:**
   a. make a payment every two years
   b. make two payments per year
   c. make two payments per month
   d. make payments every two months

By definition.

302. **Which of the following best describes what typically happens when an investor sells a bond:**
   I. the investor is reducing his ownership in the company
   II. the investor is reducing the amount lent
   III. the company repays the investor
   IV. the investor that buys the bond directly or indirectly pays the seller
   V. nothing happens

   a. I only
   b. II only
   c. I and III only
   d. II and IV only
   e. I and V only

An investor in a bond does not have ownership in the company. Typically an investor will sell a bond in the market and another investor will buy it. When the investor receives cash for the bond and no longer owns it, then that investor no longer has an outstanding loan to the bond issuer.

303. **True: In the United States, the US Department of the Treasury is responsible for issuing government debt.**

304. **True: Debt issued by the US Treasury includes T-Bills, T-Notes and T-Bonds.**

All three are government debt issued by the US Treasury on behalf of, and backed by, the US government. T-Bills mature in one year or less and they do not pay interest prior to maturity - instead they are sold at a discount to par value (like zero-coupon bonds). T-Notes have maturities between 1 and 10 years and pay interest semi-annually. T-Bonds have the longest maturities of 20 or 30 years and also pay interest semi-annually.

305. **A T-Bill in the Unites States is:**
   a. a form of equity
   b. short-term debt (maturity up to one year) issued by corporations
   c. short-term debt (maturity up to one year) issued by the US Treasury on behalf of the government
   d. long-term debt issued by the US government

This is the definition of Treasury Bills or T-Bills which we hear about frequently.

306. **Debt securities with maturities of up to one year issued by the US Treasury are known as:**
   a. Treasury Bills
   b. Treasury Notes

c. Treasury Bonds
d. Treasury Inflation Protected Securities (TIPS)

This is the definition of Treasury Bills or T-Bills which we hear about frequently.

307. Debt securities with maturities of between one year and ten years issued by the US Treasury are known as:
a. Treasury Bills
b. Treasury Notes
c. Treasury Bonds
d. Treasury Inflation Protected Securities (TIPS)

This is the definition of Treasury Notes which we hear about frequently.

308. Debt securities with maturities of over ten years issued by the US Treasury are known as:
a. Treasury Bills
b. Treasury Notes
c. Treasury Bonds
d. Treasury Inflation Protected Securities (TIPS)

This is the definition of Treasury Bonds which we hear about frequently.

309. Debt securities where the principal is adjusted by changes in the consumer price index (CPI) that are issued by the US Treasury are known as:
a. Treasury Bills
b. Treasury Notes
c. Treasury Bonds
d. Treasury Inflation Protected Securities (TIPS)

This is the definition of Treasury Inflation Protected Securities (TIPS) which we hear about frequently.

310. Which of the following have the longest maturity:
a. Treasury Bills
b. Treasury Notes
c. Treasury Bonds
d. Certificates of Deposit

They have maturities of over 10 years (20 or 30 years).

311. US government bonds are considered 'risk-free' because:
a. they can never go down in price
b. if interest rates go up, they rise in value
c. there is considered to be no risk of default
d. US Stocks are also considered 'risk-free'

The price can go up and down. When interest rates rise, the value would drop. US stocks are not risk-free. The reason that they are considered risk-free is because they are assumed to have no risk of default - it is assumed that the US government will always pay the interest and the principal.

312. A bond that is issued at a discount, that does not pay a coupon and where the return comes from the appreciation of the bond towards its principal or par value is known as:
a. a stock
b. a dividend-paying bond
c. a zero-coupon bond
d. a government bond

a. A bond can not be a stock
b. there is no such thing as a dividend-paying bond; stocks pay dividends
c. makes sense - they pay a zero-coupon (and this is a proper term for these types of bonds)
d. this is type of bond (that makes semi-annual payments) - it says nothing about zero-coupon

313. Commercial paper is:
   a. an unsecured short-term debt issued by a corporation
   b. debt issued by the government
   c. a deposit for a period of time offered by a bank
   d. a form of equity

   Commercial paper is short-term debt issued by a bank of corporation with a maturity of 1 day to less than 270 days usually.

314. **True: Corporations are able to issue different types of debt, with different maturities, depending on how they would like to repay it, market conditions, and what the funds are to be used for.**

   That is why there are many different bonds and forms of debt outstanding - more than there are stocks for example.

315. Certificates of deposit (CDs) are:
   a. an unsecured short-term debt issued by a corporation
   b. debt issued by the government
   c. a deposit for a period of time offered by a bank
   d. a form of equity

   That is the definition of a CD.

316. In the United States, certificates of deposit are:
   I. saving products offered by banks
   II. insured by the FDIC if the bank is insured by the FDIC
   III. typically for a certain time frame - they are also often referred to as 'time deposits'
   IV. potentially interesting for savers as alternatives to keeping money in a savings account
   V. potentially able to offer a higher rate of interest than a savings account where the money can be withdrawn on demand

   a. I only
   b. I and II only
   c. I, II and III only
   d. I, II, III and IV only
   e. I, II, III, IV and V

   These are all facts about CDs.

317. **True: Because there are so many different agencies that want to borrow money, and so many different situations for which they want to borrow money, and because there are also so many different ways of repaying the money, in the end there are many different types of bonds that exist and that can be created, and there is correspondingly a very large and diverse bond market.**

318. Stocks trade on a stock exchange which often has a physical location where the stocks are traded or where records are kept. Bonds trade:
   a. on a bond exchange
   b. on the same stock exchange
   c. over-the-counter: meaning by telephone and computers largely
   d. on the stock market

This is also partly due to the fact that there are so many different types outstanding each with unique characteristics.

319. To categorize bonds, bonds have different ratings that are assigned by:
   a. investors
   b. rating agencies like Moody's and S&P
   c. governments
   d. tax authorities

   Rating agencies assign ratings to bonds based on their credit worthiness - the risk that the investor will not receive coupons or the par value on the investment because of an issuer's inability to pay.

320. **True: Rating agencies rate bonds in terms of credit worthiness.**

321. **True: Rating agencies analyze bonds to the best of their abilities, but the bonds of an issuer can be downgraded when the outlook for that firm or bond changes.**

   Credit agencies can be wrong first of all, so many bond investors complement these ratings with their own analysis. Secondly, the outlook for a bond can change so the ratings also often change.

322. **False: A bond's rating is fixed and can not change.**

   Depending on the outlook for the security and the issuer, bonds can be downgraded as well as upgraded.

323. The yield or implied interest rate that longer-term government bonds provide is set by:
   a. the central bank
   b. companies
   c. governments
   d. investors who buy and sell the bonds in the market

   Central banks set short-term interest rates, or take actions to target levels for short-term interest rates. By setting the price of bonds in the market, investors set the yield for longer term bonds.

324. **True: A benefit, like a cash payment is typically worth more to us the sooner we receive it.**

   The assumption is that with positive interest rates, money that is received sooner can increase to more with time, therefore the sooner we receive it the better. This concept is referred to as the 'Time Value of Money'.

325. **True: Valuing bonds, and valuing investments in general, has a lot to do with assessing today's value of future expected cash flows.**

   Since many investments, especially bonds, can be thought of as a series of future cash flows, finding the value of the investment is about assessing the value of those potential future cash flows.

326. **True: A cash flow that we receive today is worth more than the same amount received in the future under normal circumstances.**

   The assumption is that with positive interest rates money that is received sooner can increase to become more with time, therefore having it sooner (or today) has value.

327. When interest rates for a certain period rise, the value of a fixed amount of cash to be received in the future, would be worth ________ to us today than before the interest rate rise.

a. more
b. less
c. the same
d. an equivalent amount

An investor would theoretically feel indifferent between having $1,000 today with 10% interest per year, and getting $1,100 in one year (because that $1,000 today would become $1,100 in one year with 10% interest). If interest rates were 15%, getting $1,100 in one year would not be as good as having $1,000 today, because the $1,000 today could become $1,150 ($1,000 x 1.15) in one year. Receiving the same amount of $1,100 in one year is worth less to us today, and specifically it is worth to us today:

$1,100/(1+15%) = $1,100/(1+.15) = $1,100/1.15 = $965.52.

This amount would become $1,100 in one year with interest rates of 15% (956.52 x 1.15=$1,100).

328. Normally, when the maturity of a bond or loan is longer, the interest or return is:
a. lower
b. higher
c. the same
d. all loans have the same maturity

There a number of theories behind this including the liquidity premium theory, the expectations theory and the segmentation theory.

329. Banks are theoretically able to offer a higher rate of interest when they know that they will have our deposit for longer.
a. this is true and is one of the principles behind certificates of deposit
b. this is not true
c. this is true and is one of the principles behind equity investing
d. this is true and is one of the principles behind foreign exchange

The bank can do more with the money if they know that they will have it for longer - they can often receive a better rate of interest themselves and therefore offer the saver a better rate of interest.

330. True: A bond can trade at a premium to par if interest rates change from the time the bond was issued.

For example, a bond is issued at par with a face value of $1,000 and it offers a 5% yield to maturity (i.e. 5% in coupons per year) - if interest rates change and new similar bonds are issued with a 2% yield to maturity (interest rates have gone down), then the old ones with the 5% coupon will trade at a premium to the par value (over $1,000 per bond) because they offer this higher coupon, or if we discount the cash flows of the bond using the new 2% interest rate we will arrive at a value of over $1,000 for the bond.

331. The price of a bond could fall when its yield rises because:
I. investors in new similar-risk bonds would expect a higher yield, making a bond that had a lower yield issued previously worth less
II. the discount factor that we would use to discount the bond's future cash flows rises meaning that future cash flows are worth less
III. bond prices do not fall when yields rise - the question is irrelevant
IV. the yield is a reflection of the risk of the bond -the higher yield could be caused by an increase in risk and the bond would therefore be worth less
V. when the yield rises, companies immediately cut dividends making bonds worth less

a. I only

b. II only
c. III only
d. I and V only
e. I, II and IV only

QUESTIONS 332 - 334 ARE LINKED.

332. A 5-year bond is issued with a par value of $1,000 and with a 7% semi-annual coupon. How many coupons would an investor expect to receive per year:
a. 0.5
b. 2 ***(semi-annual means two payments per year)***
c. 24
d. 6

333. Each coupon payment that the investor would expect to receive would be:
a. $70
b. $14
c. $7
d. $35

The bond would pay 7% or $70 per year in two payments. Each payment is therefore $35.

334. In total, how many coupon payments would an investor expect to receive over the entire life of the bond:
a. 2.5
b. 24
c. 10 ***(two payments per year for five years means ten payments)***
d. 1

335. When a bond becomes more risky, the return or yield that investors require is:
a. higher
b. lower
c. the same
d. not present

To compensate for the risk, or in other words, to make the bond attractive despite the higher risk.

336. Most investors that are saving and investing would have exposure to bonds by:
a. buying and selling individual bonds actively
b. buying and holding bonds to maturity
c. investing in a bond mutual fund
d. they should not have any bond exposure

Buying and selling individual bonds would require a lot of time and a large number of transactions and knowledge - also, for example, the face value of US corporate bonds is typically $1,000 or $5,000, so diversification would only be possible with a lot of capital. By buying a mutual fund, an investor can get a exposure to the asset class and to a large number of underlying securities at once (subject to the terms and the description of the mutual fund).

TOTAL: 58 ANSWERS

Equity and Stocks, Indices and Valuation

337. True: Equity relates to ownership, and stocks are slices of equity or ownership of a company, where the equity has been split into smaller pieces.

A stock is a slice or piece of the equity or ownership of a company.

338. True: The equity of a company can either be private or public depending on how widely it is available, and in particular whether it is available through a stock market.

Public equity is equity that is traded on a stock exchange. Private equity is privately held equity - i.e. it is not available though a public stock exchange.

339. A private company is typically owned by:
a. investors through the stock market
b. a limited group of investors, often including the founders of the company
c. investors who have bought bonds
d. the stock market traders

This equity is also known as private equity (private company -> private equity)

340. Which of the following statements regarding private equity is true:
I. private equity through a financial services company is typically reserved for professionals or high net worth investors
II. private equity is very illiquid and is often considered higher risk
III. private equity is equity that is not directly available through a stock exchange
IV. owners of private equity are often the founders of the company, their family and friends, perhaps some high net worth investors and potentially later on private equity funds
V. it is typically more difficult to get information regarding private companies

a. I only
b. I and II only
c. I, II and III only
d. I, II, III and IV only
e. I, II, III, IV and V

There are typically restrictions as to who can invest in private equity when offered through a financial services firm due to the higher risk. Private equity is not listed on the stock exchange by definition and private companies do not have the same disclosure or reporting requirements that public companies do; in general there is less information available publicly on them.

341. The equity of a company that is operating normally (and not close to bankruptcy) is riskier than the debt of the same company because:
I. when a company makes money, bondholders are paid first
II. when the assets of a company go down, equity is affected more
III. when the assets of a company go down, the debt is affected less
IV. in case of company bankruptcy, bondholders are typically repaid first
V. equity is considered less senior in the capital structure

a. I only
b. I and II only
c. I, II and III only
d. I, II, III and IV only
e. I, II, III, IV and V

I. we know this from the income statement
II. and III. - we saw examples of this from the balance sheet questions
IV. this is true as they are senior in the capital structure (equity more junior (V))

342. **True: Investing directly or indirectly (through funds) in stocks or shares is the most widespread way for investors to invest in the equity of companies.**

The equity of companies is much easier to access once it it public/listed on the stock exchange - these tend to be the largest companies (with the largest equities outstanding) and there tends to be the most information available on these companies.

343. **Which of the following could be an issuer of stocks:**
I. a foreign car company
II. a pharmaceutical company
III. a technology company
IV. a foreign government
V. our government

a. I only
b. I and II only
c. I, II and III only
d. I, II, III and IV only
e. I, II, III, IV and V

Governments can not sell an equity interest in themselves/issue stocks. The companies (I-III) can.

344. **True: A shareholder is a part-owner of a company.**

345. **Professional stock investors seek to allocate money:**
a. to companies that will not deliver a return
b. to companies that need it
c. based on a desire to be helpful
d. to companies that can deliver a return

That is the goal of investors - professional stock investors are paid to do this.

346. **As shareholders we might care about:**
I. company earnings
II. company profitability
III. sales growth
IV. cash flows
V. the quality of the company's management

a. I only
b. I and II only
c. I, II and III only
d. I, II, III and IV only
e. I, II, III, IV and V

All can affect the value of the company's equity which a shareholder owns a part of.

347. **While holding stocks, investors often get a return from:**
a. the coupon
b. the dividend
c. capital gains
d. depreciation

Coupons are only relevant for bonds. Capital gains might be realized when we sell a stock and not while holding it. Depreciation is an entry on the income statement and not a source of return for investors.

348. The total return to a shareholder between purchase and sale comes from:
   a. the bond yield
   b. the dividend yield
   c. the capital appreciation
   d. the dividend yield and capital appreciation

   The dividend yield relates to the dividends received while holding the stock. Capital appreciation is the difference between the price at which the stock is sold, and where it was bought.

349. True: Investors in the equity of a business should think about whether it makes sense for them to be owners or part-owners of that business.

   Investing in the equity of the company means being a part-owner of that business.

350. When a healthy business does very well, the ones that will benefit the most are the:
   a. owners or shareholders
   b. lenders or bondholders
   c. corporate bondholders
   d. government bondholders

   For a normal healthy company, the bondholders are paid a certain rate of interest. If the company's value increases greatly, the owners see the value of their stake increase greatly.

351. True: Although equityholders as a group can play a role in getting the management of a company replaced over a medium-term timeframe, for the most part they are dependent on the management to make decisions that are in the best interests of the company and its shareholders.

   Shareholders have the right to vote for directors on the company's board, which appoints and evaluates the Chief Executive of a company. Therefore a vote by a significant percentage of the shareholders can have an impact on the management of the company and even on getting the management replaced over time. In the short- to medium-term, and certainly as a very small shareholder, the investor's outcome is greatly influenced by the actions of the management - that is why stock analysis also looks at the quality of management along with valuation etc.

352. The management of a company:
   I. plays a major role in determining returns for investors
   II. could be corrupt and steal from the company at the expense of shareholders
   III. plays a major role in determining if the company is a winner or a loser in the industry
   IV. might make very bad acquisitions
   V. might have shareholders' interests at heart - or they might not

   a. I only
   b. I and II only
   c. I, II and III only
   d. I, II, III and IV only
   e. I, II, III, IV and V

   All of these are true, and in public companies there is a separation between the ownership of the company (the shareholders) and the management. That is why it is so important for shareholders to think about the quality of the management and whether its interests are aligned with those of shareholders. What the management of a company is going to do (just like what other companies

are going to do), which technologies are going to come along, and what the economy will do, are all associated with uncertainty. An investor can never be certain about what exactly will happen with a company or a stock.

353. <u>Bad company management can hurt returns for shareholders by:</u>
I. paying themselves too much - taking money out of the company that does not make it to earnings
II. making bad investment decisions
III. not retaining key staff
IV. acquiring other companies at prices that are too high
V. focussing on the wrong business activities

a. I only
b. I and II only
c. I, II and III only
d. I, II, III and IV only
e. I, II, III, IV and V

Shareholders never know exactly what the management of a company will do - smart investors try to get a sense of what the management is likely or even very likely to do, and will also look at whether the management's interests are aligned with those of shareholders.

354. <u>False: Predicting exactly what management is going to do next is very easy.</u>

Predicting exactly what the management is going to do is very difficult. That is why investors often assess the quality of the management as part of their analysis.

355. <u>A company should care about its share price for which of the following reasons:</u>
I. it creates positive publicity
II. management compensation is often linked to the share price
III. if the company wants to sell more shares, having a high share price allows more capital to be raised for the same percentage of the company that is sold
IV. if the company wants to make an acquisition, having a strong share price can be beneficial
V. companies never care about their share price

a. I only
b. I and II only
c. I, II and III only
d. I, II, III and IV only
e. I, II, III, IV and V

Looking at the interests of the management is very important in analyzing a company. Companies do care about their share prices in most cases because of I-IV.

356. <u>In a well-functioning securities market, companies and their managements should care about the performance of their shares alongside shareholders because:</u>
I. often their compensation is linked to the performance of the shares
II. they are also often shareholders
III. if the share price does not perform, the management is at risk of being relieved of their duties by shareholders as a group
IV. strong share price performance can create positive momentum for a business and affect the operations positively as well
V. the company might want to make an acquisition and use its shares to do so, in which case having highly valued shares is a big plus

a. I only
b. I and II only

c. I, II and III only
d. I, II, III and IV only
e. I, II, III, IV and V

These are all facts about the importance of the share price to a company, depending on how the incentives for the management are set up.

357. Which of the following best describes what typically happens when an investor sells a stock:
I. the investor is reducing their ownership in the company
II. the investor is reducing the amount lent to the company
III. the company repays the investor
IV. the investor will receive cash proceeds from whoever buys the stock via an intermediary system
V. nothing happens

a. I only
b. II only
c. I and III only
d. I and IV only
e. I and V only

When an investor sells a stock in the market, it is typically bought by another investor.

358. Which of the following statements regarding equity investing is true:
I. investing in the equity of a company is typically considered riskier than investing in its debt
II. investing as an owner should be based on understanding the company and its business
III. many professional equity investors spend most of their time analyzing companies
IV. the companies that are the winners in an industry often have the best share price performance
V. companies that are in a bad industry, or that are the losers in an industry, over time can go bankrupt and see their share prices go to zero

a. I only
b. I and II only
c. I, II and III only
d. I, II, III and IV only
e. I, II, III, IV and V

These are all facts related to equity investing.

359. True: There are significant groups of investors that believe that the analysis of public companies is a waste of time even for professional investors because markets have become so efficient.

Nobel prizes have been awarded for work in this area, and many books have been written about the subject, including: Winning the Loser's Game by Charles D. Ellis.

360. Good sources of information with respect to companies include:
I. annual reports
II. company websites
III. industry websites
IV. research reports
V. company press releases and filings

a. I only
b. I and II only
c. I, II and III only
d. I, II, III and IV only
e. I, II, III, IV and V

All of them can be good sources of information with respect to companies.

361. **Typical rights of a common shareholder in a company include:**
   I. a vote for company directors
   II. the right to assets during a liquidation after bondholders are paid
   III. a right to vote on major company issues
   IV. the right to the company's revenues
   V. a first claim on the company's assets

   a. I only
   b. I and II only
   c. I, II and III only
   d. I, II, III and IV only
   e. I, II, III, IV and V

   The first three are typical shareholder rights - the specific rights would be outlined in the company's charter. Shareholders do not have a right to the company's revenues - they receive that portion of earnings (revenues minus all costs) that is paid out as dividends, and they are the owners of the company. Bondholders, who are senior to equityholders, have a first claim on a company's assets if the company is liquidated - equityholders are at the bottom in this structure and get what is left over.

362. **True: A corporate raider can be described as an investor that buys the securities of a company with a view to enhancing value through some sort of action.**

   That is what a corporate raider is by definition.

363. **The difference between a very large shareholder and the holder of a single stock is:**
   I. a very large shareholder is likely to have more influence on management
   II. a very large shareholder has more shareholder votes
   III. a very large shareholder might have to declare the shareholding to regulatory authorities
   IV. a very large shareholder will take longer to sell shares and/or might move the share price more when selling
   V. a very large shareholder can make day-to-day decisions in the company

   a. I only
   b. I and II only
   c. I, II and III only
   d. I, II, III and IV only
   e. I, II, III, IV and V

   I. by having more shares, the larger shareholder has more votes - votes for the directors and on major issues
   II. more shares -> more votes
   III. different jurisdictions have different rules regarding when a larger stake has to be disclosed since it could be an indication of a planned takeover. In the US a 5% stake in a public company has to be publicly disclosed
   IV. true - when more shares are sold it could move the price down or take longer for buyers to buy them at a certain price in the market
   V. a large shareholder can try to influence the management of the company, but can not make day -to-day decisions - only the management can do that

364. **Holders of a single common stock can influence a company by:**
   I. having a shareholder vote at the annual meeting
   II. voting during the election of a board of directors

III. deciding on corporate strategy
IV. making hiring decisions
V. firing employees

a. I only
b. I and II only
c. I, II and III only
d. I, II, III and IV only
e. I, II, III, IV and V

III, IV and V are decisions taken by the management on a day-to-day basis - that is why good management is so important.

365. **True: The dividend is typically a periodic cash payment by companies to shareholders, that provides a return while the shares are held.**

366. **An investor in a single stock receives:**
a. the earnings per share of the company
b. the revenues per share of the company
c. the cash flow of the company
d. the dividends, and any capital appreciation between purchase and sale, minus taxes

367. **The amount that a company pays out from it earnings to shareholders is known as:**
a. the dividend
b. the shares
c. the earnings
d. the revenues

That is the definition of the dividend, the earnings that are not paid out are said to be retained.

368. **True: Instead of paying a dividend, companies can choose to retain earnings, in which case they would be kept within the company.**

369. **True: Companies that have less of a need to reinvest, or that are in industries that are not growing as quickly, often pay out more of their earnings in the form of dividends.**

370. **When a company's earnings drop significantly and the stock market is performing poorly, a company that wants to retain cash is most likely going to:**
a. cut its dividend
b. raise its dividend
c. buy back shares
d. decrease borrowing

All of the others do not retain cash.

371. **Companies that do not pay a dividend are:**
a. bankrupt
b. corrupt
c. cheating shareholders
d. retaining earnings

They might also not have earnings from which to pay a dividend - of the four answers, this is very much the best answer.

372. **The dividend per share divided by the earnings per share, is also known as:**
a. the dividend yield

b. the current yield
c. the payout ratio
d. the net margin

This is the percentage of earnings paid out as a dividend - in other words, the dividend as a percentage of earnings, which is the payout ratio - this can be calculated for the entire company, or on a per share basis as in this question (both will provide the same percentage).

373. The dividend per share divided by the share price, is also known as:
a. the dividend yield
b. the current yield
c. the payout ratio
d. the net margin

Dividend Yield = Dividend/Share Price in %.

374. The dividend yield is:
a. a bond yield
b. the percentage capital appreciation
c. the percentage return received in the form of dividends based on the current share price
d. the dividend divided by the earnings

Dividend Yield = Dividend/Share Price in %.

375. A company has a payout ratio of 30%; what percentage of the earnings is the company retaining:
a. 30%
b. 50%
c. 70%
d. 100%

Retained earnings = 100% of earnings - 30% paid out = 70%.

376. Which of the following is not a reason for a company to retain earnings:
a. it wants to reinvest in its business
b. it wants to avoid raising more equity or debt capital in the future
c. it has a lot of investment opportunities
d. it wants to increase its dividend yield

Retaining earnings will decrease the dividend yield.

377. It would make sense for a company to pay a larger dividend when:
I. it does not require these earnings for investment in its industry
II. shareholders have more profitable investment opportunities than the company does
III. the firm is operating in a mature industry where investment needs are low
IV. the company has more capital than it needs
V. the company is considering ways of raising capital

a. I only
b. I and II only
c. I, II and III only
d. I, II, III and IV only
e. I, II, III, IV and V

Companies should pay a larger dividend when they do not need the earnings, and/or when the earnings if they were retained can not be invested profitably.

378. <u>**Which of the following companies would be most likely to pay a dividend:**</u>
   a. a technology company
   b. a fast-growing company
   c. a utility
   d. a bond

   Utilities often have limited growth prospects. Technology companies/fast-growing companies often want to reinvest their (sometimes limited) earnings. A bond does not pay a dividend.

379. <u>**The percentage return that an investor would receive in the form of dividends is:**</u>
   a. the dividend yield - it is the dividend divided by stock price
   b. the percentage capital appreciation - it is the percentage increase in the stock price divided by the original price
   c. the bond yield - it is the coupon divided by the bond price
   d. the yield to maturity - it is the bond yield realized if the bond is held to maturity

   The percentage return that an investor receives in the form of dividends is the dividend yield as defined in a.

380. <u>**True: Companies sometimes buy back their own shares.**</u>

   This is known as a share buyback or repurchase - this could happen when a company is generating a lot of cash and the shares represent the best use of cash given their valuation in the market. Having less shares outstanding also increases the earnings per share and the returns to equityholders.

381. <u>**True: When companies buy back shares they are giving money back to shareholders. When companies pay dividends they are also giving money back to shareholders.**</u>

   Which of the two a company does often depends on tax considerations as well.

382. <u>**True: If a company feels that the market is not valuing its shares highly enough, it can buy its shares back in the market.**</u>

383. <u>**If a company makes a large extraordinary gain and it does not need or want to retain the capital, it would most likely:**</u>
   a. raise its dividend permanently
   b. pay an extraordinary dividend
   c. raise equity capital
   d. raise debt capital

   Raising the dividend permanently might require the company to lower it in the future which would not be well received by investors (a.). C. and d. would be ways of raising capital - not disbursing it.

384. <u>**Companies might buy back shares for all of the following reasons:**</u>
   I. they believe the shares are undervalued
   II. they want to signal to the market that the shares are undervalued
   III. they have excess capital
   IV. they see this as an alternative to paying a dividend
   V. they are trying to raise capital

   a. I only
   b. I and II only
   c. I, II and III only
   d. I, II, III and IV only
   e. I, II, III, IV and V

I-IV are true. Buying back shares is the opposite of raising capital - V is not true.

385. Which of the following terms might commentators use to group stocks:

I. blue-chip stocks
II. growth stocks
III. cyclical stocks
IV. defensive stocks
V. no-ownership stocks

a. I only
b. I and II only
c. I, II and III only
d. I, II, III and IV only
e. I, II, III, IV and V

There is no such thing as a no-ownership stock - all of the other ones are ways of grouping stocks. What these terms describe is provided in questions 386-389.

386. The stock of a large and well-established company could be referred to as a:

a. blue chip stock
b. growth stock
c. defensive stock
d. cyclical stock

That is the definition of a blue chip stock.

387. The stock of a company that has strong earnings and revenue growth might be referred to as a:

a. blue chip stock
b. growth stock
c. defensive stock
d. cyclical stock

That is the definition of a growth stock.

388. A stock that is very sensitive to the state of the economy could be referred to as a:

a. blue chip stock
b. growth stock
c. defensive stock
d. cyclical stock

That is the definition of a cyclical stock.

389. A stock that analysts expect to be resilient in an economic downturn could be referred to as a:

a. blue chip stock
b. growth stock
c. defensive stock
d. cyclical stock

That is the definition of a defensive stock.

390. True: Categorizing stocks as 'growth' or 'blue-chip' stocks is not without risks since companies can change quite dramatically.

The market for a growth company might mature after some time, and the company's shares might no longer perform like growth stocks for example. A blue-chip stock might significantly disappoint the market and could lose its blue-chip status.

391. **The specific area that concerns itself with how a company is run and how certain checks and balances are put in place to monitor management is known as:**
   a. government
   b. corporate action
   c. corporate governance
   d. accounting

   Corporate governance has become an important topic since it is very linked to protecting shareholder rights and ensuring that management acts in the best interests of the owners of the company - the shareholders.

392. **Public companies have a board of directors whose principal responsibility it is to:**
   a. help the company with its accounting
   b. sell the company
   c. act as a check on management
   d. invest in the company

   The board of directors is elected by shareholders to act as shareholder representatives with respect to corporate management policies, and major company issues like appointing the CEO, hiring and firing key executives, dividend policy and executive compensation.

393. **True: Public companies often have investor relations departments that communicate with investors and securities analysts, with a view to communicating information about the company, and keeping the company on investors' radar screens.**

394. **Which of the following statements about share prices and equity values is/are true:**
   I. a company can split its shares two for one - the number of shares outstanding would double (and the price would halve)
   II. a share price does not capture all of the information regarding a company's equity market value
   III. a low share price does not imply better value than a high share price
   IV. the share price multiplied by the number of shares gives the market value of the equity
   V. when share prices rise (and the number of shares is unchanged), equity market values rise

   a. I only
   b. I and II only
   c. I, II and III only
   d. I, II, III and IV only
   e. I, II, III, IV and V

   I. this is the definition of a share split
   II. the share price captures only a part of the picture - the equity market value is dependent on the number of shares outstanding as well (equity market value = share price x number of shares outstanding)
   III. a low share price in isolation does not tell investors anything about valuation. If we take the P/E ratio for example - if the share price is $2 and the earnings are $1, then the P/E ratio is 2 - if the earnings per share (EPS) were $0.10 then the P/E ratio would be 20. So even to calculate this simple way of looking at valuation we would need another piece of data (in this case the EPS)
   IV. and V. are true by definition

395. **The market-cap or market capitalization of a company can be summarized as the:**
   I. share price times the number of shares

II. market value of the company's equity
III. market value of the company's debt and equity
IV. book value of the company
V. value of the company's assets

a. I only
b. I and II only
c. I, II and III only
d. I, II and V only
e. I, II, III, IV and V

The market capitalization of a company is the market value of the company's equity - this is calculated by taking the share price and multiplying by the number of shares.

396. Which of the following does not capture the market value of the equity of a company:
a. the share price multiplied by the number of shares
b. the company's market-capitalization
c. the market value of all of the outstanding shares
d. the company's outstanding debt

A.-c. refer to the same thing - the company's outstanding debt is not related to the market value of the equity.

397. A large-cap stock, is a stock that:
a. has a high share price
b. has strong revenues
c. has a large market-capitalization
d. has strong earnings

That is the definition of a large-cap stock.

398. Terms that relate to stocks which one might find in the newspaper on a daily basis include:
I. price
II. dividend yield
III. P/E ratio
IV. name of the company
V. price change from the prior day

a. I only
b. I and II only
c. I, II and III only
d. I, II, III and IV only
e. I, II, III, IV and V

These are all typically provided in the newspaper to provide information on the stocks.

399. Which of the following could move a stock in the near-term:
I. statements by the company
II. rumors
III. a large seller
IV. a major decision by the company management
V. a change in the economic outlook from a well-recognized agency

a. I only
b. I and II only
c. I, II and III only

d. I, II, III and IV only
e. I, II, III, IV and V

All of these could move the stock price.

400. If a stock has gone down recently, we can say that:
a. it will go up again soon
b. it will probably continue to go down
c. it should stabilize next
d. we should not draw conclusions about future performance from past performance

Past performance of a stock, an index or a fund does not provide an indication of future performance.

401. A company that reported their quarterly earnings and 'beat earnings estimates':
a. reported better than expected earnings
b. delivered very poor earnings
c. grew earnings over a long period
d. delivered earnings that were higher than revenues

That is the definition of beating estimates.

402. An investor who buys a stock 'on margin' is:
I. borrowing money to buy the stock
II. using leverage
III. increasing the risk of the position
IV. magnifying returns both on the upside and downside
V. lending money

a. I only
b. I and II only
c. I, II and III only
d. I, II, III and IV only
e. I, II, III, IV and V

Buying a stock on margin means using leverage to buy the stock - the amount of own capital used, in other words the amount not borrowed, is known as the margin. The investor is borrowing money to buy the position - not lending money.

403. When an investor buys a stock on margin, the amount that the investor is putting in of his or her own money is known as:
a. the debt
b. the leverage
c. the margin
d. the stock price

The margin is the amount that the investor puts in.

404. Buying a stock on margin involves:
I. leverage
II. borrowing
III. a higher percentage loss for a given move in the stock
IV. trying to buy a fraction of a stock
V. short-selling the stock

a. I only

b. I and II only
c. I, II and III only
d. I, II, III and IV only
e. I, II, III, IV and V

Buying a stock on margin means using leverage to buy the stock - the amount of own capital used, in other words the amount not borrowed, is known as the margin. The investor is borrowing money to buy the position - not lending money. IV. and V. are incorrect.

405. <u>True: The stocks that we typically speak about are also known as a common stocks. Some companies have additional share classes beyond common stocks - such as preferred shares.</u>

Preferred shares are senior to common shares in the capital structure and might have preference over common stock for dividends. They also do not usually carry voting rights. When someone refers to stocks, they are referring to common stocks - to refer to preferred stocks, the word preferred would have to be explicitly included.

406. <u>Which of the following are characteristics of preferred shares:</u>
I. they are more senior than common stock
II. they often have a negotiated dividend amount
III. they do not carry voting rights
IV. they are not as senior as bonds
V. they can never go down

a. I only
b. I and II only
c. I, II and III only
d. I, II, III and IV only
e. I, II, III, IV and V

I-IV are very common features of preferred shares. Preferred shares can go down just like stocks and corporate bonds can go down, although they have higher seniority in the capital structure than stocks (and a lower seniority than corporate bonds), and therefore should go down less when the prospects for a healthy company worsen (and more than the corporate bonds).

407. <u>A company is considered bankrupt when:</u>
a. the company misses a dividend payment
b. it can not pay creditors and files for bankruptcy
c. the stock price loses 50% or more
d. the company loses a lot of money

Although the other three events would not be good for shareholders either - the company is only considered bankrupt when it can not pay its debts and it files for bankruptcy.

408. <u>When a company files for bankruptcy, which of the following will typically end up with more control and a greater share of the assets:</u>
a. equityholders
b. bondholders
c. management
d. stockholders

They are more senior in the capital structure.

409. <u>A company if the United States that files for bankruptcy will often be said to be:</u>
a. going into 'Chapter 0' - it refers to the chapter on very low stock prices
b. going into 'Chapter 10' - it refers to chapter 10 of the bankruptcy code

c. **going into 'Chapter 11' - it refers to chapter 11 of the bankruptcy code**
d. going into 'Chapter 12' - it refers to chapter 12 of the bankruptcy code

That is what Chapter 11 refers to.

410. **True: Under US law, if a company is so far in debt that it does not want to seek protection from creditors and try to reorganize itself, then it can elect to cease operations entirely and have a trustee sell assets - this is known as Chapter 7 of the bankruptcy code.**

411. **When a company goes bankrupt:**
I. equityholders should expect to lose all of their money
II. bondholders/creditors might be involved in the restructuring process
III. bondholders/creditors could recover some of their money
IV. there is no chance that the company will be able to continue any form of operations
V. the company will always disappear completely very shortly thereafter

a. I only
b. I and II only
c. **I, II and III only**
d. I, II, III and IV only
e. I, II, III, IV and V

A company that enters a bankruptcy restructuring process will often be able to continue some form of operations while it is protected from creditors, and will often not disappear at all. General Motors for example filed for bankruptcy under Chapter 11 of the US bankruptcy code on June 1, 2009 to give itself time to restructure. The company continued to manufacture and sell cars in the following months and actually posted greatly improved earnings in the following quarters.

412. **If we believed that picking stocks was going to help us beat the market - things that we would probably look at to determine the outlook for a company's stock would include:**
I. the quality of the management of the company
II. whether we trusted the management of the company
III. the prospects for the company
IV. the earnings and future cash flows for the company
V. the valuation of the company on various metrics

a. I only
b. I and II only
c. I, II and III only
d. I, II, III and IV only
e. **I, II, III, IV and V**

We would want to look at all of these factors in order to assess the prospects for the company.

413. **Fundamental stock analysis typically involves:**
a. **financial ratios, financial statement analysis, and modeling**
b. charts, price information, and price and volume ratios
c. an analysis of macroeconomic factors and economic forecasting
d. a quantitative analysis of government spending

Fundamental analysis involves going through the company's business, its finances and looking at various ratios to understand the operations and potential future of the company and what it might be worth.

414. **Technical stock and market analysis typically involves:**
a. financial ratios, financial statement analysis, and modeling

b. charts, price information, and price and volume ratios
c. an analysis of macroeconomic factors and economic forecasting
d. a quantitative scoring of management and key employees

Technical analysis involves looking at charts of things like the share price over time, and trading volumes with a view to making assessments about the future from this 'technical' information.

415. **True: Securities laws are set up to try and ensure that all investors have access to the same information at the same time in order to make equally informed decisions.**

This is to encourage broad-based saving and investing, and to ensure that fairness and a level playing field exist for all investors.

416. **In a properly functioning securities market, which of the following is not a common reason for an investor to sell shares in a company:**
a. his or her target price has been reached
b. they need cash
c. their view is that the shares will not perform that well
d. they know exactly what will happen in the future and no one disagrees

No one knows exactly what will happen in the future although investors clearly can have opinions. Someone that disagrees with the seller and thinks the shares are a good buy could be the buyer.

417. **One of the big conceptual elements of the Glass-Steagall act pertained to:**
a. investors not being able to invest
b. an investor in stocks not being able to hold bonds
c. a separation between commercial banking and the securities industries
d. trading on insider information

This was a very important act that was ultimately repealed, and whose repeal is often blamed for playing a role in the financial crisis linked to the securitization of sub-prime mortgage debt that started in 2007. It still is sometimes still referred to today in the context of discussions regarding what banks should, and should not be allowed to do.

418. **A well-functioning securities market has which of the following characteristics:**
I. efficiency
II. prices do not jump around by large amounts without substantial news
III. a good regulatory framework
IV. it is easy to buy and sell assets quickly
V. timely and accurate information

a. I only
b. I and II only
c. I, II and III only
d. I, II, III and IV only
e. I, II, III, IV and V

This is a list of some of the key characteristics of a well-functioning securities market.

419. **Transactions in the stock market are most likely to take place when:**
a. all investors have the same view
b. all investors have the same time horizon
c. different investors have different views and/or time horizons
d. all investors are on holiday

When different investors have different views, some will sell and some will buy, and transactions will take place.

420. True: Investors can get a sense for the movement of an entire stock market by looking at a relevant stock market index.

Stock market indices such as the S&P 500 take a number of stocks, for example all of the stocks that meet certain criteria, and look at them as a group. By following the numerical value of the index, we can follow the performance of an entire market or a segment of a market in aggregate.

421. True: A stock market index might combine information on many companies to provide a picture of how a certain market or segment of the market is behaving.

By definition.

422. True: Different indices are calculated using different methods - the differences in methods relate to how security prices are combined to arrive at the index level.

423. Price-weighted and market-capitalization weighted refer to:
  a. two different ways of calculating indices and hence two different types of indices
  b. two different types of companies
  c. two different types of bonds
  d. two different types of governments

424. True: In a price-weighted index, companies with higher share prices have a higher weighting in the index.

The value of a price-weighted stock index is calculated by adding up the share prices of the companies in the index and dividing by a fixed number (which is set at the time of the creation of the index to get a number that can be easily followed such as 1,000 or 100).

425. True: In a market-capitalization weighted index, companies that are typically considered larger will have a higher weighting.

Companies with a larger equity market capitalizations (share price x number of shares) are typically considered 'larger' - their equity is worth more. The value of a market-capitalization weighted index is calculated by adding up the market capitalizations (the market values of the equity – the share price multiplied by the number of shares) of all of the companies in that index and dividing this number by an arbitrarily selected fixed number to get the number down to an easily followed number like 1,000 when the index is started, and then continuously adding the market capitalizations together and dividing by that same fixed number to track the changes in the group of companies in aggregate.

426. Which of the following is not a stock market index:
  a. the S&P 500
  b. the Dow Jones Industrial Average
  c. the Nasdaq Composite Index
  d. the Lehman Aggregate Bond Index

d. is a bond index as the name implies.

427. True: A majority of the commonly used stock market indices are market-capitalization weighted as opposed to price-weighted.

Because the market-capitalization captures more information about the company than just the price alone.

428. **Which of the following is probably the best known example of a price-weighted index, with all of the other ones being market-capitalization weighted:**
a. the S&P 500
b. the Dow Jones Industrial Average
c. the Nasdaq Composite Index
d. the FTSE 100 Index

It is one of the few widely followed price-weighted indices - the other main one being the Nikkei 225 (Japan).

429. **Which of the following are examples of stock market indices around the world:**
I. the FTSE 100 Index
II. the CAC 40 Index
III. the Nikkei 225 Index
IV. the DAX Index
V. the Hang Seng

a. I only
b. I and II only
c. I, II and III only
d. I, II, III and IV only
e. I, II, III, IV and V

All of these are examples of commonly followed indices.

430. **If the S&P 500 is up strongly, which of the following is a safe conclusion:**
I. the market value of every US company has increased
II. the market value of all non-US companies is down
III. the share prices of the largest US companies in aggregate, weighted by size, has gone up
IV. the bond market is down
V. commodities are up

a. I only
b. I and II only
c. III only
d. I, II, III and IV only
e. I, II, III, IV and V

That is what the S&P 500 is designed to capture - some of the others may or may not be true, and would not be safe conclusions.

431. **True: Some indices capture a country's stock market performance, other indices might capture the performance of a certain industry such as the semiconductor industry.**

Indices can be set up to follow any grouping of securities that investors might have an interest in following - typically indices follow countries, regions or sectors for example - they can also follow groups of stocks by market capitalization - for example an index of small-cap stocks - a 'small-cap index'.

432. **True: The up and down movement of a technology index captures information regarding the performance of the corresponding technology sector.**

That is the reason for having indices - what exactly the index is capturing depends on what is in the index and how it is calculated - some indication of this will be given in the name. Investors can look at the index criteria and the index constituents to get a better sense of what the index is tracking.

433. A short-term down movement in a stock index could be caused by:
I. many of the largest companies in the index having their stock price decline
II. more sellers than buyers
III. news that the economy is much worse than people expect, and inflation higher
IV. investors becoming more risk-averse
V. profit warnings from a number of the largest companies in the index

a. I only
b. I and II only
c. I, II and III only
d. I, II, III and IV only
e. I, II, III, IV and V

All of these could lead to lower prices of the stocks contained in the index, or selling pressure and then lower prices.

434. False: A stock market index captures the performance of a single company's equity.

A stock market index captures the performance of a group of stocks or bonds or investments in general, allowing investors to get a sense for the performance of that group or asset class in aggregate - that is the value of an index.

435. The concept that pertains to the value of cash flows received today and those received in the future is known as:
a. the delay of money
b. the cash flows of time
c. the time value of money
d. the money value of money

The time value of money relates to how money today (the present value) relates to money in the future (the future value).

436. All future returns or yields stated for bonds or stocks are:
a. certain
b. expected
c. already realized
d. based on rumors

These might be based on analysis but the reality might still be different.

437. Security and market analysis that starts with the economy and works its way down to an individual company's financial statements is known as:
a. bottom up analysis
b. top-down analysis
c. sideways analysis
d. upside down analysis

It starts with the big picture - the economy - and then looks at the sector perhaps, and then lastly the individual company/security.

438. Security analysis that starts with, and that focuses on, the company is known as:
a. bottom up analysis
b. top-down analysis
c. sideways analysis
d. upside down analysis

The analysis of the company is also referred to as fundamental analysis.

439. **An investor might argue that valuing bonds is easier than valuing stocks because:**
   I. bondholders are more certain to be paid, since bonds are more senior in the capital structure
   II. bonds have a defined coupon and principal payment, so we have more certainty on the size of the expected cash flows and their timing
   III. the value of the stock is more dependent on the decisions of the management of the company
   IV. if we were to value both by discounting future cash flows, the discount factor would be easier to determine, or at least less variable, for the bond
   V. a stock will go to zero much earlier than the bond of the same company

   a. I only
   b. I and II only
   c. I, II and III only
   d. I, II, III and IV only
   e. I, II, III, IV and V

   These statements are all true and are all consequences of the nature of stocks and bonds, and their seniority in the capital structure.

440. **True: Valuing a bond (especially a low-risk bond or risk-free bond such as a government bond) is typically easier than valuing a stock because the cash flows are easier to project.**

   When valuing a risk-free bond, we can assume that the coupon and par value will be repaid with certainty - also we are given the timing of these cash flows. With a stock there are many uncertainties including what the earnings will be, what the dividends will be, what the competitive environment will look like etc.

QUESTIONS 441 - 453 ARE LINKED.

441. **A 5-year bond is issued with a par value of $1,000 and with a 7% annual coupon. What is the face value of the bond:**
   a. $700
   b. $70
   c. $1,000 ***(Par value and face value are the same thing)***
   d. $35

442. **What is the principal of the bond:**
   a. $700
   b. $70
   c. $1,000 ***(the principal is the amount to be repaid at maturity which in this case is $1,000)***
   d. $35

443. **What would be the payment be that the investor would expect to see annually:**
   a. $700
   b. $70 ***(7% of $1,000 is the annual coupon - this is $70)***
   c. $1,000
   d. $35

444. **This annual payment that the bond is expected to make is known as:**
   a. the bond's par value
   b. the bond's nominal value
   c. the price
   d. the coupon ***(by definition)***

445. <u>**What would happen if 5-year market interest rates rose substantially:**</u>
    a. **the price of the bond would fall**
    b. the price of the bond would rise
    c. the price of the bond would not change
    d. the price of the bond would go to 0

Because the future cash flows would be discounted at a higher rate. New bonds would also have to reflect these higher rates and would have to be issued with a higher coupon/yield, making the old ones worth less.

446. <u>**What would happen if 5-year market interest rates fell substantially:**</u>
    a. the price of the bond would fall
    b. **the price of the bond would rise**
    c. the price of the bond would not change
    d. the price of the bond would go to 0

Because the future cash flows would be discounted at a lower rate. New bonds would also have to reflect these lower rates and would be issued with a lower coupon/yield, making the old ones worth more.

447. <u>**With the substantial rise in interest rates, the coupon would:**</u>
    a. fall substantially
    b. rise substantially
    c. go to 0
    d. **remain unchanged**

The coupon of an existing bond does not change with interest rates - if the price of the bond fell, with the same coupon, the yield would become higher but not the coupon.

448. <u>**True: The coupon and principal repayment are all expected payments. If the issuer of the bonds runs into difficulty, the payments might not be realized.**</u>

All future payments are expected - if the bond is risk-free then this is not something that we have to give much thought to - with all other bonds, there is a chance that payments are not made.

449. <u>**True: The bond would be expected to make coupon payments for 5 years, and in year 5 pay the principal back along with the final coupon(s).**</u>

450. <u>**True: An investor that bought this bond some time after issue for $950 would expect a higher than 7% yield if the bond was held to maturity and all expected payments were made - he or she would expect the same annual payments - and the fact that the bond was bought below the face value of $1,000, would provide a further source of return.**</u>

The bond would be expected to pay an annual coupon of $70 which with a price of $950 means a (current) yield over 7% ($70/$950 x 100% = 7.37%); the fact that the final payment is higher than the purchase price would provide some additional return.

451. <u>**True: With the bond trading at $900, it can be said to be trading at a discount.**</u>

A bond that is trading below par value is trading at a discount; a bond that is trading above par value is trading at a premium. At any price below $1,000 the bond can be said to be trading at a discount.

452. <u>**A year after the bonds were issued interest rates have risen substantially. An issuer that comes to the market now and that wants to issue attractively priced bonds with a face value of $1,000 would have to offer coupon payments that are:**</u>

a. lower - investors expect less
b. higher - investors would expect a higher payment reflecting higher interest
c. the same - investors would not have changed their expectation
d. 0 - investors would not expect a payment any more

453. **If this bond became a lot more risky, its price would:**
a. rise
b. fall
c. stay the same
d. go to 0 immediately

Investors would pay less for a bond with the same expected cash flows but with higher risk.

454. **Which of the following completes the phrase best - the shares of a good company will be:**
a. certainly a good investment
b. certainly a bad investment
c. possibly a good investment subject to valuation
d. a good investment if the valuation is high enough

455. **False: The value of a stock can be calculated which allows all investors to know with certainty where the stock price will go to.**

We can never be certain about the exact value of a stock given all of the things that can happen in the future. The goal is potentially to have an informed view.

456. **True: There are different levels of market efficiency that professionals talk about.**

457. **A market in which historical price data can not be used to predict future prices is said to be:**
a. strong-form efficient
b. semi-strong form efficient
c. weak-form efficient
d. totally efficient

These are definitions and they are not that important.

458. **A market in which publicly available information can not be used to earn an excess return is said to be:**
a. strong-form efficient
b. semi-strong form efficient
c. weak-form efficient
d. totally efficient

These are definitions and they are not that important.

459. **A market in which insider/non-public information can not be used to earn an excess return is said to be:**
a. strong-form efficient
b. semi-strong form efficient
c. weak-form efficient
d. totally efficient

These are definitions and they are not that important.

460. **Which of the following would be most likely to have insider information about a company:**
a. an outside investor
b. a day trader

c. the government
d. the company's management

They are insiders to the company and they would have restrictions on their ability to trade the stock of their own company in many countries.

461. **True: Insider information is relevant (or material) non-public information that the company has not disclosed to investors broadly.**

462. **True: Trading on insider information is illegal in many countries.**

Because it makes the playing field uneven and favors insiders over the broader saving and investing public - fairness is important for the success of a saving and investing system.

463. **Calculating the right value for a stock is:**
a. very easy
b. just a matter of crunching a few numbers
c. filled with uncertainly - we never know exactly what will happen in the future
d. easier than calculating the value for a bond

Analysis is aimed at figuring out possible or even likely scenarios, but in the end, investors never know exactly what will happen in the future either with respect to the company, its competitors or the overall economic environment.

464. **Valuing stocks is complicated by which of the following factors:**
I. future earnings are difficult to forecast
II. company management decisions can be unpredictable
III. different valuation methods can lead to different results
IV. the competitive landscape can change dramatically
V. the future is never certain

a. I only
b. I and II only
c. I, II and III only
d. I, II, III and IV only
e. I, II, III, IV and V

All of these are true and make stock valuation an inexact science.

465. **True: Analyzing companies and stocks is a complicated process and one can never be sure exactly what will happen - by conducting detailed analysis, proponents of stock analysis try to figure out what is happening in an industry, a sector, and with a company, to determine whether the stock should be purchased.**

466. **Valuation ratios that analysts might look at in assessing a company's valuation include:**
I. the Price-to-Earnings (P/E) Ratio
II. the Price-to-Sales (P/Sales Ratio)
III. the EV/EBITDA Ratio
IV. the Price-to-Book Ratio
V. the Dividend Yield

a. I only
b. I and II only
c. I, II and III only
d. I, II, III and IV only
e. I, II, III, IV and V

All of these are ratios that analysts might look at.

467. **<u>The main advantage of the P/E ratio is:</u>**
   a. it is always accurate
   b. it takes into account many years of earnings
   c. earnings capture all of the characteristics of a firm's operations
   d. it is very easy to calculate

   This is probably the most widely known valuation measure. It divides the share price by the earnings per share or EPS. The EPS are the net income or profits per share (net income ÷ number of shares). The earnings used are either this year's earnings, next year's earnings or in some cases last year's earnings. The P/E ratio gives the same result as taking the market capitalization (share price x the number of shares) and dividing by the net income. The ratio gives the cost of each dollar of earnings, therefore a low P/E Ratio is a good thing, all other things being equal. One of the drawbacks of the P/E ratio is that it only looks at one year of earnings, and that the earnings of this one year are affected by depreciation, extraordinary charges and the growth rate of earnings, which might mean that a stock that looks expensive in one year might no longer look that way when looking at another year, or vice versa.

468. **<u>The 'P' in the P/E ratio is a:</u>**
   a. price
   b. profit
   c. earnings
   d. revenues

469. **<u>The 'E' in the P/E ratio refers to:</u>**
   a. price
   b. extraordinary profit
   c. earnings
   d. revenues

470. **<u>Earnings per share are calculated by:</u>**
   a. dividing revenues by net income
   b. dividing earnings by the number of shareholders
   c. dividing profit or earnings by the number of bonds outstanding
   d. dividing earnings by the number of shares outstanding

   By definition.

471. **<u>The P/E ratio is typically calculated by taking the price of a share and dividing by the earnings per share. It could also be calculated by taking:</u>**
   a. the revenues and dividing by the net income
   b. the operating expenses divided by the revenues
   c. the market capitalization of the company and dividing by the net income of the company
   d. the net income divided by the number of shares

   This is the same as taking the price per share and dividing by the earnings per share - it is taking the price for all of the shares/equity and dividing by all of the earnings (both the numerator and the denominator are larger by the factor of the number of shares).

472. **<u>One stock trades on a P/E ratio of 6, the other on a P/E ratio of 8. Which of the following is a prudent conclusion:</u>**
   a. the stocks with a P/E ratio of 6 is a better buy
   b. the stock with a P/E ratio of 8 is a better buy
   c. both stocks are equally valued

d. the P/E ratio alone is not enough information to draw any of the above conclusions

D. is the prudent conclusion as one valuation measure, especially in light of the arguments for efficient markets, is not enough to draw conclusions about which one is a better buy. Which one is a better buy would also need to look at earnings growth, management quality, the competitive environment etc. The stock with a P/E ratio of 6 looks cheaper on the P/E measure using the earnings of this year that is being looked at - it could be that the earnings of one of the companies are affected by one-off factors as well so that more investigation would be prudent.

473. The P/E-to-Growth ratio might be preferable to the P/E ratio when:
a. two firms have the same growth rate
b. firms have different growth rates that might help explain a part of the P/E difference
c. when P/E ratios are not available
d. when the growth is unclear

By dividing by growth, we can normalize for the growth difference, and try to look at valuation adjusted for the difference in growth, bearing in mind that we are still only looking at one year of earnings and one year of growth, with all of the drawbacks that this entails.

474. The Price-to-Sales ratio might be useful when:
I. a company does not yet have earnings
II. a company has abnormally depressed earnings
III. a company has poor earnings which should normalize to an industry average over time
IV. the company has no sales
V. the company has sales that are growing quickly

a. I only
b. I and II only
c. I, II and III only
d. I, II, III and IV only
e. I, II, III, IV and V

Many early-stage companies do not have earnings; sometimes earnings are distorted for a period of time because of extraordinary non-recurring expenses. The Price-to-Sales measure is a quick and easy-to-use valuation measure, along the lines of the P/E ratio, where companies are compared on the basis of sales. Because shareholders care about earnings and other cash flows more than sales, comparing stocks on this basis indirectly assumes that sales would translate into similar earnings if normal earnings were there. Again we are only using one year's worth of data to determine the valuation, so it has similar drawbacks to the P/E ratio in this regard.

It allows companies to be compared that do not have earnings or that have issues with respect to their earnings (I, II and III). It can not be calculated when the company has no sales, and it makes no adjustments for growth, and therefore does not offer any advantages when sales are growing quickly.

475. Which of the following is not a drawback of the P/E ratio:
a. it only takes into account one year of earnings
b. earnings are subject to accounting entries that may not reflect the actual operations of the firm
c. earnings can be distorted by write-offs
d. the price is difficult to assess

The price of a stock is one of the easiest things to find.

476. A valuation method that looks at that portion of earnings that is paid out to shareholders, and that seeks to calculate a present value for these future payments to shareholders, is known as the:
a. Discounted Cash Flow Method

b. Dividend Discount Model
c. Discounted Earnings Model
d. Cash Flow Valuation

The portion of earnings that is paid out to shareholders is the dividend; calculating a present value for these dividends is known as discounting - hence the name 'Dividend Discount Model'.

477. **True: The Price-to-Book ratio is more useful when a company has tangible assets on its balance sheet which have a value that is more easily determined.**

Tangible assets make the book value more relevant and easier to calculate.

478. **Which of the following is likely have the highest dividend yield:**
a. fast growing companies
b. technology companies
c. biotech companies
d. utility companies

Utilities are often regulated and confined to a certain market, often leading to a lower need for reinvestment and a higher dividend yield. All of the others typically have a very clear need for reinvestment.

479. **The percentage of earnings paid out as dividends to shareholders, is known as:**
a. the dividend yield
b. the earnings ratio
c. the debt/equity ratio
d. the payout ratio

By definition.

480. **Which of the following ratios tries to adjust or normalize for growth differences between stocks/ companies:**
a. price to sales ratio
b. P/E ratio
c. price to book ratio
d. P/E to growth ratio

By dividing by the growth in earnings, this ratio tries to adjust for differences in the P/E ratio due to growth rates.

481. **A market operator that buys and sells securities with a view to taking a spread between the purchase price and the sale price, and that holds the securities for short periods, also to facilitate the operation of a market in the securities, is best described as:**
a. a mutual fund
b. a long-term investor
c. a corporate raider
d. a trader

482. **True: In order to determine how currency movements will impact a company, it is necessary to look at where a company is generating its revenues and where it is incurring its costs.**

483. **True: Many of the stock market valuation measures including the P/E ratio can also be calculated for a stock market index.**

Earnings for an index can be calculated using the earnings of the companies in the index and their weights. With this a P/E ratio can be calculated for an index - other valuation metrics can be

calculated as well. Having the P/E ratio for an index allows proponents of fundamental analysis to see whether a particular stock is cheap versus its index, or whether an index is cheap versus its historical valuation for example.

484. Which of the following metrics can be used to look at the valuation of a company:

I. the P/E ratio
II. the P/Sales ratio
III. the dividend yield
IV. the discounted cash flow value
V. the price to book value

a. I only
b. I and II only
c. I, II and III only
d. I, II, III and IV only
e. I, II, III, IV and V

All of them are valid valuation measures that can be used to look at the valuation of a company - all of them provide insight into aspects of the valuation - they all have advantages and disadvantages.

485. Which of the following valuation methods looks at more than one year of data:

a. the P/E ratio
b. the P/Sales ratio
c. the dividend yield
d. the discounted cash flow method

This method involves bringing various cash flows back to the present via discounting. All of the others look at one year of data.

486. The discounted cash flow method of valuing stocks is complicated by the fact that:

I. we need cash flows for a long time into the future
II. it is difficult to know exactly what the discount factor should be
III. it requires a lot of assumptions, forecasting, and modeling
IV. it only looks at one year of data
V. it only looks at earnings

a. I only
b. I and II only
c. I, II and III only
d. I, II, III and IV only
e. I, II, III, IV and V

The discounted cash flow method should look at cash flows over the life of the company which could be a very long time, although often simplifications are made - in either case this requires assumptions, forecasting and modeling. To bring the future cash flows back to today requires the calculation of a discount factor which reflects the risk of the cash flows, which will be higher than the risk-free rate (government bond rate) since the cash flows are not certain - calculating the discount factor is subject to uncertainty as well. The method looks at many years of data and it does not look only at earnings - it looks at cash flows (IV and V).

487. In the EV/EBITDA ratio, the EV is:

a. the excess value
b. the enterprise value
c. the entrepreneur value
d. the excess vortex

EBITDA (Earnings Before Interest, Taxes, Depreciation and Amortization) is a measure of the operating earnings of a company, which go to both equity and debtholders. (Amortization is a non-cash charge similar to depreciation). The EV-to-EBITDA measure divides the Enterprise Value (the sum of the market value of the company's equity and net debt (debt minus cash)) by the EBITDA for the company; we can see how conceptually it is similar to the P/E ratio, except that it looks at more of the company, and the cash flows that go to more of the company.

488. Which of the following is the main drawback of the EV/EBITDA ratio:
   a. the EBITDA is affected by depreciation
   b. the EBITDA is affected by the tax rate
   c. the EV is difficult to calculate
   d. it only looks at one year of EBITDA

   The EBITDA looks at 'Earnings before Interest, Taxes, Depreciation and Amortization' therefore depreciation and the tax rate to not impact this number. The EV is easy to calculate. The measure only looks at one year of data (like the P/E ratio).

489. To calculate the EPS of a company, an analyst would need:
   a. the revenues of the company and the number of shares outstanding
   b. the earnings of the company and the debt/equity ratio
   c. the net income or profit of the company and the number of shares outstanding
   d. the sales of the company and the number of investors in the company

   The EPS (Earnings per Share) are calculated by taking the earnings (or net income or profit) for the company and dividing by the number of shares.

QUESTIONS 490 - 507 ARE LINKED.

Use the following data for a company to answer the next series of questions:

Revenues	$10,000,000
Net Income	$1,000,000
Number of Shares Outstanding	1,000,000
Share Price on Stock Exchange	$8.00
Average Number of Share traded per day	100,000
Dividend	$0.40

490. The earnings for this company are:
   a. $10,000,000
   b. $1,000,000 *(same as net income)*
   c. $8.00
   d. $125,000

491. The turnover for this company is:
   a. $10,000,000 *(turnover is the same as revenues)*
   b. $1,000,000
   c. $8.00
   d. $125,000

492. The top line for the company is:
   a. $10,000,000 *(top line refers to revenues)*
   b. $1,000,000
   c. $8.00

d. $125,000

493. The bottom line for the company is:
a. $10,000,000
b. $1,000,000 ***(bottom line refers to net income)***
c. $8.00
d. $125,000

494. The market capitalization for the company is:
a. $10,000,000
b. $1,000,000
c. $8,000,000 ***(share price x number of shares = $8.00 x 1,000,000)***
d. $2,000,000

495. The company is:
a. profitable ***(positive earnings)***
b. loss-making
c. bankrupt
d. not enough information has been provided to be able to tell

496. The equity of this company is:
a. private
b. public ***(a share price for the shares on the stock exchange is given)***
c. both
d. neither

497. The earnings per share for this company are:
a. $8.00
b. $10.00
c. $1.00 ***(total earnings/number of shares = $1,000,000 /1,000,000)***
d. $4.00

498. The dividend (per share) for this company is:
a. $1.00
b. $10.00
c. $4.00
d. $0.40 ***(as given in the question)***

499. The dividend yield for this company is:
a. 10%
b. 8%
c. 7%
d. 5% ***(dividend/share price = $0.40/$8.00 = 5%)***

500. The total earnings that are paid out by the company in the form of a dividend are:
a. $1,000,000
b. $8,000,000
c. $10,000,000
d. $400,000 ***(dividend/share x number of shares = $0.40 x 1,000,000)***

501. The earnings that are not paid out are referred to as, and total:
a. blown earnings and they total $1,000,000
b. spent earnings and they total $1,000,000
c. lost earnings and they total $600,000
d. retained earnings and they total $600,000 ***($1,000,000 - $600,000)***

502. <u>**The sum of retained earnings and the dividend for the entire company are referred to as:**</u>
 a. the earnings and they total $1,000,000
 b. the revenues and they total $10,000,000
 c. the number of shares and they total $1,000,000
 d. the number of shares traded and this totals $100,000

The sum of the retained earnings and the total paid out as a dividend are just the total earnings.

503. <u>**On the income statement, this company would have total costs, including cost of goods sold, operating expenses, interest expense and taxes of:**</u>
 a. $10,000,000
 b. $9,000,000 ***(revenues - all costs and expenses = net income)***
 c. $5,000,000
 d. Difficult to tell from the data provided

504. <u>**The P/E ratio for this company is:**</u>
 a. 10
 b. 12
 c. 8 ***(Price/Earnings (per share) = $8.00/$1.00)***
 d. 5

505. <u>**The Price-to-Sales ratio for this company is:**</u>
 a. 1.0
 b. 2.0
 c. 0.5
 d. 0.8 ***(Price/Sales (per share) = $8.00/($10,000,000/1,000,000))***

506. <u>**If the earnings next year were a lot higher, then the P/E ratio on next year's earnings would be:**</u>
 a. a lot higher
 b. the same
 c. a lot lower ***(would be dividing by a much larger number)***
 d. 0

507. <u>**This company is:**</u>
 a. paying out 50% of its earnings and retaining 60%
 b. paying out 50% of its earnings and retaining 50%
 c. paying out 40% of its earnings and retaining 60%
 d. paying out 60% of its earnings and retaining 40%

Paying out $0.40 of every $1.00 and retaining $0.60 - $0.40 of $1.00 is 40%; $0.60 of $1.00 is 60%.

508. <u>**A valid argument/Valid arguments for a company to retain more of its earnings would be:**</u>
 I. the company is generating very high returns on investment
 II. the company is able to do more with each dollar of earnings than an investor can elsewhere
 III. each dollar that is paid out is not likely to be invested as profitably elsewhere
 IV. the company is growing (profitably) and needs the cash
 V. the company will need capital in the next two years and retaining earnings reduces the need to sell new shares in the future

 a. I only
 b. I and II only
 c. I, II and III only
 d. I, II, III and IV only
 e. I, II, III, IV and V

Having profitable investment opportunities and having a need for the cash in the future are two main reasons for retaining earnings. The corresponding opposites of these two things are reasons for paying out earnings in the form of dividends.

509. **True: With investments, risks always need to be thought about - in order to qualify the source and nature of the risk, specific terms are sometimes used.**

There are many types of risk that investors talk about and that specify more clearly where the risk lies - more on this in question 510.

510. **Which of the following are considered risks depending on the type of investment:**
    I. interest rate risk
    II. reinvestment risk
    III. default risk
    IV. exchange rate risk
    V. market risk

    a. I only
    b. I and II only
    c. I, II and III only
    d. I, II, III and IV only
    e. I, II, III, IV and V

    I. For example, the risk that interest rates rise and that a bond is worth less
    II. For example, the risk that a bond is repaid early and that an investor can not reinvest as profitably
    III. The risk that the principal of the bond or the coupons are not paid
    IV. The risk that an investment's value drops due to currency moves
    V. The risk that the movement of a market affects the value of an investment

511. **The maximum loss for a bondholder is:**
    a. the amount invested in the bonds
    b. the total value of the bonds outstanding
    c. the net worth of the provider of capital
    d. infinite

    When an investor provides capital in the form of debt by investing in bonds, the maximum loss is the amount invested in the bonds.

512. **The maximum loss for a shareholder is:**
    a. the amount invested in the stocks
    b. the total value of the outstanding bonds
    c. the net worth of the provider of capital
    d. infinite

    When an investor provides capital in the form of equity by investing in stocks, the maximum loss is the amount invested in the stocks.

513. **A company or an individual are most likely to go bankrupt when which of the following single events occurs:**
    a. income drops a lot
    b. assets become worth a lot less
    c. they can not meet their obligations to creditors
    d. revenues drop a lot

It is not until the obligations to the creditors can not be met that there is a real risk of bankruptcy - all of the other things are bad for a company and might lead to bankruptcy, but the single event that makes bankruptcy highly likely is an inability to honor the terms of the debt.

TOTAL: 177 ANSWERS

Mutual Funds and Index Funds

514. <u>**The idea behind a mutual fund is:**</u>
   a. to pool the money of many smaller investors and invest this larger sum on their behalf
   b. to have many investors each with completely different returns
   c. to give each investor an investment in one stock
   d. to avoid diversification

   The idea of a mutual fund is to pool the money of many investors and for it to be invested on their behalf. All of the investors in the same mutual fund class will receive the same return. A mutual fund is typically designed to offer diversification and would not invest in one stock.

515. <u>**An investor that wants to buy a diversified portfolio of stocks, but does not want to manage the portfolio themselves would most likely invest in:**</u>
   a. a bond
   b. a stock
   c. a mutual fund
   d. gold

516. <u>**Which of the following statements regarding funds is true:**</u>
   I. funds typically pool the money of many investors
   II. funds often benefit from size and scale benefits over any individual investor
   III. funds will have documentation that details the characteristics of the fund
   IV. every fund is associated with a fund management or asset management company
   V. the investments of a fund could be difficult to replicate for the average investor because of the number of securities that would be required

   a. I only
   b. I and II only
   c. I, II and III only
   d. I, II, III and IV only
   e. I, II, III, IV and V

   All of these statements are true and summarize some of the characteristics and advantages of mutual funds.

517. <u>**True: For a lot of investors, mutual funds make sense over buying individual stocks or bonds.**</u>

   Advantages include: Many securities are bought with one transaction, the individual security portfolio management process is outsourced, they offer diversification over buying a small number of securities.

518. <u>**True: Each mutual fund has investment guidelines that define what the fund focuses on.**</u>

   These guidelines would be suggested potentially through the name, but can and should also be read about in the fund literature, particularly the prospectus.

519. <u>**Advantages of mutual funds can include:**</u>
   I. diversification
   II. a professional making the investment decisions
   III. professional risk management
   IV. exposure to a large number of securities through one purchase
   V. they never go down

   a. I only

b. I and II only
c. I, II and III only
d. I, II, III and IV only
e. I, II, III, IV and V

Mutual funds can clearly go down depending in part on what they are invested in (V) - all of the other statements (I-IV) are true and reflect some of the potential advantages of mutual funds.

520. **Which of the following statements regarding mutual funds is true:**
a. the guidelines and the documentation define what the fund should invest in and determine a benchmark against which the performance of the fund can be measured
b. mutual funds can typically invest in anything they like and they do not have a benchmark
c. a mutual fund that is managed by a portfolio manager is said to be passively managed
d. portfolio managers can be sure that every decision that they make is correct

They typically do have a benchmark; a fund that is managed by a portfolio manager is actively managed; portfolio managers will not be correct in every decision - that is the nature of investing - it is about increasing the likelihood of being right through analysis and thought.

521. **True: Mutual Funds are one of the main investment vehicles for private savers and investors.**

For the reasons noted above, they are one of the main ways for private savers and investors to invest.

522. **True: Mutual funds exist in various forms in many countries and they are a widespread investing vehicle. In the UK they are referred to as unit trusts.**

Instead of investing in individual debt investments or stocks directly, it is possible to get a broader exposure to equity and debt through funds, bearing in mind that although individual investments might be difficult to value, both the equity and debt markets have risen historically over time. These funds are known as mutual funds in the United States and Canada, unit trusts in Great Britain and Australia, and as public funds in some countries such as Germany (public funds because everyone is allowed to invest in them).

523. **Mutual funds would typically be available through:**
I. banks
II. asset management companies
III. mutual fund management companies
IV. public companies that the mutual fund has invested in
V. the government

a. I only
b. I and II only
c. I, II and III only
d. I, II, III and IV only
e. I, II, III, IV and V

Mutual funds are available through financial services companies that cater to retail or private clients. Some of the firms will only sell their own products, and some will have an 'open architecture' where they sell a large number of products from different providers.

524. **Which of the following statements with respect to investment regulation is true:**
a. if an investment firm is regulated, their investments never go down
b. if an investment firm is regulated, everything they say will turn out to be true
c. if an investment firm is regulated, there is no need for diversification

d. regulation means that the investment firm has met certain criteria - it does not mean that we should not look around, inform ourselves, diversify and perform reference checks

525. Which of the following statement(s) about mutual funds is/are true:
I. some mutual funds invest in US stocks
II. some mutual funds invest in European stocks
III. some mutual funds invest in Asian stocks
IV. some mutual funds invest in US government bonds
V. some mutual funds invest in the equity of the largest companies in the world

a. I only
b. I and II only
c. I, II and III only
d. I, II, III and IV only
e. I, II, III, IV and V

All of these statements are true and there is a vast array of mutual funds that exist and that target different investments.

526. True: The benchmark of a mutual fund is typically a relevant index - for example a stock market index.

This index is what the fund/fund manager is measured against.

527. True: Mutual funds can either be actively or passively managed.

Active management refers to funds that are actively managed by portfolio managers who are aiming to outperform a benchmark through active investment decisions. Passive management refers to a more automated management style where the selection of investments is directly based on their weights in an index and where the fund aims to replicate the weights in, and the performance of, the index/benchmark as closely as possible.

528. The manager of an actively managed mutual fund is known as:
a. the CEO
b. the bondholder
c. the portfolio manager
d. the lender

The portfolio manager manages the portfolio of investments.

529. When a mutual fund is managed by a portfolio manager who is trying to beat a benchmark, the fund is said to be:
a. an index fund
b. actively managed
c. passively managed
d. an exchange traded fund

Actively managed funds over- and underweight investments relative to the benchmark in order to try to beat its performance. The fund manager of an actively managed US equity fund with the S&P 500 as its benchmark for example would try to perform better than the index by making active investment decisions. He or she would weight a stock in the fund differently from the weight of that stock in the benchmark if he or she had a view on how the stock will perform. If the fund manager thinks that a stock with a 2 % weighting in the index will not perform as well as the index - that it will underperform - he or she will invest less than 2% of the fund in that stock and more in other stocks that he or she thinks will perform better. If he or she thinks that the stock will do better than the index - that it will outperform - then he or she will invest more than 2% of the fund in the stock

and less in other stocks. If these views are wrong, and the fund manager bets on the wrong stocks, then he or she will underperform the benchmark.

530. **All of the following are typical responsibilities of the portfolio manager except:**
    a. selecting the investments for the fund
    b. managing the risk of the fund
    c. selecting stocks or bonds to overweight versus the benchmark
    d. managing the day-to-day operations of the companies that the fund has invested in

    This responsibility rests with the managements of the companies themselves.

531. **An active portfolio manager is typically measured against a benchmark that he or she is trying to beat. This benchmark would usually be:**
    a. a stock
    b. a bond
    c. a commodity
    d. an index

    A mutual fund will have guidelines that dictate what the fund is supposed to invest in - the fund manager is responsible for selecting the best investments for the fund based on these guidelines. The guidelines might specify that the fund will invest in large US companies, or in large European companies, or in emerging market debt for example. Based on its guidelines, a relevant benchmark is selected against which the performance of the fund and the fund manager are measured.

532. **True: The performance of a mutual fund should be compared to an index or benchmark that is relevant for what that fund invests in.**

    That is the only way to assess the skill of the portfolio manager - if one fund is compared to another fund with a different index, or if the fund in question is compared to another index that is not relevant, this would tell us more about which asset class or index outperformed than it would about the ability of the portfolio manager to better the benchmark.

533. **True: Each stock in the S&P 500 index will have a certain percentage weight in the index.**

    Which in the case of the S&P 500 is determined by the market capitalizations of the companies.

534. **True: One of the main activities of a portfolio manager is to overweight securities versus the benchmark that the portfolio manager thinks will do better than the benchmark, and to underweight securities versus the benchmark that he or she does not think will do as well as the benchmark.**

535. **Strategies that active managers might advertise as using to try and beat the performance of an index include all of the following except:**
    a. security selection
    b. sector selection
    c. market timing
    d. spin-the-bottle

    The first three are techniques that investors can use to try and beat the market - spin-the-bottle would not be used to advertise investment skill.

536. **Skeptics of active management argue that:**
    a. markets are efficient
    b. markets are inefficient
    c. portfolio managers can successfully pick stocks that outperform the market
    d. timing the market is easy - just buy low and sell high

To argue for efficient markets means to argue that analysis can not be used to make a better return.

537. Why might actively managed mutual funds have difficulty delivering performance that is better than the benchmark:

I. there are too many people trying to do the same thing
II. the costs of active management outweigh the benefits
III. markets are efficient
IV. it is very difficult to time markets
V. any single investor can not find the inefficiencies in the market consistently

a. I only
b. I and II only
c. I, II and III only
d. I, II, III and IV only
e. I, II, III, IV and V

There are a lot of books and studies written on this and it is also explored at length in the book 'Saving and Investing' - the above list is a summary of why it is very difficult or impossible for active managers to beat their benchmark in developed markets consistently over a longer period after fees.

538. Which of the following statements is false with respect to active management:

a. active management is usually significantly higher cost than passive management
b. very few portfolio managers beat their benchmark over longer periods of time
c. because of fees, it is harder for actively managed funds to beat their benchmark
d. all portfolio managers beat their benchmark in developed markets

The evidence actually points to the opposite - that most active portfolio managers underperform the benchmark over longer periods of time, especially after fees.

539. Investors that argue that picking stocks is not a great way of beating the market are arguing for:

a. market inefficiency
b. market irrelevance
c. market efficiency
d. market relevance

Market efficiency refers to not being able to use information (and analysis) to beat the benchmark. If markets are efficient, it makes stock picking useless over just picking stocks randomly.

540. People that argue that stock-picking based on publicly available information is a waste of time, might be arguing this because they believe:

I. markets are efficient (or specifically semi-strong form efficient)
II. publicly available information is already reflected in stock prices
III. too many people are trying to do the same thing
IV. it is unlikely that any investor finds enough mispricings to outperform given the number of investors and the number of mispricings; and how many mispricings are needed to to outperform when mistakes and fees are included
V. that you can not make money by investing in stocks

a. I only
b. I and II only
c. I, II and III only
d. I, II, III and IV only
e. I, II, III, IV and V

I-IV is again a list of why stock-picking is often argued to be a waste of time. It does not mean that stocks do not offer returns, it just means that spending a lot of time picking individual stocks over others does not add additional value.

541. **True: The performance of an actively managed fund is negatively affected by trading and management costs.**

The management fees for an actively managed fund are typically higher than those of a passively managed fund - any fees reduce the net performance that an investor receives.

542. **True: The alternative to having a fund actively managed is to have it passively managed.**

These are the two types of funds.

543. **A passively managed fund is most likely to offer which of the following benefits:**

I. lower fees
II. performance that is close to the benchmark or index
III. a professional portfolio manager that makes the investment decisions
IV. capital protection
V. twice the return of other funds

a. I only
b. I and II only
c. I, II and III only
d. I, II, III and IV only
e. I, II, III, IV and V

Passively managed funds should have lower fees (always needs to be looked at) and are designed to track an index - i.e. invest passively. A passively managed fund would not have a portfolio manager that takes active investment decisions - the weighting of securities would be driven by their weight in the index for example. The fact that they are passively managed would not offer capital protection per se, and there is no reason why they should offer twice the return of other funds by definition.

544. **Which of the following is an example of a passively managed fund:**

a. a hedge fund
b. an index fund
c. a mutual fund with a star portfolio manager
d. an actively managed fund

An index fund is passive by definition.

545. **True: Funds that are passively managed aim to replicate an index and re-weight securities to stay as close to the index as possible, in a fairly automatic manner.**

That is what they are - and that is what they do.

546. **Which of the following is generally a low-cost manner of investing in the largest publicly listed companies in a developed country:**

a. a fixed income mutual fund
b. a commodities fund
c. a large-cap stock index fund
d. an art fund

By definition - large-cap refers to large market-capitalization or large-capitalization, in other words, the largest companies - investing via an index fund offers the opportunity to decrease the fees.

547. <u>The reason that index funds make sense for so many investors is because:</u>

I. it would be hard for an individual investor to buy enough securities to achieve similar diversification
II. they typically have lower fees than actively managed funds
III. they are a low-cost way of outsourcing the portfolio management process
IV. they always go up
V. they are a way of getting active management into the portfolio

a. I only
b. I and II only
c. I, II and III only
d. I, II, III and IV only
e. I, II, III, IV and V

Like other funds, they can provide exposure to a large number of securities which would be difficult for most individual investors to do to the same degree. They typically have lower management fees (always needs to be looked at closely). They do outsource the portfolio management process, and given that the merits of active management in developed markets are often questioned, they arguably do this very well. They do not always go up, and they do not get active management into the portfolio.

548. <u>Advantages of index funds include:</u>

I. typically lower cost
II. outperformance of most active managers in developed markets over longer periods
III. performance is relatively easy to track - they tend to follow the index
IV. they are risk-free
V. a professional uses his or her judgment to take investment decisions

a. I only
b. I and II only
c. I, II and III only
d. I, II, III and IV only
e. I, II, III, IV and V

I-III is a list of some of the advantages of index funds. III and IV are not true.

549. <u>True: The concept of market efficiency relates to whether information that we can get or analyze is already reflected in the prices of securities.</u>

This is another way of saying that investors/portfolio managers can not use publicly available information to select individual investments to outperform a benchmark.

550. <u>An investor that believes that markets are efficient is most likely to own:</u>

a. a single stock
b. a single bond
c. an index fund
d. a single commodity

Someone that believes that markets are efficient would most likely not engage in picking individual securities and would most likely buy an index fund.

551. <u>True: It was probably easier for a single professional investor to outperform the benchmark when a larger percentage of investors was non-professional and a smaller percentage was professional.</u>

Because these investors were not as sophisticated in valuing stocks, but also because a rational professional investor would base their buy or sell decision on valuation almost exclusively,

whereas retail investors for example might base the decision on a desire for cash at a point in time or for other personal reasons.

552. **In the US market, stocks have been observed to rise somewhat more consistently in January than in other months. If this 'January effect' was occurring consistently, it would be an example of an observable event that could be used as an example to refute efficient market theory because:**
   a. stocks should rise all year long
   b. stocks should drop in January every year
   c. everyone knows January is coming so the price rise should have taken place - it should be priced in
   d. stocks should not go up

   Market efficiency would lead us to believe that information and analysis would not lead to an improved return. The January effect would indicate that you could use information - the fact that January is coming - to improve returns. The January effect is not always observed but it has been observed, and it has therefore fueled debate on the subject - having said that, the data regarding active management in developed markets has been analyzed extensively and that is fairly compelling.

553. **If one wanted to have exposure to stock markets through a low-cost index fund that is very liquid, one should look at:**
   a. hedge funds
   b. actively managed funds
   c. gold
   d. exchange traded funds

   Exchange traded funds (ETFs) (as the name suggests) are funds that trade on an exchange like stocks and that are typically very liquid.

554. **Most exchange traded funds or ETFs are:**
   a. hedge funds
   b. actively managed
   c. passively managed
   d. destined to go to zero

   Most exchange traded funds are passively managed - they can be thought of as index funds that trade on an exchange.

555. **True: Exchange traded funds allow investors to very quickly get exposure to a particular asset class.**

   Exchange traded funds trade on exchanges and can typically be bought and sold very easily.

556. **Which of the following are advantages of exchange traded funds (ETFs):**
   I. they trade like stocks
   II. they can be bought and sold more quickly than regular mutual funds
   III. they usually have lower fees than actively managed mutual funds
   IV. they can allow an investor to get exposure to an asset class in one quick transaction
   V. they can never go down

   a. I only
   b. I and II only
   c. I, II and III only
   d. I, II, III and IV only
   e. I, II, III, IV and V

I-IV are some of the main characteristics of ETFs.

557. <u>An exchange traded fund is best described a:</u>
- a. an illiquid fund that is sold with an operating memorandum
- b. an unregulated fund often based in the Cayman Islands
- c. a fund that only buys the stocks of stock exchanges
- **d. a fund that trades on an exchange**

558. <u>A large part of the risk of buying an ETF is associated with:</u>
- a. the skills of the investment manager
- b. whether it can be sold again
- c. whether the exchange will go out of business
- **d. the risk associated with the index or benchmark that the ETF is tracking**

This is certainly the case for ETFs that are passively managed, which most are.

559. <u>A money-market mutual fund is a fund that invests in:</u>
- a. equities
- b. corporate bonds
- **c. highly rated short-term debt instruments**
- d. long-term debt

This is what the term 'money-market' refers to. What the fund can and can not invest in is discussed in the prospectus and in the documentation for the fund - this is always worth investigating.

560. <u>A 'growth' oriented mutual fund would likely invest in:</u>
- I. technology companies
- II. growing companies
- III. mature companies
- IV. bankrupt companies
- V. bonds

- a. I only
- **b. I and II only**
- c. I, II and III only
- d. I, II, III and IV only
- e. I, II, III, IV and V

It would invest in growth stocks such as the stocks of technology companies or other growing companies.

561. <u>An 'income' oriented mutual fund would most likely invest in which of the following:</u>
- I. growth stocks
- II. technology stocks
- III. high dividend paying stocks
- IV. bonds
- V. commodities

- a. I only
- b. I and II only
- c. I, II and III only
- **d. III and IV only**
- e. I, II, III, IV and V

I and II would typically pay a low dividend (therefore generating little income) because the companies would want to retain the capital for reinvestment. Commodities also do not pay an 'income'.

562. **The term 'bond fund' refers to:**
   a. a mutual fund that invests in bonds
   b. a bond of a particular company
   c. a bond of a particular government
   d. a fund that does not invest in bonds

563. **A 'sector fund' refers to a mutual fund that:**
   a. invests only in stocks
   b. invests only in bonds
   c. invests in the stocks of a certain sector - for example technology
   d. can not go down

564. **The term 'stock fund' refers to:**
   a. a mutual fund that invests in stocks
   b. the stock of a particular company
   c. the stock in a particular region
   d. a fund that does not invest in stocks

565. **A fund that invests in both stocks and bonds is known as a:**
   a. stock and bond fund
   b. balanced fund
   c. private equity fund
   d. bond fund

   This is the definition of a balanced fund.

566. **True: The name of the mutual fund will typically give some idea as to how it is managed and what its benchmark is - to get the full picture one should look at the fund documents, and in particular the prospectus.**

567. **A mutual fund that can raise money continuously is known as:**
   a. a hedge fund
   b. a closed-ended fund
   c. an open-ended fund
   d. a private equity fund

   Most mutual funds are open-ended funds - collective investment schemes that can issue and redeem shares at any time. Because they are the more common form of mutual fund, often the term 'open-ended' is just left out. Because there are also closed-end funds which make sense for less liquid investments, it is worth being aware of the distinction, and knowing which type of fund a particular fund is, given the implications. With an open-ended fund, an investor will generally purchase shares in the fund directly from the fund itself rather than from existing fund-holders. This contrasts with a closed-end fund, which typically issues all the fund units/shares it will issue at the outset, with the shares being tradable between investors thereafter.

568. **A mutual fund that can raises money only for a certain amount of time or to a certain amount, and that is aimed at a majority of investors as opposed to only very sophisticated investors is:**
   a. a hedge fund
   b. a closed-ended fund
   c. an open-ended fund
   d. a private equity fund

By definition - see also the distinction in question 567.

569. **A typical mutual fund that grows in assets as money comes into the fund from investors, and that gets smaller if assets leave the fund can also specifically be referred to as:**
   a. an open-ended mutual fund
   b. a closed-ended mutual fund
   c. a short-selling fund
   d. a bond fund

   By definition - see also the distinction in question 567.

570. **A less common mutual fund that raises money for a specific amount of time, often to invest in less liquid assets is known as:**
   a. an open-ended mutual fund
   b. a closed-ended mutual fund
   c. a short-selling fund
   d. a bond fund

   By definition - see also the distinction in question 567.

571. **The value of the investments in a mutual fund is known as the:**
   a. Management Fee
   b. Front-Load
   c. Performance Fee
   d. Net Asset Value or NAV

572. **Differences between a closed-ended and an open-ended fund include:**
   I. open-ended mutual funds can always take in money - closed-ended ones do not
   II. open-ended mutual funds typically contain liquid investments like US stocks and bonds, closed-ended funds might be justified for much less liquid investments
   III. a closed-ended fund typically takes in money for a limited time; an open-ended fund is usually continuously open for the life of the fund
   IV. an investor in an open-ended fund should be able to redeem from the fund at or very close to the NAV - this might not be the case with a closed-ended fund
   V. open-ended funds go up, closed-end funds always go down

   a. I only
   b. I and II only
   c. I, II and III only
   d. I, II, III and IV only
   e. I, II, III, IV and V

   I-IV are some of the main characteristics of open- and closed-ended mutual funds.

573. **True: Most mutual funds are open-ended.**

574. **An open-ended mutual fund should be able to take in assets continuously, and conversely return assets to investors if they want to get out of the fund. This is typically possible because the fund invests in:**
   a. liquid investments
   b. illiquid investments
   c. real estate
   d. art

   Open-ended mutual funds exist that invest in a variety of typically liquid investments.

575. <u>The manager/creator of a closed-ended mutual fund would have a valid reason to consider this structure when:</u>
   a. it makes sense to restrict inflows and outflows to the fund because the investments are less liquid
   b. there is a desire to restrict outflows from the fund even though the investments are very liquid
   c. there is a desire to allow assets to come in and out of the fund continuously
   d. performance is likely to be very bad

   Limiting outflows particularly if the investments are liquid should not be perceived well by investors.

576. <u>True: Because it is more difficult to take money out of, or to put money in to, a closed-ended mutual fund, closed-ended mutual funds are sometimes bought and sold at prices that are very different from the fund's NAV - in the case of open-ended funds this is not the case - transactions always take place at or near NAV.</u>

   With an open-ended fund, new units are constantly being created as money flows in to the fund - units are also bought back and potentially eliminated by the fund manufacturer as money flows out of the fund. With a closed-ended fund, after issue, transactions take place between different investors, and the prices that transactions take place at can be quite different from what the NAV is, especially if it is not possible to convert the fund units into the underlying investments easily.

QUESTIONS 577 - 582 ARE LINKED.

In a given year, the following performances were observed (all of the numbers are net/after fees):

S&P 500: +20.07%
FTSE 100: +10.78%
Nikkei: -5.73%

Actively managed US mutual fund with benchmark S&P 500: +18%
Actively managed UK mutual fund with benchmark FTSE 100: +9%
Actively managed Japanese mutual fund with benchmark Nikkei: -4%

The total annual fees on index funds in the three regions are: 0.3%/year

577. <u>The investor that would have had the best absolute performance over that year would have been the investor that had been invested in the:</u>
   a. actively managed US mutual fund
   b. actively managed UK mutual fund
   c. actively managed Japanese mutual fund
   d. passively managed US index fund

   The performance would have been 20.07%-0.3%=19.77%.

578. <u>The investor that would have had the worst performance in that year would have been invested solely in the:</u>
   a. actively managed US mutual fund
   b. actively managed UK mutual fund
   c. passively managed Japanese mutual fund
   d. passively managed US index fund

   The performance would have been -5.73%-.3%=-6.03%.

579. <u>Which of the following statements is true:</u>
   a. the US mutual fund manager beat the benchmark

b. the UK mutual fund manager beat the benchmark after fees
c. the Japanese mutual fund manager beat the benchmark after fees
d. none of the mutual fund managers beat their benchmarks

The Japanese manager outperformed the benchmark with a performance of -4% which is 1.73% better than the relevant index which was down 5.73%.

580. Which of the following managers has shown some skill or luck in beating their benchmark this year:
a. the US mutual fund manager
b. the UK mutual fund manager
c. the Japanese mutual fund manager
d. all of the managers

581. If an investor were to invest today (just after the above noted performance), he or she should:
a. buy the actively managed US fund - it is the best performer
b. buy the Japanese mutual fund - it is cheap
c. buy the UK mutual fund - it seems like a steady performer
d. consider a diversified portfolio of funds using dollar cost averaging knowing that past performance is not a good indicator of future performance

582. When looking at a table of actively managed mutual funds for the year in question, which of the following would definitely be the wrong conclusion(s), or based on insufficient information:
I. the US mutual fund looks good
II. the UK mutual fund looks good
III. the Japanese mutual fund looks terrible
IV. the Japanese market looks unattractive
V. the US market looks expensive

a. I only
b. I and II only
c. I, II and III only
d. I, II, III and IV only
e. I, II, III, IV and V

Both the US and UK mutual fund managers underperformed their benchmarks (I and II). The Japanese mutual fund outperformed its benchmark. We can not make any conclusions about the Japanese or US markets based on the information given (past performance does not tell us anything about future performance).

583. Which of the following statements is true:
I. what the fund invests in is a very large determinant of the fund's performance
II. comparing mutual funds that invest in different regions or that have different indices does not provide a lot of information regarding manager skill
III. the most recent year of performance for a mutual fund is not enough information to conclude whether this is a good or bad fund
IV. historical performance is not an indicator of future performance
V. in order to assess the quality of a mutual fund company, one should look at more than one year of data as well as the investment management firm

a. I only
b. I and II only
c. I, II and III only
d. I, II, III and IV only
e. I, II, III, IV and V

These are all very important considerations when looking at mutual funds.

584. **True: The guidelines of a fund, and the performance of the benchmark, are very important factors in determining the overall performance of the fund.**

What the fund invests in (largely defined by the benchmark) is typically the largest driver of performance - that is why it is not possible or useful to compare funds with different benchmarks.

585. **False: Switching between mutual funds after periods of poor performance to invest in funds that have recently done well will always lead to better overall results.**

One can not draw conclusions from past performance. Human nature can cause us to give up on an investment that has been going down, and to switch investments after a period of poor performance - potentially selling at the bottom, only to buy something else that has been performing better - potentially at a top. Keeping poor-performing investments will also not necessarily lead to better results - in general, timing entry and exit points is very difficult.

586. **True: Comparing the performance over the last year of different mutual funds that invest in different markets does not provide useful information.**

Because performance will be more driven by the nature of the assets that they invest in.

587. **True: A mutual fund or index fund should be bought from a reputable asset management/fund company.**

Yes, and we should make sure that we understand what we are buying and what the fees are. We should also look at some of the other techniques like tax savings, dollar cost averaging etc. discussed in detail later.

588. **Before purchasing a mutual fund it is worth enquiring about:**

I. the size and quality of the fund management firm
II. all of the fees associated with the fund
III. the performance of the fund(s)
IV. the amount of assets in the fund
V. the strategy of the fund and the benchmark for the fund

a. I only
b. I and II only
c. I, II and III only
d. I, II, III and IV only
e. I, II, III, IV and V

All of these things are relevant to building a view on the fund.

589. **Two reasons that the amount of assets in a fund should be above a certain minimum is that:**

I. we can be sure that others have done their homework and just invest alongside them
II. mutual fund expense ratios tend to go down as assets increase
III. we do not want to represent a large percentage of a fund
IV. larger funds always outperform
V. larger funds do not charge management fees

a. I and II
b. I and III
c. II and III
d. II and IV
e. I. II and V

I. we should still look at the fund ourselves and draw our own conclusions
II. some costs are spread across more assets, so on a percentage basis they should decrease
III. this might raise some flags as to whether we have missed something (perhaps the company is just starting out), but it could also make selling our investment more difficult depending on what the fund invests in
IV. there is no evidence to support this
V. that is not true

590. True: Index funds often represent a great option for mutual fund investors.

Because in developed markets most actively managed funds underperform index funds over time after fees.

TOTAL: 77 ANSWERS

HEDGE FUNDS

591. True: Hedge funds share with mutual funds the characteristic that an investment manager invests a pool of money, typically on behalf of a number of investors in the fund.

This is a characteristic common to funds in general - it could theoretically be just one investor, but one of the reasons for setting up a fund structure is to raise capital from many investors.

592. Which of the following statements is typically true:

I. hedge funds are often less regulated than mutual funds
II. one of the keys to evaluating hedge funds is to assess the investment manager
III. hedge funds can employ more leverage than mutual funds
IV. hedge funds are typically less restricted in what they can buy or sell than mutual funds
V. a hedge fund can be invested in with very small sums of money by all investors

a. I only
b. I and II only
c. I, II and III only
d. I, II, III and IV only
e. I, II, III, IV and V

There are usually investment minimums, and investors often have to qualify by having a certain net worth and/or income to invest directly in a hedge fund. I-IV are some of the main characteristics of hedge funds.

593. Which of the following statements is false:

a. hedge funds traditionally targeted sophisticated investors and/or high net worth individuals
b. mutual funds are distributed widely - most banks will offer them
c. mutual funds have no risk
d. different mutual funds invest in different markets - there is a very wide range of them

Mutual funds do have risks - risks that are in part very related to what the fund invests in.

594. Which of the following statements apply to hedge funds:

I. hedge funds are more flexible in what they invest in and often do not have a benchmark
II. instead of aiming to beat a benchmark, hedge funds often focus on absolute returns
III. hedge funds often employ strategies that hedge risks
IV. many hedge funds are theoretically in a position to make money whatever the market is doing
V. hedge funds often employ leverage to increase their returns

a. I only
b. I and II only
c. I, II and III only
d. I, II, III and IV only
e. I, II, III, IV and V

These are common traits of hedge funds.

595. Differences between mutual funds and hedge funds include:

I. mutual funds have a more clearly defined benchmark
II. hedge funds are less regulated
III. hedge funds often employ leverage
IV. mutual funds typically do not short-sell securities
V. hedge funds are often reserved for more sophisticated and/or high net worth investors

a. I only
b. I and II only
c. I, II and III only
d. I, II, III and IV only
e. I, II, III, IV and V

These are some of the main differences between hedge funds and mutual funds.

596. **Which of the following statement(s) with respect to hedge funds and mutual funds is/are true:**
I. hedge funds tend not to have a benchmark against which they are measured
II. hedge funds are usually reserved for sophisticated or high net worth investors
III. hedge funds are often less regulated, so assessing the fund management institution is crucial
IV. mutual funds track the performance of an index more closely and the performance of the benchmark or index can be a very important driver of overall absolute performance
V. hedge funds never go down

a. I only
b. I and II only
c. I, II and III only
d. I, II, III and IV only
e. I, II, III, IV and V

I-IV are some of the key features of hedge funds. Hedge funds can go down and some have gone down very significantly in some years.

597. **True: The risk of a particular hedge fund can be more difficult to assess than the risk of investing in a particular mutual fund.**

The risk of investing in a hedge fund has a lot to do with the investment manager and what the investment manager does. Because even actively managed funds do not deviate that much from their benchmark typically, and because the investment manager is typically more regulated, the risk is more linked to what the fund invests in. So, for example, a good hedge fund might not lose money when the market crashes, but a bad hedge fund could lose a lot of money even though the market does well. The risk of fraud can also be much larger with a hedge fund for example.

598. **When an investor claims to be able to 'generate alpha', this refers to an ability to:**
a. pick the right markets to be in
b. pick stocks that will outperform the broader market
c. never lose money
d. get out of the market at the right time

That is the definition of generating alpha.

599. **True: The 'beta' of a stock compares the historical volatility of that stock to that of the index. A beta greater than one means that the stock is more volatile than the index.**

600. **Selling a stock without actually owning it is referred to as:**
a. long-selling
b. short-selling
c. same-selling
d. selling at a loss

Short-selling involves borrowing a stock from another entity that owns it, usually via an intermediary, and then selling it in the market. After the stock is bought back (hopefully at a lower price), it is returned to the owner.

601. <u>**Short-selling is often associated with hedge funds. If a hedge fund sold a stock short, the hedge fund would:**</u>
   a. benefit from a rise in the share price
   b. would not benefit whether the share fell or rose
   c. benefit from a fall in the share price
   d. lend the stock that it owned

   For example, a hedge fund might borrow a stock and sell it in the market at $10. If the hedge fund buys it back at $8, and if the costs for the borrow and all transaction fees are $.50, then the profit would be the $10 received when the stock is sold minus the $8 paid to buy the stock back minus the fees of $0.50, giving a profit of $1.50.

602. <u>**True: Selling securities short requires a party that holds the stock to be prepared to lend it to the short-seller.**</u>

   In order for the short-seller to sell the stock, it has to be borrowed from a party (often via an intermediary like an investment bank) that lends it.

603. <u>**Short-selling allows hedge funds to:**</u>
   a. make money from investments that rise in value
   b. make money from securities that fall in value
   c. sell investments that they own
   d. guarantee strong performance to investors

   As per the example in question 601.

604. <u>**Mutual funds might be prepared to lend their stocks out because they:**</u>
   a. want the stocks to go down
   b. want to be nice to short-sellers
   c. get paid for lending them
   d. don't want to hold them

   They might either want to hold a stock because it is part of the benchmark, or because they have the view that it will go up - by lending the stock they make additional money while owning the stock (and if the stock rises in value, they will make this money too).

605. <u>**A mutual fund has made its portfolio of stocks available to an investment bank that will then use some of their stocks for lending to short-sellers. One of these stocks was lent to hedge fund that then sold the stock short. Which of the following could happen after that:**</u>
   I. the stock could go down
   II. the stock could go up
   III. the mutual fund is compensated for lending it
   IV. the hedge fund pays a borrowing cost
   V. the hedge fund decides to buy back the stock and it is ultimately returned to the mutual fund

   a. I only
   b. I and II only
   c. I, II and III only
   d. I, II, III and IV only
   e. I, II, III, IV and V

   All of these could happen and all of them are very common elements of a short-selling transaction.

606. <u>**Short-selling allows a hedge fund to benefit from:**</u>
   a. a rise in the share price
   b. an unchanged share price

c. a fall in the share price
d. shares just existing

607. <u>**In order for a hedge fund to be able to short-sell a stock, the following has to be true:**</u>
a. someone has to be willing to lend the stock
b. the stock has to be that of a US company
c. the stock must be of an oil company
d. the stock price has to be high

The other three are not true. Selling a stock without having the borrow arranged is known as a naked short-sale and is illegal in many countries.

608. <u>**A fund holds a very liquid stock that they believe will rise in value. If they make the stock available for short-selling they could be considered:**</u>
a. foolish, because it is only going down and we can be sure about that
b. smart, because they are getting paid for lending it
c. foolish, because selling-short and lending stocks is always illegal
d. smart, because the lender will benefit from a fall in the share price

This is in addition of course to any appreciation if they are right with respect to the share price rising. If the share price falls then at least they got paid for lending it.

609. <u>**A certain hedge fund might:**</u>
I. buy a stock
II. short-sell a stock
III. buy a bond
IV. short-sell a bond
V. use leverage

a. I only
b. I and II only
c. I, II and III only
d. I, II, III and IV only
e. I, II, III, IV and V

These are all things that hedge funds do.

610. <u>**A hedge fund that believed a certain stock would do very well, certainly versus the S&P 500 index, but that was worried about the broader market, should:**</u>
a. buy the S& P 500 index
b. sell the stock
c. buy the stock
d. buy the stock and sell (sell-short) the S&P 500 index

They would buy the stock to benefit from a potential rise in the share price, and sell-short the S&P 500 index in order to benefit from/or not be hurt by, a fall in the S&P 500.

611. <u>**Which of the following, in relation to short-selling, would be of greatest concern to stock market regulators if it were to happen:**</u>
a. stocks declining in price gradually in light of deteriorating operating conditions
b. a number of large hedge funds short-selling a single company's stock very aggressively at the same time to the point that it begins to impact the company's operations
c. mutual fund companies making money through stock lending
d. stocks declining on poor earnings

If a number of large hedge funds sold a single company's stock very aggressively at the same time, the share price could end up artificially depressed . This can make the firm more vulnerable to a takeover - it can reduce the ease with which the firm can borrow - it can impact employee compensation - and it can fuel rumors regarding the company's viability - not to mention that it can be very alarming for other investors and management. That is not to say that share prices should not go down aggressively - regulators get concerned when it is happening in the absence of news, or because of a co-ordinated effort to make the shares go down. These are reasons why naked short-selling (selling a stock where a borrow has not been arranged) is illegal and why the uptick rule (discussed in question 612) is sometimes applied..

612. The 'uptick rule' when in effect relates to:
   a. selling a stock that is held by a mutual fund (a long position)
   b. buying stocks
   c. that a short-sale can only take place at a stock price higher than the last trade, or if the last trade was higher than the preceding trade
   d. investment banking rules regarding mergers and acquisitions

613. Which of the following is not a hedge fund strategy or type:
   a. opportunistic hedge funds
   b. event-driven funds
   c. relative value funds
   d. mutual funds

   a. this strategy includes long/short equity and macro funds. Long/short equity funds buy (or 'go long') stocks that they think will go up, and sell short (or 'go short') stocks that they think will go down. Macro funds aim to generate returns by capitalizing on macroeconomic factors such as interest rate differences, currency anomalies or inflation trends
   b. these funds seek to benefit from valuation differences between different securities surrounding an event like a merger, a spin-off or a restructuring. Merger arbitrage funds for example seek to benefit from the price difference between the stock of the company that is being bought, and that of the acquirer, when there is uncertainty whether the deal will go through. Distressed security funds buy the securities (often the bonds) of companies that are near bankruptcy on the belief that the company will be able to avoid some of the financial difficulties that the market expects
   c. these funds try to profit from differences in valuation between different securities that provide a similar economic position. For example, a convertible bond can be replicated with a combination of bonds and stocks. A hedge fund could buy a convertible bond and sell short the appropriate combination of stocks and bonds to exploit a valuation difference between the two economically similar positions
   d. mutual funds are not a type of hedge fund, and there are important differences between hedge funds and mutual funds

614. A fund that invests in other hedge funds is knows as a:
   a. mutual fund
   b. an index fund
   c. a fund of fund of funds
   d. a fund of funds

   Or alternatively, as a fund of hedge funds.

615. A fund of hedge funds can be best described as a fund that:
   a. invests in a number of hedge funds to diversify the risk
   b. buys stocks and bonds
   c. invests in money
   d. buys corporate and government bonds

616. **Funds of hedge funds are often tailored to private investors and typically have lower minimum investment requirements than single hedge funds. Which other advantages might a fund of funds offer:**

I. diversification
II. a professional selecting the individual hedge fund managers
III. outsourcing of the due diligence
IV. easier to access than certain hedge funds
V. lower fees

a. I only
b. I and II only
c. I, II and III only
d. I, II, III and IV only
e. I, II, III, IV and V

The first four are definitely potential advantages of funds of hedge funds. Because the fund of hedge funds also charges fees, there is an additional layer of fees on top, leading to a double layer of fees (higher fees).

TOTAL: 26 ANSWERS

Real Estate

617. **Which of the following can be considered real estate:**
   I. undeveloped land
   II. single family homes
   III. office buildings
   IV. condominiums
   V. warehouses

   a. I only
   b. I and II only
   c. I, II and III only
   d. I, II, III and IV only
   e. I, II, III, IV and V

   These are all categories of real estate.

618. **True: One way of splitting the overall real estate market is into residential real estate and commercial real estate.**

   Residential real estate includes single family homes and apartments. Commercial real estate includes office buildings, warehouses etc.

619. **Which of the following statements with respect to real estate investing is true:**
   a. real estate never goes down
   b. real estate markets are less liquid than the securities markets of developed countries
   c. real estate cycles are very short
   d. buying real estate property outright is known as indirect real estate investing

   a. real estate can go down
   b. a securities market like the stock market in a developed country like the US is much more liquid
   c. real estate cycles tend to be quite long
   d. buying real estate directly and without a fund structure is known as direct real estate investing

620. **Which factor(s) is/are likely to have an impact on the price of real estate in a particular area:**
   I. the economy
   II. interest rates
   III. demographic/employment factors
   IV. transportation related factors
   V. supply

   a. I only
   b. I and II only
   c. I, II and III only
   d. I, II, III and IV only
   e. I, II, III, IV and V

   All of these factors impact real estate prices because they impact supply, demand, or the cost of borrowing and therefore the affordability of real estate.

621. **True: A mortgage is in effect a form of leverage, in that the buyer's money is augmented with borrowed money to make an investment that is larger than the equity capital contributed.**

   The equity is the ownership that we would have in our homes. The mortgage is debt.

622. **True: Mortgage interest rates are lower than many other interest rates especially credit card rates, because the money is being borrowed against an asset (a house) that can be sold, that can be repossessed, and that typically does not depreciate as quickly as consumable items.**

Although real estate clearly can depreciate, when compared with clothing for example which is almost worthless in many cases a few weeks after being bought, it holds its value much better - importantly real estate can also be found and repossessed more easily, further reducing the risk for the lender.

623. **True: There is often a difference in the way that we are taxed on our primary residence versus how we might be taxed on an investment property.**

Governments very frequently want to incentivize home ownership, and provide tax incentives to promote home ownership.

624. **Real estate tax incentives for private individuals would most likely focus on:**

I. home ownership
II. redevelopment or improvement of run-down areas
III. environmentally friendly initiatives
IV. speculation on luxury apartments
V. rental of commercial property

a. I only
b. I and II only
c. I, II and III only
d. I, II, III and IV only
e. I, II, III, IV and V

As with many other tax incentives, the government tries to incentivize behaviors that they feel will be good for society as a whole.

625. **The value of a property minus the debts including mortgages on the property is known as:**

a. the equity in the property
b. the debt of the property
c. the value of the property
d. the commission

The equity that we have in the property is the value of the property less all debts on the property. We can also think of the house as the only asset on a balance sheet - the equity equals the value of the asset minus the debt, and it is the equity or ownership that we have in the property.

626. **Sometimes the value of a property falls below the amount of the mortgage or the amount borrowed to purchase it. This is referred to as:**

a. positive equity
b. positive reinforcement
c. negative reinforcement
d. negative equity

In this case, when we subtract the debt/mortgage from the value of the property, we end up with a negative number.

627. **Which of the following statements is false:**

a. two main sources of return for a real estate investor are rental income and capital appreciation
b. real estate investing requires analysis, as does all investing
c. real estate never goes down
d. governments often incentivize home ownership - they typically do not incentivize speculation

628. <u>Professional real estate investors often do more than buy properties and wait. Professional real estate investing can involve which of the following:</u>
   I. renovating run-down properties
   II. splitting properties into multiple units
   III. making use of government programs
   IV. financial engineering
   V. understanding local regulations and planning permissions

   a. I only
   b. I and II only
   c. I, II and III only
   d. I, II, III and IV only
   e. I, II, III, IV and V

   These are strategies that professional real estate investors use to try to add value to real estate. They are also strategies that can help explain why some professional investors might make money even if the real estate market is not rising. Having said that, because real estate investing almost always involves leverage, sometimes significant amounts of leverage, when the market goes down significantly or things do not turn out as planned, the returns can be very poor (although the losses might be slightly mitigated by the value that was added by the investor). The fact that professional real estate investors often use these strategies also means that the returns that they achieve are not representative of what an individual investor might achieve by just buying and holding on to a property.

629. <u>Buying real estate though a fund is also known as:</u>
   a. direct real estate investment
   b. indirect real estate investment
   c. real real estate investment
   d. upside down real estate investment

   In contrast to buying the property directly which is known as direct real estate investment.

630. <u>False: In the United States, the UK, and Canada, real estate funds tend to invest in residential real estate - in particular single family homes.</u>

   In these three countries, and in developed countries in general, real estate funds invest in commercial real estate much more often than in residential real estate. Commercial real estate properties tend to be much larger, making the large investment required more suited to a fund structure. Furthermore, investors can benefit because costs such as management costs can be spread amongst multiple larger properties, allowing economies of scale to be realized. Also, the purchase of a home for personal use is often tax-incentivized by the government as we said - this makes the returns potentially better for an individual investor buying a house, than for a fund buying a house, so the fund would potentially be at an immediate disadvantage in terms of the return it would ultimately offer an individual investor. In emerging economies, because of a fast growing need for housing, a higher percentage of funds might look at residential real estate although this would depend on the country - the government might event incentivize investment in this area if there is a drastic need for housing.

631. <u>Real estate cycles are typically:</u>
   a. very short
   b. long
   c. not something that has been observed over history
   d. too short to notice

Real estate cycles can be very long because economic cycles that impact real estate are also typically long-term - interest rates can go one way for a long time and demographics and employment trends are also usually very long-term trends. It can also take a long time for buyers and/or sellers to adjust their expectations.

632. **Real estate should be thought of as:**
   a. a long-term investment
   b. a short-term investment
   c. a permanently good investment
   d. a permanently bad investment

   For some of the reasons noted in question 631.

633. **Advantages of a professionally managed real estate fund can include:**
   I. each investor only needs to contribute a fraction of the overall sum or price of any property
   II. a professional makes the investment decisions
   III. some of the costs can be allocated across multiple projects
   IV. a property fund can in some cases be more easily sold than a property
   V. these funds can provide access real estate that would otherwise be difficult for an individual investor to purchase

   a. I only
   b. I and II only
   c. I, II and III only
   d. I, II, III and IV only
   e. I, II, III, IV and V

   This is effectively a list of some of the key features and advantages of real estate funds.

634. **Which of the following would be an example of an indirect real estate investment:**
   a. buying a principal residence
   b. buying a real estate investment property
   c. investing in a stock mutual fund
   d. investing in a REIT

   REIT: A Real Estate Investment Trust - a trust that manages a pool of capital of many investors (like a fund) to purchase real estate investments such as income properties or mortgage loans. REITs are listed and trade like stocks.

635. **Governments generally provide incentives to promote:**
   a. real estate speculation
   b. home ownership
   c. flipping of real estate properties
   d. renting real estate

   The government uses taxes to encourage certain behaviors. They often offer tax reductions for homeowners because they want to encourage home ownership and the financial responsibility that comes with this.

636. **Which of the following statements about real estate is true:**
   I. residential real estate refers to housing and apartments that people live in
   II. commercial real estate includes office buildings
   III. real estate always goes up
   IV. real estate speculation is something that the government wants to encourage
   V. real estate cycles are typically very short

a. I only
b. I and II only
c. I, II and III only
d. I, II, III and IV only
e. I, II, III, IV and V

637. **Which of the following costs would be relevant to the analysis of a real estate investment and the potential for making a return:**
I. property taxes
II. interest expense
III. maintenance fees
IV. capital gains taxes
V. taxes on rental income

a. I only
b. I and II only
c. I, II and III only
d. I, II, III and IV only
e. I, II, III, IV and V

All of them can affect the return.

638. **Which of the following statements makes the most sense:**
a. real estate tends to perform well when the economy is weak therefore it is a great diversifier
b. real estate tend to perform poorly when the economy is weak therefore it is a great diversifier
c. real estate tends to perform great when the economy is weak therefore it is a poor diversifier
d. real estate tends to perform poorly when the economy is weak and this makes it an ok diversifier

When the economy is weak, the stock market might go down - how it would perform would depend on many other factors and would be difficult to predict. Because real estate might also go down, it is an ok diversifier - a great diversifier would be one that would definitely go in the opposite direction in the short term.

639. **True: An investment in real estate, unlike an investment in stocks in developed markets, can have significant carrying costs associated with it.**

These costs can include maintenance costs, communal property management fees, property taxes amongst others.

640. **False: Transaction costs associated with buying and selling real estate are lower than those associated with stocks in developed markets.**

They are typically higher.

641. **The rental yield is defined as:**
a. the annual rent on a property divided by the number of months
b. the annual rent on a property divided by the value of the real estate object
c. the price of a property divided by the number of months
d. the price of a property divided by the annual rent

A yield is typically a return divided by a price or market value usually over a year. The rental yield is b. - the rent divided by the value (market value) of the real estate object.

642. **If an investor wanted to know the annual percentage return based on the rent received and less any expenses, the appropriate single measure to look at would be the:**

a. occupancy rate
b. maintenance costs
c. gross rental yield
d. net rental yield

We know that the yield expresses the percentage return based on the amount invested or the market value. The net figure will take into account expenses and taxes etc.

643. The annual rent received divided by the current market value is known as the:
a. net rental yield
b. annual bond yield
c. dividend yield
d. gross rental yield

Gross means before expenses.

TOTAL: 27 ANSWERS

Commodities

644. **True: The word 'commoditization' is very closely linked to commodities - it refers to a loss of differentiation as a product for example becomes more generic.**

By definition.

645. **The best definition for a commodity is:**
   a. something that comes out of the ground
   b. a product for which there is no qualitative differentiation across a market
   c. a product that is based on something living
   d. a stock

   a. it does not have to come out of ground - corn, pork bellies for example do not
   b. this is a very good definition for what a commodity is
   c. it does not have to be based on something living - for example gold or oil are not living
   d. it is not a stock

646. **True: Cars, phones or clothes from different manufacturers typically differ quite a bit from one another. With commodities, many producers produce an effectively identical product.**

This is the case for a certain type of oil, a grade of silver or gold, or even types of agricultural commodities - the producer is largely irrelevant as a certain grade of the commodity is the same irrespective of where it came from.

647. **Which of the following are typically considered commodities:**
   I. gold
   II. wheat
   III. corn
   IV. coffee
   V. oil

   a. I only
   b. I and II only
   c. I, II and III only
   d. I, II, III and IV only
   e. I, II, III, IV and V

   These are all examples of commodities.

648. **Which of the following are typically considered commodities:**
   I. corn
   II. oil stocks
   III. gold stocks
   IV. mining companies
   V. farming companies

   a. I only
   b. I and II only
   c. I, II and III only
   d. I, II, III and IV only
   e. I, II, III, IV and V

As soon as we are talking about investing in stocks or companies, we are no longer talking purely about investing in commodities, but rather about investing in the equity of companies that are involved in the commodities business, which is very different.

649. True: Supply and demand play a very large role in determining commodity prices.

When we provide capital to a company, the capital is used to fund that company's business - what the capital grows to can depend greatly on how that company develops its business, particularly if the capital is provided in the form of equity. When an investor invests in commodities, the investment is in a product that most likely will be used to produce something else, and where nothing much happens with the commodity other than it being used in the production of something else. Supply and demand play a very large role in determining the commodity price.

650. True: Commodity prices tend to rise during periods of strong economic growth.

It can take some time to increase the productive capacity, and in the meantime demand is often stronger with similar levels of supply, meaning that prices often rise.

651. True: When there are concerns about the value of money potentially because monetary policy is very loose and/or investors are looking for safety, investors often look to gold to preserve investment values.

Gold is often thought of as a safe haven, and if the value of money declines, then gold is often looked at as a potential store of value.

652. False: Trading commodities is easy - just buy low and sell high.

Timing any market with many participants is not straightforward.

653. True: Commodities can provide diversification because they often perform well when inflation is high - stocks and bonds often do not perform well in a high-inflation environment.

This has historically been one of the main arguments for adding commodities to an investment portfolio. In a high-inflation environment with potentially rising interest rates, stocks and bonds tend not to perform well (one reason: interest rates up->discount factors up->present values down). With high inflation (prices rising), commodity prices rise almost by definition. As the number of investors that have diversified with commodities has increased, the diversification benefits of this strategy have decreased slightly - when these investors sell investments, they might sell them all at the same time, meaning that they move more together, thereby decreasing the diversification benefit.

654. True: Agricultural commodity prices can be affected by weather which is difficult to predict.

The amount of agriculture produced in a certain area is greatly affected by the weather.

655. True: There is a difference between investing in the equity of companies that are involved in the commodities business, and investing in the commodities themselves.

The equities are invariably affected by equity market factors and company specific factors, in addition to commodity prices.

656. The ownership of commodities among institutional and private investors has become more widespread over the last ten years. What would this mean in terms of the diversification benefits of adding commodities to a traditional portfolio of stocks and bonds:
   a. the diversification benefits would be unchanged
   b. the diversification benefits would increase
   c. the diversification benefits would decrease

d. the diversification benefits would greatly increase

As similar investors took more similar actions, the investments would be more likely to move together.

657. **True: Many investors trade in the commodity markets through funds, exchange traded funds or derivatives such as futures, as opposed to trading the physical commodities themselves.**

Partly because of storage costs, a lot of trading in commodities does not take place in the actual physical market.

658. **True: As many different types of commodities become easier to access for many investors, through ETFs and other derivatives, their diversification benefits would be expected to decrease.**

If the investors are the same, then the likelihood of them selling at the same time (or buying at the same time) increases, and the diversification benefits would be reduced.

659. **Which of the following would typically drive the demand for certain commodities higher:**
I. strong demand for products that use a particular commodity in their manufacture
II. strong economic growth
III. increased use of a commodity in the manufacture of certain products
IV. fear about the value of money
V. less use of the commodity in manufacturing

a. I only
b. I and II only
c. I, II and III only
d. I. II, III and IV only
e. V only

Fear about the value of money typically drives the price of gold and potentially other precious metals commodities higher. Less use of a commodity in manufacturing would be expected to lower the demand for the commodity.

660. **True: Commodity producers might sell their production forward in order to lock in a price in the future - on the other side of this trade, there could be a speculator who is betting on a higher price in the future.**

The producer would lock in a sales price and be protected from a decline in price. The speculator locks in a purchase price.

661. **Which of the following sectors have a close commodities link:**
I. agriculture
II. energy
III. mining
IV. technology
V. telecommunications

a. I only
b. I and II only
c. I, II and III only
d. I. II, III and IV only
e. I. II, III, IV and V

Agriculture, energy and mining are businesses that are very linked to one or more commodities. Although commodities might be used in the technology and telecommunications sectors, these

business are really about the added value that takes place - the concepts, the designs, the manufacture and marketing.

662. Higher oil prices will most likely lead to:

I. higher costs for oil producers
II. higher revenues for oil producers
III. higher costs for companies that use oil
IV. higher revenues for companies that use oil
V. lower revenues for oil producers

a. I only
b. I and II
c. III only
d. II and III
e. V only

663. True: Commodities are a major input cost for many other industries including most manufacturing and transportation. That is why commodity price rises can be a concern.

This means that higher commodity prices can lead to higher inflation across the economy.

664. True: Soft commodities are commodities like coffee, sugar and soybean - they share the characteristic that they are grown and not mined.

This is effectively the definition of soft commodities.

665. True: Hard commodities include metals and coal - they share the characteristic that they are mined and not grown.

This is effectively the definition of hard commodities.

666. Gold has tended to perform well as an investment when:

I. investors were seeking a safe haven
II. there were concerns about the value of money perhaps due to very loose fiscal or monetary policy
III. there are inflation concerns
IV. the cost of extracting gold drops
V. a number of very large gold discoveries have recently been made

a. I only
b. I and II only
c. I, II and III only
d. I. II, III and IV only
e. I. II, III, IV and V

Gold has historically done well when I-III have taken place. If the cost of extracting gold falls, this should not lead to an increase in the price of gold as it would make more gold extraction and mining feasible. More large discoveries would mean more supply - this would also be more likely to lower prices.

TOTAL: 23 ANSWERS

OTHER INVESTMENTS & TERMINOLOGY

667. **If an investment certificate provides a large percentage of the upside of a stock index, and protects capital on the downside, why might this not be a no-brainer:**
   I. it could involve credit risk with the counter-party that is issuing the certificates
   II. the investment might not provide the dividend yield
   III. there might be hidden costs associated with the capital protection
   IV. anything that sounds too good to be true should be looked at very carefully
   V. there is no such thing as a good investment

   a. I only
   b. I and II only
   c. I, II and III only
   d. I, II, III and IV only
   e. I, II, III, IV and V

   Capital-protected notes or certificates are often offered to retail investors and they often come with hidden costs like the ones noted above - that is why they have to be looked at very carefully.

668. **True: Futures allow speculators to take a view on price movements and they allow hedgers to protect themselves from price movements.**

   A futures contract is an obligation to buy or sell something at a certain price and at a certain time in the future, thereby eliminating the risk of a price movement between where it is sold today in the futures market, and the price at which it could be sold at in the future. Futures contracts are like forward contracts - additionally futures contracts are standardized and they trade on an exchange.

669. **Who might be a user of futures contracts to protect from price movements:**
   I. an oil company that sells oil
   II. a car company that buys large quantities of steel
   III. a multinational company that has a lot of earnings in foreign currencies
   IV. a coffee company that sells coffee
   V. a chain of cafés that buys a lot of coffee

   a. I only
   b. I and II only
   c. I, II and III only
   d. I, II, III and IV only
   e. I, II, III, IV and V

   All of them could use futures contracts to lock in prices for the products that they buy or sell.

670. **True: Forward contracts and futures contracts have a very similar function - both allow the contract-holder to buy or sell an asset at a specific price and at a specific time in the future. The main difference between them is that futures contracts are standardized and trade on an exchange.**

671. **One of the main differences between futures and options is that:**
   a. futures are about things in the future, options are about things in the past
   b. futures are bought, options are sold
   c. futures are for speculation, options for hedging
   d. the buyer of a futures contract has an obligation, the buyer of an option has an option

   The owner of an option can choose to exercise the option if that is profitable. In the case of futures, the transaction must take place.

672. <u>The primary function of lotteries is to:</u>
   a. provide a viable saving and investing alternative
   b. allow many people to get wealthy
   c. distribute the government's wealth
   d. raise money for various agencies including governments in many cases

   Lotteries take in more money than they pay out and are often run by the government, or on behalf of the government, to raise money. They are often considered a form of taxation.

673. <u>Casinos are most likely to go bankrupt when:</u>
   a. too many people go to the casino
   b. too many people win at the casino
   c. too few people go and therefore less wealth is transferred to the casino
   d. people realize that this is the best way to build wealth

674. <u>The reason that casinos are often housed in very elegant buildings and in some cases can even provide free drinks is because:</u>
   a. they are like charities - they want to make people happy
   b. they are always running at a loss to provide a service
   c. in aggregate the people that go there lose significant sums of money to the casino
   d. they can afford to because the government supports them - people need to gamble

675. <u>It is not sensible to rely on the lottery to achieve our saving and investing goals because:</u>
   I. the odds are against us
   II. the outcome is too much out of our control
   III. we are likely to end up too rich
   IV. it is too easy
   V. it is sensible to rely on the lottery

   a. I only
   b. I and II only
   c. I, II and III only
   d. I, II, III and IV only
   e. I, II, III, IV and V

676. <u>True: Credit card companies can securitize the loans they have made to individual credit card holders by packaging the loans, describing them and parcelling them into securities that can be sold to other investors who then own credit card loans. This is referred to as securitization.</u>

   The securities are referred to as asset backed securities and are backed by the credit card loans.

677. <u>True: Securitization is best described as pooling and repackaging future cash flows to convert the cash flows into tradable securities.</u>

678. <u>Which of the following are often securitized:</u>
   a. credit card loans
   b. auto loans
   c. mortgages
   d. all of the above

679. <u>A financing company might securitize some of its loans for which of the following reasons:</u>
   I. it removes them from the asset side of the balance sheet
   II. it raises cash for the financing company
   III. it can make it easier to issue more loans
   IV. it transfers the risk of owning the loans to someone else
   V. it makes their loans assets more liquid

a. I only
b. I and II only
c. I, II and III only
d. I, II, III and IV only
e. I, II, III, IV and V

Securitization is very common, largely because of I-V. It has also gotten a lot of press, especially in the context of sub-prime debt securitization, and the financial crisis that started in 2007. Asset-backed securities are not typically bought by individual investors and are not offered by retail banks - they require a lot of sophisticated analysis (analysis that the ratings agencies and many sophisticated investors clearly got wrong clearly during the crisis, hence the losses). They are mentioned here only because they have been spoken about so much, and because it is worth knowing what they are, and what is being spoken about.

680. Many financial firms had large losses related to sub-prime mortgages in 2008. How could securitization have played a role in this situation:
I. the companies making the loans wanted to make as many as possible
II. the companies issuing the loans were not the ones that would get hurt if there were a lot of defaults
III. the loans were restructured and repackaged - this makes analysis even more difficult
IV. the loans were not securitized
V. securitization turned out to be illegal

a. I only
b. I and II only
c. I, II and III only
d. I, II, III and IV only
e. I, II, III, IV and V

I-III are all reasons why the securitization led to large losses.

681. True: Securitization, or the process of creating a security out of something, refers to taking a certain set of future cash flows and creating a tradable instrument out of them that can be sold (and bought).

This is the definition of securitization.

682. True: A collateralized debt obligation (CDO) is a type of asset backed security where different ratings are assigned to the different tranches based on their seniority.

This is what a CDO is. They are split into different risk classes or tranches, and senior tranches are considered the safest securities because they receive cash flows from the underlying assets first.

683. Investments that appear too good to be true:
a. should be bought immediately
b. probably are, and need to be looked at very carefully
c. are never a scam
d. will never go down

That is also partly why it is so important to have some level of financial literacy - to be able to assess any investments to see how they work, what the premise is, and what the fees are etc..

684. A bank that assists companies in making mergers and acquisitions, that trades in stocks and bonds, and that helps users of capital issue stocks and bonds, would be best describes as:
a. a private bank
b. a commercial bank

c. a retail bank
d. an investment bank

This is what investment banks do - unlike retail banks that have retail branches and will deal with private individuals.

685. **Which of the following would most likely have a large network of branches to deal with some wealthy clients, but also many other types of customers:**
a. an investment bank
b. a retail bank
c. private bank
d. a central bank

Retail banks deal with private individuals, also known as retail customers. This is in contrast to corporate customers (companies).

686. **Underwriting of securities refers to:**
a. a process of creating insurance that a stock will never go down
b. making sure that investors have a diversified portfolio
c. a way of raising capital for companies and governments with investors
d. a way of taking the risk out of a portfolio

Underwriting of securities refers to the process of raising capital for companies through the issue of stocks or bonds, or for governments through the issue of bonds.

TOTAL: 20 ANSWERS

THE ECONOMY

687. **The system that relates to the production, distribution and consumption of goods and services in a nation is broadly referred to as the:**
   a. bond market
   b. stock market
   c. economy
   d. trade deficit

   This is the definition of what the economy is.

688. **The size of an economy can be measured through the:**
   a. Gross Domestic Product (GDP)
   b. Great Domestic Product (GDP)
   c. Gross Dominion Product (GDP)
   d. Gross Domestic Produce (GDP)

   The Gross Domestic Product is a measure of a country's overall official economic output. It is the value of all the goods produced, and all of the value that is added by production, in a particular country. The countries with the largest GDPs are the countries with the largest economies, and these are currently the United States, China, Japan and India. Yearly changes in GDP are very interesting to follow because they indicate how quickly the economy of a country is growing, whether growth is slowing, or even whether an economy is shrinking.

689. **True: Labour and capital are two main inputs into the economy.**

   Labour and capital are two main inputs that affect the GDP of a country. Typically as GDP rises, the rate of unemployment falls as companies employ more people to produce more goods. When the unemployment rate falls, consumers typically feel better and consumer confidence often rises. With respect to capital, when GDP is growing, companies increase production, and the level at which they use their plant and equipment increases – this level of use is known as the capacity utilization. The level of industrial economic activity is also quantified through industrial production numbers that measure the total output generated from mines and factories.

690. **True: There are many surveys that are carried out to assess the state of the economy.**

   These surveys can assist investors, governments and companies understand the state of the economy and potentially plan for the future.

691. **Which of the following groups might care about the state of the economy:**
   I. news agencies
   II. investors
   III. companies
   IV. governments
   V. central banks

   a. I only
   b. I and II only
   c. I, II and III only
   d. I, II, III and IV only
   e. I, II, III, IV and V

   All of them would have an interest in knowing what the state of the economy is.

692. **Which of the following statements about economic data is/are true:**

I. economic data typically captures data about the past
II. economic forecasts can be wrong
III. economic surveys depend on the views of those reporting to the surveys
IV. GDP growth can slow down
V. one can never be certain about the future

a. I only
b. I and II only
c. I, II and III only
d. I, II, III and IV only
e. I, II, III, IV and V

These are some of the issues associated with economic data and why for example central banks or governments might not always get it right when they take certain actions based on economic data.

693. **True: There are different ways of looking at certain parts of the economy - for example, one could look at the manufacturing sector, or exports, or employment, specifically - with each area being a part of the overall picture and helping form a view on the overall picture.**

694. **Which of the following statistics could be important to assessing the state of the economy:**
I. GDP growth
II. unemployment
III. industrial production
IV. retail sales
V. manufacturing surveys

a. I only
b. I and II only
c. I, II and III only
d. I, II, III and IV only
e. I, II, III, IV and V

They all provide insight into different parts of the economy.

695. **The increase in prices of goods and services in an economy is known as:**
a. inflation
b. deflation
c. recession
d. depression

This is the definition of inflation, and because it means that our money will buy less as prices rise, most central banks have as one of their main goals, if not the main goal, targeting inflation.

696. **Which of the following would typically not lead to an increase in the prices of goods and services:**
a. stronger growth
b. a disruption in the supply of goods and services
c. weaker growth
d. a lack of goods and services

Weaker growth typically means less demand - less demand typically means lower prices. The other three would likely lead to an increase in prices - a. because of higher demand, b. and d. because of lower supply.

697. **Inflation is an area that governments and central banks care about because it:**
a. causes growth
b. raises prices and therefore reduces purchasing power

c. reduces the cost of goods and services
d. can lead to deflation

It reduces purchasing power because each dollar or unit of money will buy less. Governments care about inflation, especially very high inflation, because it devalues money and cash savings which has a very negative impact (especially for retirees for example) - furthermore, it can lead the general public to save less as money becomes worth less, or even to hoard as prices of goods rise, leading potentially to shortages. Price instability which is linked to inflation also makes planning by consumers and companies more difficult leading to inefficiencies.

698. Inflationary pressure is most likely to occur when:
a. the economy is slowing
b. the economy is in recession
c. banks are tightening their lending practices
d. growth is high and/or when banks are loosening their lending practices

When growth is high, demand is typically strong and inflationary pressure can be a direct consequence. When banks are loosening their lending practices, individuals and companies have greater access to capital and therefore more money can be used for purchases - demand for goods and services is likely to increase, putting upward pressure on prices.

699. When setting interest rate policy, the central bank of any particular country faces numerous challenges. These challenges include:
a. how other countries/the global economic environment will affect that country can be difficult to predict
b. there is always uncertainty when it comes to the future
c. economic data is generally historical and therefore there can be delays in perceiving changes in the state of the economy
d. all of the above

Ideally of course central banks would like to keep the economy in the perfect sweet spot of moderate inflation and good growth. That is what would make consumers, businesses and the government the happiest, and it would avoid economic cycles entirely. Unfortunately this is difficult to do. First of all, the central bank will use its tools based on the data and analysis that it has available, and sometimes different pieces of economic data can be inconsistent. Furthermore, no one knows exactly what will happen in the future, which is where the changes that the central bank makes will have impact. Economic data about the past and present is easy to get, but forecasts for the future always come with uncertainty. Furthermore, when things are going well, in many industries, companies often overbuild capacity to go for available market share – taking the future impact of this into account can be difficult. International trade also connects the economies of many regions to such an extent, that any individual central bank can not account for the impact of what is going to happen in another region exactly. The Bank of England or the Federal Reserve (The Fed) might be right on target, but if there is a massive crisis in a certain region or very strong growth in another region, their efforts might not yield the desired results.

700. True: The real return is defined as the nominal return (which is the return by name and that we see on paper) minus inflation.

The real return measures the return after adjusting for inflation - for example, if the return is 3% and if inflation is also 3% then the nominal growth of the money at 3% is not giving us more spending power since the price of goods and services is also rising by 3% per year (the real return in this case is 0% (3% - 3%).

701. True: Central banks in the US, the UK and Europe play a major role in ensuring that inflation does not become too much of a concern.

For most central banks, keeping inflation in check is one of the main objectives, if not the main objective.

702. **Central banks control the availability of money and the cost of money in an economy. This is known as:**
   a. fiscal policy
   b. monetary policy
   c. trade policy
   d. defense policy

   This is the definition of monetary policy.

703. **The main tool for controlling inflation and stimulating the economy under normal circumstances is:**
   a. fiscal policy
   b. foreign policy
   c. defense policy
   d. monetary policy

   Interest rates and other central bank monetary policy initiatives can be changed more quickly than fiscal policy (consisting of tax policy and government spending), furthermore changes to monetary policy are less politically sensitive. For example, in the US, the budget is prepared once per year, whereas interest rate decisions are taken on a monthly basis; raising taxes (fiscal policy) is also often very unpopular.

704. **As the economy slows and inflation drops, which of the following would be likely to happen:**
   I. company revenues would be likely to go down
   II. earnings would likely go down for many companies
   III. unemployment might rise
   IV. interest rates might be cut
   V. interest rates might be raised

   a. I only
   b. I and II only
   c. I, II and III only
   d. I, II, III and IV only
   e. I, II, III, IV and V

   As the economy slows and inflation drops - a need to raise interest rates would rarely exist. Raising interest rates would slow the economy further and reduce inflation further typically (unless that particular central bank focused on exchange rates or other non-growth oriented metrics).

705. **Excessive inflation is considered undesirable because it:**
   I. reduces purchasing power
   II. means that our existing savings will buy less
   III. can lead to price instability
   IV. reduces prices
   V. leads to interest rate cuts

   a. I only
   b. I and II only
   c. I, II and III only
   d. I, II, III and IV only
   e. I, II, III, IV and V

   Excessive inflation raises prices and often leads to interest rate hikes (increases).

706. Inflation can also be thought of as:
a. a price level
b. an old price level
c. a new price level
d. a change in price levels

By definition a change in price levels that is an increase is known as inflation - a change in price levels that represents a decrease is known as deflation.

707. The return that an investor achieves after adjusting for the effect of inflation is known as the:
a. nominal return
b. real return
c. inflation rate
d. interest rate

That is the definition of the real return.

708. Higher interest rates:
a. make borrowing cheaper and stimulate the economy
b. make borrowing more expensive and slow the economy
c. mean higher taxes
d. are aimed at raising inflation

709. If the Central Bank lowered interest rates by a 'quarter point', interest rates would be reduced by:
a. 25%
b. 2.5%
c. .25%
d. .025%

A quarter point refers to a quarter of a per cent or 0.25%.

710. If the central bank lowered interest rates by 50 basis points, interest rates would be reduced by:
a. 50%
b. 5.0%
c. .50%
d. .050%

A basis point is defined as one one-hundredth of a per cent. 100 basis points is 1%; 50 basis points is .50%; 25 basis points is .25%.

711. A basis point can be best described as:
a. a percentage point
b. ten percentage points
c. a tenth of a percentage point
d. one hundredth of a percentage point

712. Central banks, when they change interest rates, directly change:
a. very short-term interest rates that will first affect banks and credit institutions
b. the dividend companies pay
c. long-term government bond yields
d. the return for long-term bond investors

713. Which of the following is not a central bank:
a. the European Central Bank
b. the Fed (The Federal Reserve System) in the US
c. the Bank of Japan

d. a bank that provides saving and deposit accounts

714. <u>A central bank can be described as:</u>
   a. banks that provide investment banking services
   b. banks that individual consumers would use
   c. a bank for other banks and for the government
   d. a bank that provides commercial mortgages

   By definition.

715. **<u>True: When the central bank changes interest rates, it affects short-term interest rates for banks and credit institutions first, who then pass the changes in their situation on to their customers.</u>**

   If the central bank comes to the conclusion that growth is too fast and/or that inflation is a risk, it adjusts monetary policy either by changing interest rates, or by changing the amount of money in circulation in the economy. Changing interest rates is the most significant mechanism by which central banks influence the growth of the economy and inflation. The central bank typically sets the interest rate that other banks or major private sector institutions have to pay when they borrow money overnight from the central bank. This rate is a benchmark for other interest rates, and ultimately trickles through the economy and causes banks to adjust the rates at which consumers and businesses can borrow. Anyone that relies on debt as a source of funding realizes that the cost of financing has gone up when the central bank raises interest rates. Faced with a higher interest cost, companies and consumers typically adjust their spending downwards and the overall economy begins to slow, easing the pressure on inflation. Central banks can also control the amount of cash in the economy by buying and selling financial assets - these operations are referred to as open market operations. If the central bank for example buys government bonds in the market (using cash), then the amount of money is increased in the economy and this represents a loosening of monetary policy and would stimulate the economy and potentially increase growth and inflation. They can also sell financial assets to slow the economy.

716. <u>Interest rates for longer periods such as a year or even multiple years are to a large extent set by:</u>
   a. central banks
   b. investment banks
   c. commercial banks
   d. fixed income markets

   These longer-term rates are set by buyers and sellers of bonds and other fixed income instruments in the market - they are not set by banks in the first instance (although banks often then use these rates in setting their interest rates for example for mortgages and other products). Investors value and set the price of fixed income instruments like bonds and thereby define the yield or required return/interest rate for different time periods in the market. Although the rates for loans for example might be set by a bank, this rate is priced off of the rate that is set by the financial market.

   Central banks play a role in where the market thinks these rates should be. They set short-term interest rates and also make statements regarding the economy and where they think interest rates might go in the future. This is important, because these statements affect longer-term risk-free rates by affecting investors' expectations. According to the expectations theory which is one of the ways of looking at interest rates - the longer-term is a product of all of the shorter time periods between now and the end of the longer-term. For example, a two-year interest rate is [1+the one-year rate] multiplied by [1+the one year rate, one year from now] annualized to give a percentage; the three year rate is [1+the one-year rate] multiplied by [1+the one-year rate, one year from now] multiplied by [1+the one-year rate, two years from now] annualized to give a percentage, or alternatively [1+the two-year rate] multiplied by [1+the one-year rate, two years from now] annualized to give a percentage and so on.

If the central bank says that inflation pressure is expected to rise and that they will need to make adjustments in the future that are more aggressive than people expect, short-term interest rates would be expected to rise in the future and therefore longer-term rates would rise today. As these longer-term interest rates rise, longer-term borrowing costs rise and the economy would typically slow as companies and consumers borrow less. As these longer-term risk-free rates rise, government bond prices would also fall.

717. **True: The key goal of most central banks today is price stability, which is another way of saying that they focus on keeping inflation (and deflation) under control.**

718. **Central banks can ultimately affect which of the following through their actions:**
    I. inflation
    II. deflation
    III. growth
    IV. employment
    V. currency exchange rates

    a. I only
    b. I and II only
    c. I, II and III only
    d. I, II, III and IV only
    e. I, II, III, IV and V

    Changes in interest rates can affect all of the above, although the primary goal for the central bank might only be one of these elements (for example, inflation).

719. **Falling prices for goods and services is also known as:**
    a. inflation
    b. deflation
    c. leverage
    d. normal

    By definition.

720. **The agency that is responsible for setting interest rates in Europe is the:**
    a. Fed
    b. European Government
    c. European Central Bank
    d. French Government

    This is the Central Bank for Europe - its name is abbreviated as the 'ECB'.

721. **The agency that is responsible for setting interest rates in the USA is the:**
    a. Fed
    b. European Government
    c. European Central Bank
    d. French Government

    Also known as the Federal Reserve System - the Central Bank for the US.

722. **Government spending on public projects and taxation are elements of:**
    a. monetary policy
    b. fiscal policy
    c. trade policy
    d. defense policy

Fiscal policy is the policy of government spending and taxation. If the government is spending more than it is receiving, it is said to be running a deficit. A government that is running a deficit will need to borrow more money in the bond market than it otherwise would. With this deficit, the government's debt would increase, and at some point in the future they would be expected to repay the debt as it matures to the bondholders that bought it. Fiscal policy is also important because it can affect the economy. Taxes for companies, known as corporate taxes, affect company spending. Income taxes and other consumer taxes affect how we as consumers spend. How companies and consumers are taxed, and what the government spends on parts of the economy, clearly affect growth, inflation and ultimately the overall economy. If the government raises taxes for companies and individuals, both have less money to spend, and growth and inflation should decrease. When taxes are lowered, parts of the economy might receive a boost because companies and/or individuals have more money to spend. Therefore fiscal and monetary policies are usually coordinated - when the government implements tax changes, the central bank will be sure to monitor the impact of these changes to ensure that the policy goals of low and stable inflation and a well functioning economy continue to be met.

723. Changing short-term interest rates that banks pay is a part of:
 a. monetary policy
 b. fiscal policy
 c. trade policy
 d. defense policy

 By definition.

724. Putting a tariff or charge on imported goods to protect domestic industries is a part of:
 a. monetary policy
 b. fiscal policy
 c. trade policy
 d. defense policy

 By definition.

725. True: Both monetary and fiscal policies impact the economy.

726. Which of the following policies would not stimulate the economy in the near term:
 a. lowering interest rates
 b. increased government spending
 c. increased taxes
 d. a looser monetary policy

 Increased taxes would take money away from spenders and would be a part of a tighter fiscal policy that would be more likely to slow the economy.

727. True: A government can spend more than it receives in tax revenue - it can make up for the shortfall by borrowing.

 This is very common and governments issue bonds (government bonds) to borrow.

728. Which of the following statements is false:
 a. a government that spends more than it takes in is said to be running a deficit
 b. a budget surplus exists when the government takes in more than it spends
 c. when the government needs to borrow, it typically issues government bonds
 d. governments borrow through corporate bonds

 Companies issue corporate bonds to borrow - governments issue government bonds.

729. **All of the following make setting monetary policy in a particular country a challenge except:**
a. what is going on in other countries affects growth and that can be difficult to predict
b. the central bank is trying to target the future and that is never an exact science
c. economic surveys are never 100% exact
d. there is too much corruption in the central bank and they never do what they say

Answer d. is certainly not universally true - the other answers are there to illustrate some of the challenges of setting monetary policy.

730. **Central banks cut interest rates with an ultimate view to:**
I. making borrowing cheaper
II. making borrowing feasible for more companies
III. stimulating the economy
IV. making debt cheaper
V. decreasing the cost of money

a. I only
b. I and II only
c. I, II and III only
d. I, II, III and IV only
e. I, II, III, IV and V

These are all reasons for and/or direct results from cutting interest rates.

731. **Sectors that are generally considered to be very sensitive to the economy include the:**
I. automotive sector
II. retail sector
III. biotech sector
IV. defense sector
V. utility sector

a. I only
b. I and II only
c. I, II and III only
d. I, II, III and IV only
e. I, II, III, IV and V

I and II are typically discretionary purchases. This is much less the case for spending on biotech, defense and utilities.

732. **A sector that is considered defensive would be the:**
a. automotive sector
b. retail sector
c. utility sector
d. technology sector

733. **An significant and sustained increase in the price of oil will most likely:**
I. increase the revenues of companies that sell oil
II. increase the cost of goods sold of companies that use oil to manufacture something else
III. lead to an increase in the price of gasoline
IV. lead to a transfer of wealth to nations or states that produce the world's oil
V. be good for the average consumer

a. I only
b. I and II only
c. I, II and III only

d. I, II, III and IV only
e. I, II, III, IV and V

The average consumer would have less disposable income and it would not be good for him/her.

734. **Countries that export more than they import have a:**
a. budget surplus
b. budget deficit
c. trade surplus
d. trade deficit

By definition.

735. **Governments that spend more than they take in have a:**
a. budget surplus
b. budget deficit
c. trade surplus
d. trade deficit

By definition.

736. **Countries that import more than they export have a:**
a. budget surplus
b. budget deficit
c. trade surplus
d. trade deficit

By definition.

737. **Governments that spend less than they take in have a:**
a. budget surplus
b. budget deficit
c. trade surplus
d. trade deficit

By definition.

738. **True: Governments that spend more than they take in will often borrow. This borrowing ultimately has to be repaid, and in order to repay it they may have to raise taxes or cut spending.**

739. **Which of the following statements is true when the central bank is independent of the government:**
a. monetary policy always takes fiscal policy into account because they are both the responsibility of the government
b. monetary policy always takes fiscal policy into account because they are both the responsibility of the central bank
c. monetary policy should take fiscal policy into account because they both impact the economy
d. monetary and fiscal policy never take one another into account

Even though the Fed, the Bank of England, and the European Central Bank are independent of the respective governments, the two policies should take each other into account. For example an economy that is going to be slowed through fiscal policy will for example have less of a need to be slowed through monetary policy etc. The two types of policies may have similar effects and should be coordinated to be proportionate and effective.

740. **True: Governments create tax incentives to encourage behavior that they feel is in society's best interest.**

For example, to stimulate saving and investing.

741. **True: Governments as elected entities, should have society's well-being as one of their main considerations.**

742. **Which of the following are elements of government fiscal policy:**
I. government spending
II. taxation
III. the government budget
IV. interest rates
V. currency exchange rates

a. I only
b. I and II only
c. I, II and III only
d. I, II, III and V only
e. I, II, III, IV and V

IV and V are considered elements of monetary policy.

743. **A government entity might issue bonds for which of the following reasons:**
I. they have a budget deficit
II. they need capital for a major project
III. tax revenues are falling short of their spending requirements
IV. they are looking to start a major investment period
V. they want to sell an equity stake in themselves

a. I only
b. I and II only
c. I, II and III only
d. I, II, III and IV only
e. I, II, III, IV and V

I-IV are true. Governments can not sell an equity stake in themselves (also bonds are lending/ borrowing instruments, not ownership/equity instruments).

744. **True: A slowing economy can decrease the revenues of companies that are economically sensitive.**

745. **Which of the following is most likely to lead to higher asset prices:**
a. lower interest rates and easier borrowing
b. higher interest rates and more difficult borrowing
c. a recession
d. high unemployment and lower spending

More capital is available and it is more affordable to borrow (or for the same interest cost, more can be borrowed) - so for example, with lower interest rates people would be able to afford larger homes and spend more leading to higher prices.

746. **An industry where there is only one provider of a good or service is known as:**
a. competition
b. an oligopoly
c. a monopoly
d. a duopoly

By definition.

747. An industry where there are only two providers of a good or service is known as:
   a. competition
   b. an oligopoly
   c. a monopoly
   d. a duopoly

   By definition.

748. An industry where there are a small number of providers of a good or service is known as:
   a. competition
   b. an oligopoly
   c. a monopoly
   d. a duopoly

   By definition.

749. Money can be thought of all of the following except a:
   a. medium of exchange
   b. means of storing value - a store of value
   c. unit of account
   d. a stock in a company

   A.-c. are considered the three main functions of money:
   a. it is a medium of exchange, meaning that it is used to buy and sell goods so that they are not directly traded one for another - in other words we are not bartering some goods for other goods, for example trading a chicken for a visit to the dentist etc.
   b. meaning that it is a way of storing value and it represents value even though money consists of pieces of paper and coins with numbers and words on them
   c. meaning that it is a way of measuring the cost of something that can be counted, added up and divided into smaller units and that provides us with a way of describing prices
   d. it is not a stock

750. **True: Economists argue that some goods and services should be provided by the government because private companies can not deliver these goods and services at prices that consumers would buy them at, because only a part of the the value associated with them goes to the purchaser, while the rest goes to society as a whole, including to many consumers that are not paying for the good or service. These types of goods are often referred to as 'public goods'.**

   An example of a public good that is sometimes cited is national defense which benefits the entire country. It is a service that everyone can 'use' or benefit from, and the fact that our neighbor is protected by the national defense does not mean that we are less protected. The fact that no one is excluded (non-excludability) and the fact that no one benefits less because someone else is benefitting (non-rivalry), are the two key characteristics of public goods.

751. A discussion of public goods and externalities would be most likely to start in the context of:
   a. pollution and lighthouses
   b. cars
   c. food
   d. clothing

   If we pollute less, everyone benefits. A lighthouse is good for all ships and cargo transport in general - who should pay for the lighthouse?

752. **True: All other things being equal, investors might be more likely to want to hold a certain currency when deposits in that currency earn a higher interest rate.**

Although often this higher interest rate could be counteracted by a depreciation of the currency.

753. <u>High levels of unemployment could lead to the following:</u>

I. lower tax revenues for the government
II. higher social security and welfare benefit payments by the government
III. a rise in the levels of crime
IV. lower consumption
V. higher levels of homelessness

a. I only
b. I and II only
c. I, II and III only
d. I, II, III and IV only
e. I, II, III, IV and V

That is why governments care so much about employment - unemployment has a lot of negative side effects.

754. <u>A government that cuts taxes and spends heavily is likely to:</u>

I. stimulate the economy
II. reduce its budget surplus or even run a budget deficit
III. need to increase its tax revenues and/or reduce spending at some point in the future
IV. be able to continue to do this forever
V. cause a recession immediately

a. I only
b. I and II only
c. I, II and III only
d. I, II, III and IV only
e. I, II, III, IV and V

This would be considered a loose or stimulative fiscal policy - i.e. it is intended to stimulate growth - clearly this will cost the government money while it is keeping more money in the economy by not taxing as highly, and by spending heavily. Because of the costs, the government will not be able to do this forever. It should stimulate growth and not cause a recession immediately.

755. <u>The 'public sector' refers to:</u>

a. companies
b. the government
c. schools that are not private
d. the insurance industry

By definition.

756. <u>The 'private sector' refers to:</u>

a. companies
b. the government
c. schools that are not private
d. the insurance industry

By definition.

757. <u>A capitalist system versus a communist system is intended to achieve which of the following:</u>

I. meritocracy
II. a more efficient allocation of resources

III. competition
IV. a government that allocates resources on behalf of society
V. similar benefits for everyone

a. I only
b. I and II only
c. I, II and III only
d. I, II, III and IV only
e. I, II, III, IV and V

We have spoken quite a bit about the allocation of capital and how providers of capital seek out profitable investment opportunities and try to allocate capital to companies and governments that are able to provide a return - those companies will be the ones that consumers prefer - consumers will pay for their goods and services because they represent the best value for money or their best choice.

758. The idea that a capitalist system is preferable to a communist or socialist system is consistent with which of the following ideas:
a. the government is best placed to allocate resources
b. everyone should receive similar rewards irrespective of effort or ability
c. financial markets are the best allocator of capital, the private sector is the best provider of most goods and services
d. stock markets are bad

759. In many Western European countries during the second half of the 1990s, the country's government-owned telephone and telecommunications company was privatized, and the ownership of the company was in each case transferred from the government or its agencies (the public sector), to investors that purchased shares/stocks in the company as the company was in each case listed on the stock market. This was done with a view to achieving which of the following:
I. decreasing government debt
II. stimulating competition
III. reducing the cost of telephone and telecommunications services for companies and individuals
IV. promoting an equity culture
V. reducing the quality of these services

a. I only
b. I and II only
c. I, II and III only
d. I, II, III and IV only
e. I, II, III, IV and V

This was done with a view to achieving I-IV. By stimulating competition and offering consumers choice, the fate of the companies is determined by what consumers choose - they are forced to become more efficient and to think about the products that they should offer consumers. Only those companies that can offer a good service at the right price will be able to generate profits and deliver returns to shareholders and pay interest on their debt, and therefore only these companies will have access to capital over the long-term - this is not the case if the government provides the service. Reducing the quality of these services was not a goal (V) - and in fact usually the very opposite happened.

760. True: Governments tax certain items very heavily to receive tax revenues, and to discourage their consumption - examples of this include taxes on cigarettes, alcohol and gasoline.

This is what tax incentives and tax disincentives are about.

761. **True: Governments play a role in the allocation of capital alongside financial markets - they do this via their fiscal policy initiatives.**

This is true, although in most capitalist countries it is believed that most goods and services are best provided by private companies where there is competition and where there are incentives for the companies to try and do well - this competition and the incentives are very difficult to replicate without financial markets and if the government provides them.

762. **The reason that the US government does not just print dollars to pay off all of its debt and then secondly share some of the money with all US passport-holders is because it would:**
   a. be too easy
   b. eliminate a lot of jobs in the accounting and financial services profession
   c. decrease the value of the dollar greatly and lead to very high inflation
   d. not be possible to print money

Printing a lot of money would make the money worth less - i.e. a greater number of dollars would exist chasing goods and services, and prices would rise (inflation), and each dollar would buy less.

763. **Stagflation refers to an environment in which growth is:**
   a. strong and prices are dropping
   b. weak and prices are dropping
   c. strong and prices are rising
   d. weak and prices are rising

By definition.

764. **Stagflation has historically been very rare although some inflation is very common. The fundamental reason that stagflation is a very worrying scenario is because prices are:**
   a. rising with strong growth, cutting interest rates will not work
   b. rising with weak growth, the normal policy measures can not be implemented as easily
   c. falling with weak growth, cutting interest rates will not work
   d. falling with strong growth, raising interest rates does not make sense

For example, the fact that there is inflation might lead the central bank to raise interest rates - this would however slow growth further with potentially other bad side effects like companies going out of business and higher unemployment. If the central bank lowered interest rates to address the weak growth, inflation might rise further which would also be a concern. That is why stagflation is hard to deal with and why traditional policy might be harder to implement.

765. **True: The most common technical definition of a recession is a period of decline in economic activity as measured by negative GDP growth lasting at least two quarters.**

This is the technical definition of a recession.

766. **The government can be said to have balanced the budget when:**
   a. interest rates are 0
   b. when imports equal exports
   c. when net tax revenues equal government expenditure
   d. when growth is constant

This is the definition of a balanced budget.

767. **The phrase 'economies of scale' refers to:**
   a. the economies of large countries
   b. the budget surplus of large governments
   c. producing something more cheaply on a per unit basis when many units are made

d. cost cutting at a company

This is what economies of scale refers to. For example, management costs and marketing costs do not usually increase in proportion to the number of units sold, in which case, with more units sold these costs can be spread across more units, decreasing the cost allocated to each unit and therefore the cost per unit.

768. **When a company is nationalized:**

I. the company is being listed on the stock market
II. the company will be held by shareholders
III. the company is going public
IV. the company is no longer controlled as other listed companies typically are
V. the government is taking over ownership of the company

a. I only
b. I and II only
c. I, II and III only
d. I, II, III and IV only
e. IV and V only

A company is nationalized when the government takes ownership of the company.

769. **When a company is privatized:**

I. the company is being listed on the stock market
II. the company will be held by shareholders
III. the company is going public
IV. the company is no longer controlled as other listed companies typically are
V. the government is taking over ownership of the company

a. I only
b. I and II only
c. I, II and III only
d. I, II, III and IV only
e. IV and V only

By definition.

770. **Which of the following could play a role when a company is nationalized:**

I. the company is on the brink of failure
II. the company is strategically important
III. the government does not want the company to fail
IV. the government believes it should play a role in the management of this company
V. the failure of this company could cause problems for other significant firms

a. I only
b. I and II only
c. I, II and III only
d. I, II, III and IV only
e. I, II, III, IV and V

All of these could play a role. If the government believed that saving this company was a priority, then the likelihood of it being nationalized would rise greatly.

771. **Proponents of widespread nationalization of businesses typically believe that:**

a. companies are better held by outside shareholders
b. private control is better for companies

c. **the government is a better allocator of resources and manager of goods and services**
d. only a capitalist system will allow a proper allocation of capital and companies to prosper and fail as required

TOTAL: 85 ANSWERS

<u>Saving and Investing in Practice - Introduction</u>

772. <u>Thinking about financial matters is something we should do:</u>

a. once in a while
b. naturally as part of everyday life
c. never do
d. only when forced to by a lack of money

It is such an important topic - it affects so much of what goes on around us, and it is spoken about so much - that it should be something that we think about regularly and naturally as a part of everyday life. When it makes sense, we will think about it more regularly as a part of everyday life.

773. <u>An often quoted Wall Street saying is:</u>

a. there is always a free lunch
b. there is no such thing as a free lunch
c. dinner is on me
d. breakfast is the most important meal of the day

The saying has a lot to do with the idea that if something looks too good to be true, then it probably is. That does not mean that there are no good investment ideas, it just means that there are no short-cuts, that investments often involve risk, and that there might not be a single perfect investment idea. Importantly it also means that diversification, dollar cost averaging, tax savings, knowledge and effort all can play a role in improving the outcome.

774. <u>Saving can be best described as:</u>

a. earning more than spending
b. spending more than earning
c. earning more than investing
d. investing

In theory saving is not that difficult - monitoring what we spend and reducing unnecessary expenses clearly play a role in ensuring that we are saving.

775. <u>Investing can be best described as:</u>

a. following the latest fashion
b. going with the crowd
c. gambling
d. allocating capital based on analysis, bearing in mind diversification, risk-management, tax considerations, time horizons among other fundamental saving and investing principles

A.-c. are definitely not good ways of thinking about investing - d. is.

776. <u>One of the byproducts of knowing about saving and investing is that:</u>

I. we can understand what is being spoken about in the press
II. we have a better chance of not falling victim to bad financial ideas
III. we can have a dialogue with a financial adviser and it will not seem like a foreign language
IV. we can think for ourselves and not always follow the crowd blindly
V. every investment we are involved in will be fantastic

a. I only
b. I and II only
c. I, II and III only
d. I, II, III and IV only
e. I, II, III, IV and V

I-IV are some of the main reasons for knowing about saving and investing - unfortunately not every investment is sure to be fantastic, some will be better than others - the key is to increase the odds of getting more of them right, and to use things that we can be sure about like tax savings, dollar cost averaging and diversification.

777. **Which of the following statements with respect to saving and investing in practice is true:**
   I. having an understanding of this subject can improve our understanding of available alternatives
   II. ideally saving and investing is not a process of high-risk trial and error
   III. making use of things we can be sure about is a good start
   IV. managing risk has to be a key element of any saving and investing plan
   V. this subject is to a large extent based on fairly simple concepts

   a. I only
   b. I and II only
   c. I, II and III only
   d. I, II, III and IV only
   e. I, II, III, IV and V

   These are some of the key reasons for learning about saving and investing, and some of the key aspects of a saving and investing plan.

778. **To save and invest intelligently, we need to:**
   a. dedicate a lot of time to the project
   b. just let someone else do it
   c. develop an understanding and automate what we can
   d. give up before we start

779. **Investing is mostly about:**
   a. being right all of the time - one less than satisfactory investment will always wipe us out
   b. never making mistakes - why bother
   c. taking huge bets - otherwise it is not worth it
   d. making informed decisions, taking thought-out action and managing risk

   We should clearly not set ourselves up so that one less than satisfactory investment wipes us out. There is always some uncertainty when it comes to thinking about the future, so it is possible (and even fairly likely) that some investments turn out to be mistakes. Taking huge bets is also not what saving and investing is about for most of us.

780. **True: When it comes to investing, there are some things we can be certain about, and others that are inherently filled with uncertainty. Good investors will make use of all of the things they feel certain about and try to minimize the risk with things that they feel uncertain about.**

781. **In investing, things that we can be certain about include:**
   I. saving tax on the annual returns helps improve the return over the long term significantly
   II. the effect of compounding at 5% every year is affected dramatically by the length of time that the compounding takes place
   III. when any single investment has some risk, diversification is a good idea
   IV. for an asset that moves up and down on a monthly basis, but up over the long-term, dollar cost averaging can decrease the purchase price
   V. some people argue that developed markets are efficient and this makes market timing and stock picking very difficult

   a. I only
   b. I and II only
   c. I, II and III only
   d. I, II, III and IV only

e. I, II, III, IV and V

782. Things that we can not be certain about include:

I. next year's stock market performance
II. the performance of a single stock
III. the exact growth of the economy
IV. where interest rates will be exactly in 12 months
V. what exchange rates will be for certain currencies

a. I only
b. I and II only
c. I, II and III only
d. I, II, III and IV only
e. I, II, III, IV and V

783. Successful investors are:

a. never wrong
b. never right
c. never investing
d. right more often than wrong and managing risk

By making informed decision, automating parts of the process, making use of things that one can be sure about, trying to be right more often then wrong, and managing risk.

TOTAL: 12 ANSWERS

THE IMPACT OF TIME

784. Which of the following statements is true with respect to stocks, bonds and cash:
   a. **investments that have historically had higher returns have tended to have higher volatility**
   b. investments with higher returns have tended to have lower volatility
   c. the volatility of all investments is the same
   d. volatility is higher when our time horizon is higher

   Higher volatility is almost like a cost for the higher return. Stocks which have had the highest returns of the three historically (between stocks, bonds and cash) have also had the highest volatility.

785. Which of the following statements about the US stock market is false:
   a. the stock market has tended to go up over long time periods
   b. the stock market is very volatile over any one-year period, less so over the longer term
   c. the return of the stock market has been more steady over longer periods
   d. **the stock market return is very predictable if investing for a shorter period**

   The stock market return is not very predictable if investing for a shorter period because of this higher volatility. The other three statements are true.

786. True: The day-to-day, or even the year-to-year, fluctuations become less relevant if our time horizon is longer (as long as the investment is solid etc.).

   Unless we have to sell, we do not care that much about the short-term performance when compared with the long-term performance - although it can be hard to stomach high volatility.

787. True: One of the implications of short-term stock market volatility is that investors with longer time horizons would be the ones with more stock market investments typically.

   And conversely investors with shorter time horizons would have less stock market investments because the movement of these investments is more difficult to predict in the short-term.

788. True: If we felt that we could be more certain that an investment was going to rise in the long-term, but we were less certain that it would do so in the short-term, it would make sense to think of this as a potential long-term investment.

   Thereby increasing the likelihood of a positive outcome.

789. True: The time horizon that we have for our investments is one of the most important considerations when it comes to thinking about saving and investing.

   The time horizon is influenced by when we need the money, our age, our retirement plans etc.

790. Rank the following investments in terms of expected volatility:
   I. short-term US government debt (Treasury Bills)
   II. 5-year US government notes (Treasury Notes)
   III. 5-year corporate bonds
   IV. US stocks

   a. IV. III, II, I
   b. IV, II, III, I
   c. II, IV, III, I
   d. **I, II, III, IV**

791. Past performance is most likely to be:

a. a very good guide to future performance
b. a great indicator of future performance
c. the best indicator of future performance
d. a poor indicator of future performance

792. **A 'five-bagger' is a investment that:**
a. trades at $5
b. has a yield of 5%
c. whose price has gone up five-fold
d. has dropped 50%

This is just a term that is thrown around in the press sometimes.

793. **An investor that had a long time horizon would typically hold more:**
a. bonds
b. cash
c. stocks
d. commodities

Because the result would be more predictable over the long-term.

794. **False: As we get older, it makes more sense to have money that we need for retirement in stocks.**

It makes sense to have more of our investments in less volatile assets as we get older because our time horizon is shorter. We would not want to sell right after a major decline for example (even though this would not say much about the future). Since the retirement money becomes very important to us as we get older, and because we are getting closer to needing the money, less risky/volatile investments make sense despite lower observed long-term returns.

795. **True: An investor that has a longer time horizon would typically have more stocks than one who has a very short time horizon.**

As per the above. In fact, in retirement, wealth preservation is so much more important than seeking a return, that often holding very high levels of cash and government debt is a good idea.

796. **Which of the following should have some impact on the time horizon for our investments, or the time horizon for some of our investments, and correspondingly how we think about asset allocation:**
I. our age
II. when we expect to retire
III. when our kids go off to college
IV. upcoming major expenditures
V. our market outlook for the next week

a. I only
b. I and II only
c. I, II and III only
d. I, II, III and IV only
e. I, II, III, IV and V

Our market outlook is filled with uncertainty and not a key element of making a long-term financial plan.

797. **A 20-year old college graduate and a 65-year old retiree are most likely to:**
a. have the same investment objectives and the same investments
b. have different investment objectives but should invest in the same way

c. have the same investment objectives but very different investment approaches
d. have different investment objectives and potentially very different investment approaches

The 20-year old graduate most likely wants to accumulate wealth, save for the future, build a nest-egg, buy a home etc. The 65-year old retiree will most likely want to preserve a nest-egg and live well in retirement on savings of the past. These different objectives will clearly manifest themselves in the saving and investing approaches.

798. Someone that is 64 years old and one year away from retirement, compared to a 23-year old college graduate starting a first job, is likely to have have more of which of the following assets in his or her portfolio:
a. cash and other very low-risk investments
b. emerging market stock mutual funds
c. passively managed Asian stock mutual funds
d. MSCI World ETFs

799. False: An investor that wants to invest for the long term should put all of his or her money into the US stock market.

This would not offer enough diversification. Even if the investor has a long-term time horizon, there should be diversification into investments other than stocks - other asset classes: bonds, commodities, real estate, cash. Secondly, the investments should include regions other than the US - Europe, Asia, emerging markets etc.

TOTAL: 16 ANSWERS

Timing Investments and Dollar Cost Averaging

800. Following the crowd blindly is not a good strategy because:
a. everyone is an idiot
b. prices often already reflect the expectations of the crowd
c. crowds can trample you
d. it is guaranteed to make money - but investing is not about making money

If everyone expects house prices to rise, then sellers will ask for more money, and buyers would be prepared to pay more as well. In general, security/asset prices will reflect the expectations.

801. Human psychology - especially greed and fear are most likely to:
a. help us with our investments
b. be a hindrance - we might buy for fear of missing something and/or sell at the bottom
c. help us with our relationships
d. make us be great investors

802. True: Human nature can lead to poor investment decisions.

803. Buying an investment that everyone is buying:
a. ensures a lower price
b. can lead to too high a price
c. means not following the crowd
d. always leads to excellent returns

Being aware of investor behavior is useful in understanding some of the pitfalls that we might fall into. For example, investor behavior in the short term is often influenced by headlines such as: 'the real estate market is hot and is expected to go higher', 'stocks are performing well and should continue to rally' splashed across the front pages of the newspaper. When we hear things like this, we should always think about what this means in terms of the expectations that investors have. If everyone thinks real estate is going higher, then probably either sellers would wait to sell, or they would sell at a higher price today reflecting the fact that they think the asset will be more expensive soon. Buyers, would probably be prepared to pay higher prices today as well, for fear of having to pay more soon. Therefore the expectation of higher prices often means that prices are already high. This does not leave much room for the good news to impact prices positively in the short term. The good news will already be in the price, and when good news does come out, the asset price might not even go up because it was so widely expected. If anything, very positive expectations leave room for disappointment – disappointments that can cause asset prices to drop dramatically when everyone has been anticipating good news. Conversely, if everyone thinks that an investment will continue to go down, expectations might be so low that negative news will no longer impact the price of the investment, and any positive news might cause a very positive stock price reaction.

804. True: Emotions and what we hear can influence our investment decisions.

805. Selling when everyone else is selling is potentially a bad idea because:
a. prices will be higher
b. prices will be lower
c. it is all about being different
d. it will be too easy to sell

As per the answer to question 803 as well.

806. Which of the following investments is most likely to fall a lot in the short term:
a. a much loved investment with good news that were expected

b. a much loved investment with slightly disappointing news
c. an unloved investment with news that were expected
d. an unloved investment with good news

The disappointment (and surprise) is greatest - if everyone already hates an investment, bad news would not make it go down as much in the short-term because expectations were already low.

807. <u>When good news is priced into an investment and everyone loves it, the biggest risk is that:</u>
a. the investment disappoints slightly versus these very high expectations
b. more investors start to like the investment and the price rises
c. even expected news makes the investment rise strongly
d. the investment is not really there

Given the role of expectations, smart investors spend a lot of time trying to figure out things that might be unexpected by the majority of investors. In the stock market, they try to think about things that are not on the front page of the newspaper and that might not be reflected in prices. In the real estate market, they might look for well-located properties in an overlooked area that would probably have more potential than properties in an area that everyone is focused on, certainly in the short-term. It is worth bearing expectations in mind, especially when assessing what the short-term performance might be, or whether going with the crowd blindly is a good idea.

808. <u>Which of the following investments is most likely to rise a lot in the short term:</u>
a. a much loved investment with news that were expected
b. a much loved investment with good news
c. an unloved investment with news that were expected
d. an unloved investment with better than expected news

809. <u>Anchoring is a mental process by which we fix our minds on the price that something traded at in the past - for example a higher price than where we bought it, and a price that is higher than where we could sell it now. Knowing this, anchoring is most likely to:</u>
a. stop us from selling an investment even though we should
b. make us sell investments that have not gone down
c. help us deal with our investments without any emotion whatsoever
d. help us with our other emotional problems

This is a commonly observed process that it is worth being aware of.

810. <u>In order to be effective, saving and investing should be:</u>
a. fun, not too time consuming, and sensible
b. stressful and high risk
c. a bloodbath
d. risky - to the point of risking our entire existence

Things are more likely to be stressful when we are not adequately prepared and/or when we feel we are losing control. Starting early, getting information, making use of automation and well-founded techniques is intended to avoid some of this stress.

811. <u>Smart professional investors:</u>
I. always follow the crowd
II. believe everything they read
III. think for themselves
IV. try to figure out things that are not priced into investments or generally recognized
V. believe in doing their homework before investing

a. I only
b. I and II only

c. III and IV only
d. III, IV and V only
e. I, II, III, IV and V

812. **True: The less people are following a potential investment or asset, and the less people there are rigorously analyzing the data, the higher the likelihood of mispricings.**

When something is 'undiscovered' and there are not a lot of buyers chasing that item, the likelihood of having mispricings is much greater. Conversely, if there are too many investors chasing the same investment this is less likely to be the case.

813. **The greater fool theory incorporates the concept of:**
a. fundamental value
b. buying sound companies at the right price
c. short-term market timing
a. being able to find someone that will pay more irrespective of value

Throughout history, situations have arisen where investors got caught up in frenzies and blindly expected positive performance to continue. Looking back on this now, it seems that the only reason investors could have justified buying the investments is because they thought that the investments could be resold at a higher price in the future to someone else that was caught up in the frenzy. Neither the price at which they bought the investment, nor the higher price at which they expected to sell it, appear linked to the value of the item. This is sometimes referred to as the greater fool theory – investors expect a 'greater fool' to purchase the investment from them. At some point investors come to their senses and recognize the discrepancy between the price of the asset and its true value. The bubble bursts as buyers disappear and sellers are unable to sell; since prices are often so far above real values, they can fall significantly and quickly.

An example of this would be the share prices of technology companies in the late 1990s. Valuing stocks as it had been done up until then was largely ignored or revised. It was argued that things were different this time and that traditional valuation models were no longer relevant. Unfortunately for many, the same old valuation methods soon became relevant again and prices began to drop. When prices began to drop, there was no reason left to buy the stocks – why buy a stock that is not going up and that doesn't look cheap? Many companies lost more than 90% of their value over the twelve months that followed March 2000.

814. **When everyone loves a certain investment, and everyone is speaking about it, and it is on the front page of the newspapers, we should be most concerned about:**
a. buying the investment too cheaply
b. whether we might be overpaying for the investment and what the impact of a small change in perception might be
c. not following the crowd
d. interest rates

As per the above, with respect to much loved investments.

815. **One way to avoid letting emotions drive our investment decisions is to:**
a. day-trade like a maniac
b. go with what we feel like
c. automate the investment process
d. give up, start again, give up, start again etc.

Apart from the fact that it saves us a lot of time, automating a part of the process avoids making reactive decisions, and poor decisions that human nature would sometimes lead us to make.

816. **Prices that get completely out of line with reality and fundamentals are a feature of:**

a. troubles
b. bubbles
c. soaps
d. hills

817. **Bubbles are most likely to be the result of:**
a. sellers asking too high prices
b. buyers wanting too low prices
c. individual thinking by investors based on their own analysis
d. a herd mentality - everyone doing the same thing and often ignoring fundamentals

818. **Timing the stock market can be best described as:**
a. straightforward, just buy low and sell high
b. straightforward, that is why most traders make money in all market conditions
c. difficult, too many people are doing the same thing and markets are fairly efficient
d. neither straightforward nor difficult - time is just an illusion

819. **Which of the following statements about timing the markets is true:**
I. buying after the market has gone down ensures that it will go up again
II. buying after the market has started going up ensures that the trend will continue
III. selling after the market has risen by at least 10% is a good strategy
IV. most long-term investors rely on timing the market for a majority of their returns
V. we can be sure about the past, but not so certain about the future, and timing buys and sells is a waste of time for most investors

a. I only
b. I and II only
c. I, II and III only
d. I, II, III and IV only
e. V only

820. **True: An alternative to trying to time the market is to automate regular investments thereby avoiding timing decisions and ensuring that the savings are set aside and that the investments are made consistently and not skipped based on a feeling regarding the market. This also gives us more time to focus on other things.**

821. **Day-traders are most likely to get involved in the stock market and make money:**
a. when the market is falling
b. all of the time - they will make money under all conditions typically
c. during a bull market
d. during a bear market

The number of people that make money in a bear market is much less; the focus of the press is much greater on markets during a bull market and a lot more people jump in.

822. **Dollar cost averaging refers to:**
a. buying the same number of shares periodically (for example every month)
b. buying the same number of bonds every month
c. buying different investments every month - each time with a similar amount of money
d. investing the same sum of money periodically (for example every month) in the same investment

This is the definition of dollar cost averaging.

823. **The best way of describing why dollar cost averaging works is by saying that buying:**
a. the same amount periodically ensures that the average price is lower

b. less when the price is low ensures a lower average price
c. more when the price if high, ensures a lower average price
d. more when the price is low, and less when the price is high, leads to a lower average price

By investing the same dollar (or other currency) amount, this ensures that more units are bought when the price is low, and less when the price is high. For example, if a fund trades at $10 in Month 1, and $20 in Month 2, then the average price over those two months is $15 [($10+$20)/2]. If an investor had invested $60 each month (the same amount), he or she would have bought 6 units in Month 1 ($60/$10) and 3 units in Month 2 ($60/$20), for a total of 9 (6+3) units and $120 invested ($60/month for two months). The average price paid over the two months was therefore $120/9 = $13.33 - a lower average price was achieved (when compared with the $15 average price if the same number of units had been bought in both months) by investing the same amount and therefore automatically buying more at the lower price, and less at the higher price. The result would be the same if this were done over more months with a volatile but long-term rising asset.

824. **Dollar cost averaging implicitly recognizes that:**
a. timing markets is difficult, and a waste of time for most investors
b. timing markets is highly profitable
c. timing markets is difficult but by automating the timing we have a shot
d. we can time markets as long as we remember to buy high and sell low

825. **An advantage of dollar cost averaging is that it:**
a. requires very little attention once an automated process is set up
b. allows us to become full-time day-traders
c. ensures higher purchase prices
d. ensures investments never go down

826. **A method that can be used to make contributions of equal sums periodically is known as:**
a. anchoring
b. dollar cost averaging
c. timing investments
d. active mutual fund management

827. **Dollar cost averaging can:**
I. avoid market timing
II. bring the average cost of investments down
III. automate a part of the investment process
IV. allow a part of saving and investing plan run itself
V. avoid all losses

a. I only
b. I and II only
c. I, II and III only
d. I, II, III and IV only
e. I, II, III, IV and V

Dollar cost averaging can help lower the average purchase price, and when done over long periods of time can be a very powerful way to increase returns. By automating the investment process, dollar cost averaging also helps avoid some of the traps that human nature would otherwise let us fall into (and it saves time). Dollar cost averaging can not avoid all losses especially over the short term.

TOTAL: 28 ANSWERS

TAXES AND COMPOUNDING

828. <u>True: Governments often put in place policies that are aimed at improving the quality of lives for voters and the public in a country. The government can use the budget to achieve this.</u>

The government uses taxes to encourage certain behaviors. Tax reductions that are intended to promote certain actions are known as tax incentives. Because saving and investing is so important, and because savers and investors play such an important role in the economy as providers of capital, governments provide tax incentives to encourage us to save and invest.

829. <u>Tax incentives are best described as:</u>
a. higher taxes for good ideas
b. lower taxes for behavior that the government is trying to discourage
c. lower taxes for behavior that the government wants to encourage
d. higher taxes for behaviors that governments want to encourage

830. <u>Governments often provide tax incentives that relate to saving and investing for which of the following reasons:</u>
I. having retirees with adequate savings is in the government's best interest
II. savers and investors play a role in providing capital to companies and governments
III. the government wants to encourage saving and investing
IV. the government wants to discourage saving and investing
V. governments want people to be poor

a. I only
b. I and II only
c. I, II and III only
d. IV only
e. III, IV and V only

831. <u>Government tax incentives to promote saving and investing are:</u>
a. illegal
b. worth investigating
c. unheard of
d. never available

Saving taxes on income or on an investment can increase returns greatly especially over the long-term.

832. <u>The government is least likely to incentivize:</u>
a. spending on a home purchase
b. spending on education
c. credit card spending on clothes
d. charitable giving

833. <u>Saving tax on the annual return each year would lead to savings that end up growing:</u>
a. similarly
b. less
c. slightly more
d. much more

Increasing the return each year somewhat by saving the taxes increases the return after many years greatly.

834. <u>**True: Tax considerations are a legitimate consideration when it comes to investing. Total returns are the final objective - minimizing taxes can play a role in this. Minimizing taxes should not be the only or main concern as this by itself does not necessarily ensure the best return.**</u>

835. <u>**True: Many countries have created a system whereby money can be set aside on a tax-free basis and is allowed to grow on a tax-free basis to provide savings for retirement.**</u>

The specifics of the plans will vary from country to country and often change over time, but many countries have set up systems to incorporate this philosophy - including in many countries through the pension plan system.

836. <u>**True: The idea behind most pension plans and retirement plans is to provide savings and/or an income for when someone is no longer working.**</u>

And the rules are typically set up to reflect this objective - i.e. saving tax on contribution, saving of tax on returns and a way of taking the money out after retirement with lower taxes.

837. <u>**True: Having a robust pension and retirement planning system is in the best interests of society, and therefore ultimately of government, typically, as well.**</u>

838. <u>**Which of the following might be benefits of a well-functioning pension or retirement system:**</u>

I. adequate savings for more retirees
II. large pools of capital that are invested in the financial markets to fund companies and governments
III. a lower percentage of retirees living in poverty
IV. governments do not have to provide welfare benefits to retirees to the same extent
V. guaranteed returns each year for all investors

a. I only
b. I and II only
c. I, II and III only
d. I, II, III and IV only
e. I, II, III, IV and V

839. <u>**True: The two main types of pension plans are known as defined benefit and defined contribution (plans).**</u>

With a defined benefit plan, it is the benefit in retirement that is defined. Defined benefit plans are also sometimes known as final salary plans, dollar times service plans or final average pay plans. Each of these is a type of defined benefit plan, with a slightly different way of calculating the benefit. With a defined contribution plan, the contribution is set (often by the plan participant), and the amount that is paid out in retirement is the result of the contributions and the returns that take place.

With a defined benefit plan, it is difficult to know how much money needs to be set aside - it depends on the number of retirees, their expected lifespans in retirement, the returns that will be possible. If there is too little money in the end, because there are too many retirees, or because their lifespans are too long, then the plan is said to be underfunded. In order to shift this burden of trying to provide a defined benefit for retirees, most new plans in companies today are defined contribution.

840. <u>**The vast majority of company pension plans that employees can join today in the United States are:**</u>

a. defined contribution plans
b. defined benefit plans
c. defined return plans
d. none of the above

Guaranteeing a defined benefit comes with a lot of risks for the plan sponsor (the company or agency providing the plan) (and for the employees if the plan ends up underfunded). Most new plans today are defined contribution plans.

841. **When the media speaks about pension plans that are 'underfunded' they are speaking about:**
   a. defined contribution plans
   b. defined benefit plans
   c. defined return plans
   d. none of the above

842. **True: With a defined benefit pension plan, the worker - also known as the plan participant - does not play a role in choosing the investments.**

   They are based on asset-liability studies that aim to ensure that there are enough assets in the plan to pay the retirees their defined benefit.

843. **True: In the United States, the UK and Canada (among many others), defined benefit pension plans were common in the past - today, almost all new company pension plans are defined contribution plans. Defined benefit plans are still common in the public sector (government.**

844. **Which of the following statements is/are true and is/are illustrative of some of the differences between defined benefit and defined contribution plans:**
   I. defined benefit plans 'define the benefit', often based on a multiplier of final years' salaries
   II. defined contribution plans focus on the contribution - the benefit is then determined by the amount contributed and the performance of the assets invested in
   III. in a defined benefit plan the investment decisions are not made by the employee - they involve complicated calculations (made by actuaries) regarding future potential liabilities
   IV. in a defined contribution plan, the plan member (the employee) decides to a large extent how much to contribute and how the funds are to be invested
   V. a defined contribution plan typically requires a bit more initiative on the part of the employee, but it also provides more control and will not end up 'underfunded' (because there is no promised benefit) if the employer gets into trouble or does not set aside sufficient contributions

   a. I only
   b. I and II only
   c. I, II and III only
   d. I, II, III and IV only
   e. I, II, III, IV and V

   I-V are some of the key characteristics of defined benefit and defined contribution plans.

845. **A 401k in the United States is a:**
   a. mutual fund
   b. stock fund
   c. bond fund
   d. retirement savings plan

   And it is a type of defined contribution retirement savings plan.

846. **A pension plan that pays the retiree based on their earnings in the years preceding retirement is a type of:**
   a. defined benefit plan
   b. defined contribution plan
   c. savings plan
   d. mutual fund plan

Defined benefit plans define the benefit - often based on final years' salaries.

847. A pension plan that pays retirement benefits based on what the retiree contributed and the returns that were achieved is known as a:
   a. defined benefit plan
   b. defined contribution plan
   c. savings plan
   d. mutual fund plan

848. A 401k plan is a type of:
   a. defined benefit plan
   b. defined contribution plan
   c. chequing account
   d. mutual fund

849. Stories of companies that are unable to meet the pension plan obligations of plans that were often set up some time ago, usually relate to:
   a. defined benefit plans
   b. defined contribution plans
   c. savings plans
   d. mutual fund plans

   This happens when there are too many retirees compared to the number of people still paying into the plan and/or when the returns were not as expected.

850. Which of the following statements is true:
   a. a 401k plan is the same thing as a stock
   b. a mutual fund is by definition a tax efficient wrapper and we can buy lot of 401k plans
   c. a 401k plan is a mutual fund by definition
   d. a 401k plan can be considered a tax efficient wrapper which can invest in mutual funds

   Because the money goes in on a tax-free basis and compounds inside the plan on a tax-free basis. Depending on the specifics of the plan, the money can then be invested in a variety of investments including mutual funds and/or index funds. Other techniques like dollar cost averaging and diversification can also be used.

851. True: A defined benefit plan is a liability of the plan 'sponsor' - the company or government offering the plan - if the sponsor runs into financial difficulties, the benefits for retirees could be impacted.

852. A company might opt for a defined contribution plan over a defined benefit plan because:
   I. it does not want to have a liability for retirees in the future
   II. it does not want to have the burden of predicting how much needs to be set aside
   III. it is difficult to predict how the number of employees paying into the plan will develop
   IV. it wants the employees to have more say in how the money is managed
   V. it wants to make use of the 401k structure

   a. I only
   b. I and II only
   c. I, II and III only
   d. I, II, III and IV only
   e. I, II, III, IV and V

853. True: The assets of some long-established defined benefit plans are insufficient to cover the defined benefits partly because the number of retirees has gone up a lot, while the number of people paying in to the plan has decreased greatly.

854. **True: A defined benefit plan involves assumptions regarding lifespans and investment returns, as well as detailed calculations to try to assess how much money needs to be in the plan.**

855. **A defined benefit plan with insufficient assets to cover the defined benefits is:**
   a. overfunded
   b. underfunded
   c. funded
   d. not funded

   By definition.

856. **In the UK, a government sponsored structure that allows after-tax money to be set aside in order to grow tax-free, is known as a:**
   a. defined benefit pension plan
   b. 401k
   c. an ISA - an Individual Savings Account
   d. a checking account

   It is not any of the other three - it is known as an ISA - an Individual Savings Account.

857. **True: A money purchase plan is a type of defined contribution pension plan.**

858. **True: Pension laws and contribution rules vary between countries and can change over time, but the generic structures, the plans, and their characteristics can be understood by knowing a few key concepts, and then looking at the plans in more detail.**

   Pension plans differ between countries and the rules also change over time - often employers also play a role in defining the offering. Being aware of the options and being able to assess them is very important especially over the long-term and in planning for retirement. Key elements to think about are:
   - ***the value of saving tax on contributions to the plan;***
   - ***the existence of any other incentives to save, either provided by the government or by the employer;***
   - ***the difference that compounding without taxes can make;***
   - ***the nature of defined contribution and defined benefit type plans;***
   - ***the role that the other key concepts like dollar cost averaging and diversification that can play a key role in a long-term pension plan savings structure.***

TOTAL: 31 ANSWERS

DIVERSIFICATION

859. True: Diversification can be described as mixing different investments that do not move perfectly together in order to spread risk.

Diversification means not putting all of our eggs into one basket. Research has shown that when we invest in multiple things that do not move perfectly together over the short-term (but where we believe that they will go up over the long-term), that the risk/reward relationship can be improved. This is relevant when we buy more than one stock, multiple bonds, a mixture of stocks and bonds, or a mixture of stocks, bonds and commodities. The less the assets move together in the short-term, the better the diversification effect.

860. Diversification can be best thought of as:
   a. a leveraging of returns
   b. a means of guaranteeing returns
   c. a way of borrowing against future returns
   d. a risk management technique

861. Diversification is achieved by:
   a. adding more of the same investments to a portfolio
   b. adding leverage to a portfolio
   c. mixing different investments within a portfolio
   d. selling the entire portfolio

862. Which of the following statements with respect to diversification is/are true:
   I. diversification is an important part of a successful saving and investing plan
   II. diversification can also be referred to as 'not putting all your eggs in one basket'
   III. diversification aims to ensure that some investments go up while others are going down
   IV. diversification relies on all investments moving together
   V. diversification depends on some investments going to zero

   a. I only
   b. I and II only
   c. I, II and III only
   d. I, II, III and IV only
   e. I, II, III, IV and V

Diversification relies on investments not moving together. Although diversification would dampen the impact of some investments going to zero, this would still have a negative impact and diversification certainly does not rely on it.

863. Diversification when properly executed can theoretically do all of the following except:
   a. obtain a higher return for a similar level of risk
   b. reduce the level of risk for a given expected return
   c. limit the impact of a single investment going down a lot
   d. ensure we never lose money

It can reduce the risk of losing money, but not ensure that we never lose money (especially over short time periods).

864. Investing in international stocks is:
   a. a crazy idea - most other countries are uncivilized
   b. a potentially good way to diversify and get access to some market-leading companies
   c. a bad idea - we should always put all of our eggs in one basket
   d. not even worth considering

865. True: Sometimes investments that appear to have nothing to do with each other might move together nonetheless because they are owned by the same investors.

Having the same investors can increase the amount by which investments move together - since the likelihood of the investors acting in a similar manner is increased, leading to a higher correlation.

866. The more two different investments move together, the more they can be said to be:

a. coordinated
b. correlated
c. concentrated
d. cultivated

That is what correlation is by definition - the amount by which different investments move together.

867. True: Diversification makes a case for combining investments that do not move perfectly together.

This is the key underlying fundamental concept behind diversification.

868. True: Investments that do not appear to move together under normal market conditions, might move together more under extreme market conditions when all investors are selling them as a group.

869. In extreme market conditions, for example major market corrections, the following would be most likely to happen:

a. diversification benefits would increase and investments would move more independently
b. diversification benefits would decrease and investments are at risk of going down together
c. investments would go up in value
d. investments would not move in value

During an extreme market correction, there would be more widespread panic selling, causing more investments to move together. To the extent possible, this has to be factored in - for example by holding more cash when we are closer to needing the money, and diversifying enough to take an extreme scenario into account as well.

870. Which pairs below are more diversified than either item in each pair alone:

I. stocks and bonds
II. US stocks and International stocks
III. international stocks and US government bonds
IV. bonds and commodities
V. a US portfolio containing the 500 largest US companies and an S&P 500 index fund

a. I only
b. I and II only
c. I, II and III only
d. I, II, III and IV only
e. I, II, III, IV and V

Choice V contains two groups that are very similar, and therefore the two together would not be much more diversified than either of them alone - this is not the case in the other examples.

871. Which of the following investments can help achieve diversification:

I. stocks
II. bonds
III. commodities

IV. real estate
V. international stocks

a. I only
b. I and II only
c. I, II and III only
d. I, II, III and IV only
e. I, II, III, IV and V

All of these when added to other assets can provide some diversification benefits.

872. True: Funds (mutual, index, exchange traded) provide an increased level of diversification over holding a small number of securities. In fact, often funds hold more securities than it would be possible for a single individual to own - this has contributed to the popularity of funds.

This is one of the key attractions of funds.

873. True: Cash should also be considered an asset class for diversification purposes.

874. True: Diversification can take place across securities, across asset classes and across geographic regions.

875. Which of the following would be considered an asset class:

I. stocks
II. bonds
III. commodities
IV. cash
V. real estate

a. I only
b. I and II only
c. I, II and III only
d. I, II, III and IV only
e. I, II, III, IV and V

These are all major asset classes and an investor would diversify further within each asset class.

876. Diversification often has something to do with which of the following:

a. leverage
b. fees
c. asset allocation
d. accounting

The exercise of selecting different assets to invest in is known as asset allocation. Because to a large extent, individual stock selection, sector selection, and active management in general, are so difficult, and as many researchers argue, a waste of time, asset allocation is probably the most important decision that we can make when it comes to investing. Ideally, the best assets are the ones with the highest return and the lowest risk. Given that there is usually 'no free lunch', unfortunately a higher return usually comes with higher risk (and volatility) - this is where diversification becomes very important in that it can reduce the risk for a similar level of return by combining different asset classes.

877. Which of the following statements is true:

I. professional investors will use diversification
II. there are solid mathematical principles behind the theory of diversification
III. diversification is a part of prudent portfolio management

IV. the level of diversification varies amongst investors, however some level of diversification is present with almost all investors
V. diversification is only for very risk-averse investors

a. I only
b. I and II only
c. I, II and III only
d. I, II, III and IV only
e. I, II, III, IV and V

878. **Two stock markets on two continents have very different fundamentals in terms of country growth, demographics, exports versus imports, dominant industries, government policy and earnings. As investors in these two continents diversify their investments and become investors in both countries (as do investors from other countries), the correlation (the amount by which these two countries' markets move together) would be expected to:**
a. go down
b. stay the same
c. increase
d. stay the same or go down

879. **Two different stocks might move together or be correlated because:**
I. they are in the same industry
II. they sell the same products
III. they buy the same raw materials
IV. they are in the same index
V. they are owned by similar groups of investors

a. I only
b. I and II only
c. I, II and III only
d. I, II, III and IV only
e. I, II, III, IV and V

TOTAL: 21 ANSWERS

Transaction Costs

880. <u>An investment firm or bank typically gets paid:</u>
- a. when we get rich
- b. if we have a great saving and investing plan
- **c. on the products they sell, per transaction and as a percentage of assets they manage**
- d. only if we end up 100% satisfied over the very long term

We can see how our interests (a., b. and c.) might be slightly different than those of the service provider. Having said that, most businesses get paid for the products and services that they sell - the problem here is that the investor does not know the value or merit of the product until many years later potentially, and that the fee structure can be more difficult to understand in some cases.

881. <u>True: Investment products can have explicit fees or hidden fees.</u>

As an investor of course, we care about all of the fees.

882. <u>True: An annual fee that reduces our percentage return by a few percent each year can have a large impact over the long term.</u>

Because compounding with a lower return has a very big impact after many years.

883. <u>When it comes to fees and transaction costs on investments, a reasonable philosophy might be summarized as:</u>
- a. never pay transaction costs
- b. pay the highest fees possible
- c. always go for the lowest cost service
- **d. try to understand what the fees relate to and pay those that make sense - avoid others**

884. <u>True: Unnecessary fees and transaction costs can hurt our return over the long-term significantly.</u>

Because they reduce the annual return, which with many years of compounding has significant impact.

885. <u>In order to save on fees, fund investors would be least likely to focus on:</u>
- a. index funds
- b. ETFs
- c. passively managed funds
- **d. actively managed funds**

Actively managed funds typically have higher fees than all of the others. If an investor felt that active management had some merit (particularly perhaps because this market is less mature and perhaps less efficient), he or she might consider active management - but not to save on fees in the first instance. The fees in all cases have to be looked at and investigated and compared along with other characteristics of the funds.

886. <u>True: An investor should understand all transaction fees, management fees and other potential fees associated with an investment prior to making the investment.</u>

887. <u>Mutual fund fees could include:</u>
- I. sales loads, sales charges on purchases and deferred sales charges
- II. redemption fees, account fees and purchase fees
- III. management fees
- IV. distribution fees
- V. other expenses

a. I only
b. I and II only
c. I, II and III only
d. I, II, III and IV only
e. I, II, III, IV and V

888. False: A no-load mutual fund will not have any expenses.

A no-load fund can have many other kinds of expenses - they just do not have what are known as load fees.

889. When it comes to mutual funds, which fees should we care about:
a. sales fees
b. sales loads
c. annual operating expenses including the management fee
d. all of the fees as they all reduce return

890. True: In the US, a good source of unbiased consumer information regarding mutual fund charges and fees is the US Securities and Exchange Commission (SEC).

There are similar other agencies in many other countries.

891. If a mutual fund is described as a no-load fund, which of the following statements is true:
a. it will certainly have no fees associated with it
b. it has a sales load
c. it has a redemption load
d. it will not have a sales or redemption load but could have many other charges

This terminology is prevalent in the US and highlights one of the issues with fees - that we have to look at this ourselves to understand the fees. Similar principles apply in other countries.

892. A fund is a no-load fund. This fund might have the following other fees or charges:
I. redemption fees
II. purchase fees
III. account fees
IV. annual operating expenses
V. sales load fees

a. I only
b. I and II only
c. I, II and III only
d. I, II, III and IV only
e. I, II, III, IV and V

Purchase and redemption fees are not considered load fees although charged in a similar way (on purchase and redemption) - account fees and operating expenses are other types of fees. The only fees that a no-load fund will not charge are explicit load fees.

893. Which of the following statements regarding expense ratios is/are true:
I. they are the operating expenses as a % of assets
II. they are also sometimes referred to as the management expense ratio or MER
III. they do not include sales loads or redemption fees
IV. they include all expenses and fees
V. a higher expense ratio is always better

a. I only

b. I and II only
c. I, II and III only
d. I, II, III and IV only
e. I, II, III, IV and V

The expense ratio typically does not include the load fees for example - it focuses on the operating expenses paid out of the fund, and the load fees are paid by the investor to the broker - as such, one can not conclude that expense ratios include all fees - looking at the prospectus is very important. Higher expenses ratios are clearly not better, all other things being equal.

894. True: A great place to find detailed information regarding a funds fees and characteristics is in the prospectus.

The prospectus will contain the fine print and the all of the legal details.

895. True: A 1% difference in the annual return over 10 or 20 years or more can have a very large impact on the amount that we end up with.

- $10,000 compounding for 30 years at 6% grows to $57,434.91
- $10,000 compounding for 30 years at 7% grows to $76,122.55
- $10,000 compounding also for 30 years but with an 8% return grows to $100,626.57

Compounding $10,000 at 7% or 8% versus 6% significantly increases the amount that the money grows to over a longer period - in this case 30 years. We could look at many other compounding examples to illustrate the fact that a small percentage difference per year, can make a very large difference over the long-term.

896. True: Index funds tend to have the lowest fees and can be an excellent alternative for investors in developed markets.

Because they tend to have these lower fees (always needs to be looked at) and because most actively managed mutual funds in developed markets underperform the index over the longer term, index funds can provide a better net percentage return per year in many cases, meaning that the return over the long-term with the effects of compounding can be much greater.

897. True: Load fees typically go to a selling broker and not to the fund management firm.

This is the case in the US where the capital markets are very well-developed and a lot of literature is available on capital markets - similar principles apply in other countries.

898. True: Some fees are avoidable - on that basis we can often increase returns without compromising quality.

A clear example of this might be the load fees that go to the broker.

899. In the context of mutual funds, a front-end load is:
a. an annual management fee for the fund
b. a fee that the investor pays when the fund is purchased
c. a fee that the investor pays when the fund is sold
d. a fee that the investor never has to pay

This is the case in the US where the capital markets are very well-developed and a lot of literature is available on capital markets - similar principles apply in other countries.

900. In the context of mutual funds, a back-end load is:
a. an annual management fee for the fund

b. a fee that the investor pays when the fund is purchased
c. a fee that the investor pays when the fund is sold
d. a fee that the investor never has to pay

This is the case in the US where the capital markets are very well-developed and a lot of literature is available on capital markets - similar principles apply in other countries.

901. Front-end loads and back-end loads typically go to:
a. the fund
b. the fund manager's private bank account
c. the fund management company
d. the broker or introducer

So these fees do not necessarily have any impact on the quality of the product and might be avoidable - another product with lower fees might be completely substitutable.

902. A no-load fund, does not charge:
a. any fees
b. load fees
c. management fees
d. account fees

It does not mean that they do not charge a lot of other fees - that is why this needs to be looked at in detail.

903. True: Even though a mutual fund might not have load fees, it could still have a number of other fees.

904. True: The business of mutual funds has become a fairly mature and competitive business - correspondingly there might be opportunities to reduce fees in some cases without compromising quality.

This is definitely true and is the reason for looking around for a reputable firm that provides a high quality offering at reasonable fees.

905. True: Smart investors look at fees and try to assess which ones are justified and which ones are not.

906. Performance after fees is referred to as:
a. gross performance
b. levered performance
c. future performance
d. net performance

907. True: Structured products including capital-guaranteed products are prime targets for hidden fees because of their complexity.

TOTAL: 28 ANSWERS

GETTING STARTED

908. <u>**If we were to start thinking about implementing a saving and investing plan, the best first two things to do would be to:**</u>
   a. start investing and take big bets
   b. start investing and monitor investments
   c. monitor investments and take big bets
   d. take stock of our finances and gather information

909. <u>**Which of the following can be objectives of a financial plan:**</u>
   I. capital preservation
   II. capital appreciation
   III. current income
   IV. total return
   V. interest rates

   a. I only
   b. I and II only
   c. I, II and III only
   d. I, II, III and IV only
   e. I, II, III, IV and V

   And as we saw, depending on age, risk tolerance, preferences, and financial responsibilities, different plans can and will have quite different objectives. Interest rates are out of our control.

910. <u>**True: The objectives of a financial plan should be defined before starting any thought on investment selection.**</u>

   The objectives of the investment plan have huge impact on the investment selection.

911. <u>**An investment plan might operate within certain constraints. Constraints of this type could include:**</u>
   I. liquidity issues
   II. time horizon
   III. tax issues
   IV. legal and regulatory factors
   V. unique needs and preferences

   a. I only
   b. I and II only
   c. I, II and III only
   d. I, II, III and IV only
   e. I, II, III, IV and V

   Depending on the specific needs and preferences of the person in question.

912. <u>**A financial plan begins with:**</u>
   a. an analysis of investments
   b. selection of investments
   c. purchase of investments
   d. an understanding of risk tolerance, goals, time horizon etc.

913. <u>**A good saving and investing plan:**</u>
   I. can run itself to a large extent
   II. makes use of things we can be sure about
   III. is tax efficient

IV. takes huge risks and gambles
V. pays out a lot of fees

a. I only
b. I and II only
c. I, II and III only
d. I, II, III and IV only
e. I, II, III, IV and V

914. The decision to invest in stocks versus bonds versus cash versus commodities and real estate is known as:
a. stock picking
b. asset allocation
c. liability management
d. capital structure

915. True: Asset allocation is more important than stock selection to an investor over a long period of time and in varying market conditions.

916. True: Preparing a balance sheet for ourselves or for our families is a good way of taking stock and seeing where we are.

917. Which of the following items would be included on our personal or on our family balance sheet:
I. cash in bank account
II. our investments
III. any debts
IV. property investments
V. mutual funds

a. I only
b. I and II only
c. I, II and III only
d. I, II, III and IV only
e. I, II, III, IV and V

918. On our personal balance sheet, the assets minus the liabilities would be:
a. what we owe, our debts or our liabilities
b. what we make, our income or our revenues
c. what we own, our equity or our net worth
d. what we paid, our cost or our total expenditure

This is just a review of the previous section on balance sheets, and the main point there.

919. On a personal balance sheet, liabilities would include which of the following:
I. mortgages
II. credit card debts
III. a loan to a friend
IV. a school loan
V. our investments

a. I only
b. I and II only
c. I, II and III only
d. I, II, III and IV only
e. I, II, III, IV and V

Our investments would be assets on our balance sheet.

920. **True: It is possible to prepare a personal income statement for ourselves.**

921. **Which of the following items would be included on our personal or on our family income statement:**
   I. our income
   II. property taxes
   III. gasoline expenses
   IV. dividends we receive
   V. the value of our investments

   a. I only
   b. I and II only
   c. I, II and III only
   d. I, II, III and IV only
   e. I, II, III, IV and V

   Our investments would be assets on our balance sheet.

922. **With our personal income statement, we could figure out:**
   a. how we are invested
   b. how much money we owe
   c. whether our investments are going up
   d. how we are spending our money

923. **The purpose of preparing our personal balance sheet would be to figure out:**
   a. how much we make
   b. how much we spend
   c. how much we are saving
   d. our net worth

   Items a.-c. would be figured out from an income statement.

924. **True: A balance sheet is a snapshot at a point in time, whereas an income statement is a summary of events over a period of time.**

925. **True: In a personal income statement, revenues would include:**
   a. a salary received
   b. expenses
   c. investments owned
   d. debt/liabilities

926. **Which of the following are good reasons to set money for savings aside first:**
   I. it ensures that the money is saved
   II. it effectively simulates a lower income
   III. it can be a part of automating the process
   IV. it can be a part of using dollar cost averaging
   V. it ensures that the investments never go down

   a. I only
   b. I and II only
   c. I, II and III only
   d. I, II, III and IV only
   e. I, II, III, IV and V

927. **True: An cash fund for emergencies is a good idea.**

For a worst case scenario.

928. In order to track spending, which of the following prepared in detailed form would be most useful:
    a. a balance sheet
    b. an income statement
    c. a credit card statement
    d. a bank statement

929. In order to track net worth, investments and liabilities, which of the following prepared in detailed form would be most useful:
    a. a balance sheet
    b. an income statement
    c. a credit card statement
    d. a bank statement

930. A budget for a family showing expenses on a monthly basis would most resemble:
    a. a balance sheet
    b. an income statement
    c. a credit card statement
    d. a bank statement

931. After an analysis of our own finances, a likely first step would be:
    a. paying down high interest credit card debt
    b. investing in stocks immediately
    c. increasing our debt levels
    d. quitting our jobs

    Because of the high interest rates, this can be the most painful liability we have, certainly of those choices presented in the question.

932. **True: In a fairly priced market, a large part of investing refers to selecting appropriate investments and managing risk. It is not that stocks are necessarily better investments than bonds or vice versa in all circumstances - a large part of investing is about making sensible investments based on individual time horizons, risk tolerances and preferences.**

933. **True: The solidity and integrity of the counter-party is one of the most important considerations before considering any financial transaction.**

934. Of the following alternatives, which is likely to be the most sensible saving and investing program:
    a. buying a single stock periodically using dollar cost averaging
    b. buying an S&P 500 ETF in one lump sum
    c. investing in stocks globally, bonds, commodities, cash and real estate with small contributions over the long-term using dollar cost averaging, tax savings and diversification
    d. buying a lottery ticket and hoping

935. An investor buys the stock of a single company as a complement to a diversified portfolio of index funds and other investments. He or she would theoretically be most likely to be successful with this investment in a stock when he or she:
    a. is buying it because everyone says it is a great idea
    b. is buying it with no knowledge of the company
    c. knows the company well and has good reason to believe that the company will deliver better results than investors in general expect
    d. knows the company well and believes that the company will disappoint the market

936. A financial scheme that promises to triple our money with no risk is likely to be:

a. a great idea
b. a very good idea
c. a scam
d. an idea worth putting all of our money into

937. <u>When looking at investments, it might be useful to think about:</u>
I. why the investment might make sense
II. whether we are we dealing with a trustworthy counter-party
III. how the counter-party being paid
IV. why everyone isn't doing this
V. what the worst-case outcome could be (the absolute worst case)

a. I only
b. I and II only
c. I, II and III only
d. I, II, III and IV only
e. I, II, III, IV and V

TOTAL: 30 ANSWERS

This book has focused on fundamental concepts that exist in our financial world - concepts that to a large extent have withstood the test of time because, for example, they provide the basis for a mutually beneficial interaction - for example the one which can take place between providers and users of capital through equity and debt. Understanding these concepts and some of the terms is what financial literacy is all about - and it is financial literacy that allows us to interpret new information, understand what is being spoken about, have a dialogue with others about financial matters and potentially get on the road to realizing our own saving and investing desires.

* * * * *

If we choose to, by understanding and applying the concepts detailed in this book, it is possible to travel far down the road to making better investment decisions and towards financial freedom. Ultimately, we will have to take decisions ourselves about what we are going to do with this knowledge, and potentially take action based on our means, our goals and our preferences. For each one of us this will probably mean slightly different things; each one of us has also probably been doing some things well, and others not so well - and each one of us might have a good understanding of certain matters, and less of some others.

For most of us, we could safely do a lot of what is required to be effective savers ourselves. We can eliminate high interest rate debt, start saving through regular automatic contributions, use index funds, make use of tax savings, diversify our investments and so on. Getting on the road to financial freedom will take a few decisions and a very manageable amount of set-up time. All we have to do is be proactive and take some action.

Choosing to start saving in a proper manner today will have huge impact on our lives in twenty years' time. Just as starting a healthier lifestyle today will have huge impact on our lives in twenty years as well. We can not get to all of our goals overnight, but we can certainly set the foundation for attaining them, take small steps on a regular basis, and see the a huge improvement over time.

Keeping a long-term focus is crucial. The long-term is where we are going to end up by definition. Our worst decisions will be made by acting without thinking first, or by letting a moment of fear or greed determine what we do.

Fear and greed definitely lead to some of the worst investment decisions. So much so that scams and get-rich-quick schemes that are doomed to fail play on exactly these two emotions. The fear of missing something, an empty promise of riches with no effort – if it were that easy, there would be no point in making any effort, and the people touting these schemes would probably be on a beach somewhere, as opposed to wasting their time trying to sell something to us. On the other hand, fundamentally valid investment concepts that we have learned about will withstand the test of time - so much so that they are to a large extent the very basis of how our society interacts.